# Chil... ...ok

. . . . . . . . . . . . . . . . . . . . . . . . . . . . . . . . . . . . . . . .

**28th edi...**

Mark Brou...

Child Pove...

Child Poverty Action Group works on behalf of the more than one in four children in the UK growing up in poverty. It does not have to be like this. We use our understanding of what causes poverty and the impact it has on children's lives to campaign for policies that will prevent and solve poverty – for good. We provide training, advice and information to make sure hard-up families get the financial support they need. We also carry out high-profile legal work to establish and protect families' rights. If you are not already supporting us, please consider making a donation, or ask for details of our membership schemes, training courses and publications.

Published by Child Poverty Action Group
30 Micawber Street, London N1 7TB
Tel: 020 7837 7979
staff@cpag.org.uk
cpag.org.uk

A CIP record for this book is available from the British Library

ISBN: 978 1 910715 61 1

Child Poverty Action Group is a charity registered in England and Wales (registration number 294841) and in Scotland (registration number SC039339), and is a company limited by guarantee, registered in England (registration number 1993854). VAT number: 690 808117

Cover design by Colorido Studios
Internal design by Devious Designs
Content management system by Konnect Soft
Typeset by DLxml, a division of RefineCatch Limited, Bungay, Suffolk
Printed in the UK by CPI Group (UK) Ltd, Croydon CR0 4YY

# The author

**Mark Brough** is a freelance writer. He previously worked for many years as a welfare rights adviser for people with learning disabilities.

# Acknowledgements

A huge debt is owed to all the authors and checkers of previous editions and, in particular, to Will Hadwen and Nick Turnill.

Many thanks to Anne Ketley for compiling the index and Kathleen Armstrong for proofreading the text.

Finally, thanks are also due to officials at the Department for Work and Pensions for patiently answering queries and providing helpful information.

The law described in this book was correct at 1 May 2020.

# Contents

# Abbreviations

| | |
|---|---|
| CMS | Child Maintenance Service |
| CSA | Child Support Agency |
| DfC | Department for Communities (Northern Ireland) |
| DLA | disability living allowance |
| DWP | Department for Work and Pensions |
| ESA | employment and support allowance |
| EU | European Union |
| HMCTS | HM Courts and Tribunals Service |
| HMRC | HM Revenue and Customs |
| IB | incapacity benefit |
| ICE | Independent Case Examiner |
| IS | income support |
| JSA | jobseeker's allowance |
| NI | national insurance |
| PAYE | pay as you earn |
| PC | pension credit |
| PIP | personal independence payment |
| UC | universal credit |

# Chapter 1

# Introduction

**This chapter covers:**
1. What is child support (below)
2. The statutory child support scheme (below)
3. Responsibility for the child support scheme (p2)
4. Arrangements in Northern Ireland (p3)
5. Using this *Handbook* (p4)

## 1. What is child support

All parents have a legal responsibility to support their children financially until they are 16 and, in some circumstances, until they are 20.[1] Child maintenance paid by parents who do not live with their children is intended to reflect this. Some people make voluntary arrangements to pay maintenance, others have arrangements made by a court order, and some people have maintenance calculated and enforced under the statutory child support scheme run by the Department for Work and Pensions. Some people may pay or receive child maintenance in more than one of these ways.

This *Handbook* explains how the statutory scheme operates. We use the term 'child support' to refer to maintenance calculated and enforced under the statutory scheme. 'Child maintenance' is used as a generic term for all types of child maintenance, including child support, voluntary arrangements and payments made under a court order.

## 2. The statutory child support scheme

The statutory child support scheme calculates the amount of child support people have to pay. It has been in operation since 1993, but has changed significantly since then.

The current system of calculating child support was introduced on 10 December 2012. Since 25 November 2013, all new applications have been dealt with under this system. It is sometimes referred to as the '**2012 rules**' or the 'gross income' scheme. There are four rates of child support, depending on the parent's gross income (see Chapter 4). The calculation can be varied in certain circumstances (see Chapter 5). Fees may be charged for some aspects of the administration of the system (see p24, p138 and p187).

There are two previous schemes. The original scheme, introduced in 1993, is usually referred to as the '**1993 rules**'. In 2003, this scheme was replaced by a simpler calculation, usually referred to as the '**2003 rules**'.

Both these previous schemes are now closed – ie, it is not possible to make new applications under them. Most cases that began under these schemes have now been closed. The only cases that remain are ones where there are still arrears due, but no ongoing liability to pay child support .[2] All child support cases with ongoing liability are now dealt with under the '2012 rules'.

If you are a party in a case that has been closed and want to stay in the statutory scheme, you must apply under the '2012 rules' (see Chapter 2).

For full details of the '1993 rules' and '2003 rules' and the process of closing these cases, see previous editions of this *Handbook*.

# 3. **Responsibility for the child support scheme**

The Department for Work and Pensions (DWP) is responsible for the statutory child support system in Great Britain.

The child support scheme is administered by the **Child Maintenance Service** (CMS), staffed by the DWP.

The DWP is also responsible for the **Child Maintenance Options** service (see below), which provides information and support.

**Note:** previous cases were dealt with by the Child Support Agency (CSA). The CSA continues to deal with arrears arising from previous '1993 rules' and '2003 rules' cases.

## **The Child Maintenance Service**

The CMS is responsible for calculating child support payments and, in some cases, collecting and enforcing them. This includes tracing non-resident parents and investigating parents' financial circumstances.

The CMS has wide powers to gather information. These are covered in Chapter 3. If you think that a child support decision is wrong, you may be able to challenge it (see Chapters 9 and 10). If you are unhappy with the service provided by the CMS, you can make a complaint (see Chapter 11).

## **Child Maintenance Options**

The DWP is responsible for the Child Maintenance Options service, which is intended to be the first port of call for anyone seeking information on child maintenance. Parents must contact Child Maintenance Options before making an application for child support (see p24).

Child Maintenance Options offers information and support to help parents make informed choices about child maintenance arrangements. It can be used by separating and separated parents, as well as by family, friends, guardians and anyone with an interest in child maintenance.

Child Maintenance Options can provide information and assistance with:
- setting up a child maintenance arrangement following separation;
- establishing child maintenance arrangements for parents who are not in a relationship;
- switching from a voluntary arrangement to an application under the statutory scheme, or vice versa; *and*
- situations in which an existing child maintenance agreement has broken down or is not working well.

The service is free and is delivered by telephone, through a web-chat service or by filling in an online enquiry form.[3] If you have difficulty using any of these methods, a face-to-face meeting may be arranged. See Appendix 1 for contact details. Child Maintenance Options aims to encourage voluntary maintenance arrangements by providing estimated calculations based on the statutory scheme, and other guidance to help parents decide on maintenance arrangements and amounts. It also provides information on other related areas, such as housing, employment and money, and can put people in touch with specialist advice agencies.

Child Maintenance Options can be used anonymously and records are not linked, so if two people contact the service independently in relation to the same child(ren), no information about one person will be divulged to the other. Child Maintenance Options no longer has its own website. If you want to know anything about how it operates (for example, how personal information is used and kept secure) ask for details. If you are not happy with the service you receive, you can complain (see Chapter 11).

# 4. **Arrangements in Northern Ireland**

The child support system is largely the same throughout the UK, but Great Britain and Northern Ireland are treated as two separate territories for child support purposes.

There is a separate agency for Northern Ireland, also known as the Child Maintenance Service. It is part of the Department for Communities (DfC), and has the same powers as the Child Maintenance Service in England, Scotland and Wales. There is also an information and support service, known as Child

Maintenance Choices, providing information and support in a similar way to Child Maintenance Options.

If this *Handbook* is being used in Northern Ireland, references to the Department for Work and Pensions should be read as references to the DfC. **Note:** some legislative references are different in Northern Ireland.

If an application is made to the statutory child support scheme and the person with care (see p11), non-resident parent (see p12) and qualifying child (see p8) do not all reside in the same territory, there are special rules to determine how the application is dealt with.

New applications are generally dealt with by the agency of the territory where the non-resident parent named in the application lives. They are dealt with by the territory in which the applicant lives until the address of the non-resident parent is verified and, if the applicant lives in Great Britain, any application fee (see p24) due is paid.

Outstanding arrears under the '1993 rules' and '2003 rules' are dealt with by the agency of the territory where the person with care lives.[4]

Any calculation made must take into account the rules of the other territory.[5] Because the rules for calculating child support in the two territories are very similar, this should not make any difference in practice.

# 5. **Using this *Handbook***

This *Handbook* explains the rules of the statutory child support scheme and how it is administered by the Child Maintenance Service (CMS). It is intended to help parents who use this scheme and their advisers. It covers the child support scheme in England, Wales and Scotland as at 1 May 2020.

This *Handbook* deals with the current '2012 rules' scheme. In a few places, it highlights important older rules where these are different. For full details of the previous '1993 rules' and '2003 rules' schemes, see the 2014/15 edition of this *Handbook*.

Much of the caselaw relevant to child support was established under the '1993 rules' and '2003 rules'. However, many of the principles still apply to '2012 rules' cases. Where there are likely to be differences in interpretation or difficulties in applying previous caselaw to the '2012 rules', this is explained.

Around 95 per cent of people who apply for child support are women. However, the rules apply in the same way whatever the gender of the person with care of the child or the paying parent, including if both parents are men or both are women. The various parties are therefore referred to in a gender-neutral way in this *Handbook* wherever possible.

## Structure of the book

**Chapter 1** is an introduction to child support. It explains how to use this *Handbook*.

**Chapter 2** explains how applications are made and **Chapter 3** covers how the CMS seeks information. Once all the information is available, the amount of child support can be worked out. **Chapter 4** explains how this is done, and **Chapter 5** explains how the amount can be varied in certain circumstances. **Chapter 6** covers decisions. **Chapter 7** explains how child support is collected and paid. **Chapter 8** explains how child support arrears are dealt with and enforced. **Chapters 9 and 10** explain how to change, query or challenge a decision. **Chapter 11** explains how to complain about anything to do with child support.

The **appendices** contain useful addresses and information about reference materials.

The best way to find the information you need is to use the **index** at the back of the book.

## Endnotes

Each chapter has endnotes that contain the legal sources, relevant caselaw and other information that support the text. These can be quoted to the CMS if the statement in the text is disputed. Appendix 5 explains the abbreviations used in the endnotes, with information on how to obtain the sources.

The Department for Work and Pensions (DWP) does not currently publish the guidance used in making child support decisions. As the guidance is not readily available, this *Handbook* generally avoids using it as a source. The guidance can, however, be obtained by making a request to the DWP under the Freedom of Information Act 2000. Anyone concerned about the application of a particular aspect of the law may wish to ask the CMS to provide a copy of any guidance it has taken into account when making the decision.

# Notes

### 1. What is child support
1   s1(1) CSA 1991

### 2. The statutory child support scheme
2   DWP/Office for National Statistics, *Child Support Agency Quarterly Summary of Statistics: data to September 2019December 2018*, January 2020February 2019

### 3. Responsibility for the child support scheme
3   gov.uk/making-child-maintenance-arrangement/arrange-child-maintenance-yourself

### 4. Arrangements in Northern Ireland
4   Sch 1 Art 5(5) CS(NIRA) Regs
5   Sch 1 Art 5(4) and (7) CS(NIRA) Regs

# Chapter 2

# Applications

This chapter covers:
1. Who can apply for child support (below)
2. When an application can be accepted (p16)
3. How to apply (p24)
4. Withdrawing or cancelling an application (p28)
5. Multiple applications (p28)
6. Communicating with the Child Maintenance Service (p29)

## 1. Who can apply for child support

Both parents (see p9) of a child have a legal duty to contribute to the maintenance of that child.[1] A parent who is not living in the same household as her/his child (a 'non-resident parent' – see p12) may be required to pay child support to the person who is the child's main carer (a 'person with care' – see p11). In most cases, this is the child's other parent, but could be another person – eg, the child's grandparent.

The following people can apply to the Child Maintenance Service (CMS) for child support for a 'qualifying child' (see p8):
- a person with care (see p11);
- a non-resident parent (see p12);
- in Scotland, a child aged 12 or over (provided no application has been made, or is treated as having been made, by the person with care or the non-resident parent).[2]

Child support can only be paid to one person with care of a qualifying child. If there is more than one person with care and they both/all apply for child support, the person whose application is accepted (see p28) receives all the child support. There is an order of priority that the CMS must consider when deciding which application to accept (see p28).

If two or more people in different households care for a qualifying child and at least one, but not all, of them has parental responsibility (see p10) for the child, only those with parental responsibility can apply for child support.[3] For example, if a child is cared for partly by her/his mother who has parental responsibility and partly by her/his grandmother who does not have parental responsibility, only the mother can apply. This means that if the person with parental responsibility decides not to apply, another person with care could lose out on child support.

## Who is a qualifying child

Child support is only payable for a 'qualifying child'. A child is only a **'qualifying child'** if one or both of her/his parents are non-resident parents (see p12).[4]

A **'child'** is defined as a person who is:

- under 16 years of age; *or*
- a young person aged 16–19 inclusive and is a 'qualifying young person' for the purposes of child benefit.

Even if someone is in one of the above groups, s/he is not a child if s/he is, or has been, married or in a civil partnership. This applies even if the marriage or civil partnership has been annulled or was never valid – eg, because s/he was under 16.[5]

The main condition for being a 'qualifying young person' for the purposes of child benefit is to be receiving full-time, non-advanced education (see below) or undertaking certain approved training. See CPAG's *Welfare Benefits and Tax Credits Handbook* for full details of the rules on child benefit.

### Full-time, non-advanced education

A course is **non-advanced** if it is up to A level or Higher or Advanced Higher Scottish National Qualifications, or NVQ and SVQ level 3 and below. Courses of degree level and above, Diploma of Higher Education, Higher National Diploma or Higher National Certificate, Diploma of Higher Education, or NVQ and SVQ level 4 and above count as advanced education.[6]

The young person must attend a recognised educational establishment (such as a school, college or university). If s/he is educated elsewhere (eg, at home), the education must be recognised by the CMS. The CMS can normally only recognise such other education if it was being provided for the young person immediately before s/he reached 16.[7]

The CMS must treat a young person as receiving **full-time** education if s/he attends a course with more than 12 hours of weekly contact time. 'Contact time' includes teaching, supervised study, exams and practical or project work which are part of the course. It does not include meal times or unsupervised study, whether on or off school premises. It is the hours of education received that count, not the hours of attendance.[8]

If a young person is not attending such a course (eg, if the contact time is 12 hours or less), the CMS must look at all the facts and decide whether the education is full time.[9]

After leaving school or college, a young person still counts as being in full-time education until child benefit stops being paid.

A young person at school or college can still count as a qualifying child if there is a temporary break in full-time education. It does not matter whether s/he is under or over 16 when her/his education is interrupted. A break of up to six months can be allowed. The CMS can allow longer if the break is due to an illness or disability of the young person. For someone to continue to count as a qualifying child, any breaks in full-time education must not be followed by a period during which child benefit stops being payable.[10]

## Who is a parent

A '**parent**' is a person who is legally the mother or father of the child.[11] This includes:

- a biological parent;
- a parent by adoption;[12]
- a parent under a parental order (used in surrogacy cases).[13]

If a child was conceived by artificial insemination or in vitro fertilisation:

- the mother is the woman who gave birth to the child, unless an adoption order or parental order is made;[14]
- the father is the man who provided the sperm (but see below).

If the insemination or in vitro fertilisation took place on or after 1 August 1991 but before 6 April 2009, the father is:

- the mother's husband, unless he did not consent to,[15] or died before, insemination;[16] *or*
- if the insemination was during licensed treatment services provided for the mother and a man, that man.[17] The man and woman must have received treatment services together.[18] This rule does not apply if the woman was inseminated or fertilised outside the UK.[19]

From 6 April 2009, in the case of assisted reproduction:[20]

- a man who is married to, or is a civil partner of, the mother is the father, unless he did not consent;
- if a man and woman are not married or in a civil parntership and the woman has a child as a result of licensed treatment, the man is the father if there is a notice of consent between them.

Two women who are married or civil partners are treated in the same way as a man and woman who are married or civil partners – ie, if one partner gives birth to a child as a result of donor insemination, she is the mother of the child and her partner is automatically the other parent, unless she did not consent to the mother's treatment.[21] If two women are not married or in a civil partnership and one woman has a child as a result of licensed treatment, the other woman can be treated as a parent of the child if no man is treated as the father and there is a notice of consent between the two women.[22]

If someone who is married to or in a civil partnership with the mother at the time of creation of an embryo using donor sperm dies before the embryo is placed in the mother, that partner can be treated as the other parent for the purposes of birth registration if that person consented to the treatment, provided no one else is legally treated as the parent of the child.[23]

An **adoption order** means the child is legally the child of the adopter(s).[24] The liability of a biological parent to maintain her/his child ends on adoption, and the parent(s) by adoption become the only person/people liable to maintain the child.

**Note:** a person who has legal parental responsibility (see below)[25] is not necessarily a parent for child support purposes.[26] For example, a step-parent who has acquired parental responsibility (except one assumed to be a parent – see p44) cannot be required to pay child support.[27] However, the courts could order her/him to pay maintenance.

A **foster parent** is not a parent for child support purposes because the child has been placed with her/him by a local authority (see p11).

**Note:** the information above is summary and is not intended to be a statement of the law. If you have any queries about how you are affected, seek legal advice.

## Parental responsibility

A mother automatically has parental responsibility for her child from birth. Parents who were married to, or in a civil partnership with, each other when the child was born both automatically have parental responsibility. This continues even if they later divorce or the civil partnership is dissolved.[28] If the mother is not married or in a civil partnership with her partner, she can make a formal agreement giving her partner parental responsibility.[29]

In addition, in England and Wales, if a child's parent is married to or in a civil partnership with someone who is not the child's other parent (ie, a step-parent), s/he (or if both biological parents have parental responsibility, both parents) can make a parental responsibility agreement with the step-parent, giving her/him parental responsibility for the child.[30] The courts can also give parental responsibility to a person, including a non-parent or step-parent, who applies for parental responsibility.[31]

In England and Wales, if the name of a father who is not married to or in a civil partnership with the mother appears on a birth certificate on or after 1 December 2003, he automatically has parental responsibility.[32] In Scotland, this applies if an unmarried father jointly registers a birth on or after 4 May 2006. (**Note:** changes to the law in Scotland relating to civil partnerships between different sex couples are proposed but not yet enacted.[33]) Unmarried fathers who signed a birth certificate before these dates cannot acquire parental responsibility without going through one of the other routes – ie, arranging a formal agreement with the mother or applying for a court order.

A female partner of the mother of a child conceived on or after 6 April 2009 automatically has parental responsibility if her details are included in the birth registration on or after 1 September 2009.[34]

If a birth certificate was issued before these dates, a female partner can only acquire parental reponsibility through one of the other routes.

## Who is a person with care

A '**person with care**' is a person with whom a child has her/his home (see below) and who usually provides 'day-to-day care' (see below) for the child.[35]

If the person with care is the child's parent, s/he is known as the '**parent with care**'.[36] **Note:** the CMS uses the term '**receiving parent**', rather than 'person with care', in its leaflets and letters.

*Home*

A '**home**' is the physical place where the child lives. It is different from a household (see p13). Although there is no specific definition of 'home' in the child support rules, the child's home is usually clear. A child may have more than one home – in which case, the CMS decides which is her/his principal home.

The person with care is usually the child's parent or another individual who provides day-to-day care for her/him, but could also be, for example, an organisation such as a children's home. However, a local authority *cannot* be a person with care, nor can someone who is looking after a child who has been placed with her/him by the local authority (including, in Scotland, someone who is providing 'continuing care' to a young person after s/he reaches age 16[37]). In England and Wales, a person with whom a local authority has placed a child can be a person with care if s/he is the child's parent and the local authority has allowed the child to live with her/him.[38]

Child support can only be paid to one person with care in respect of each qualifying child. If there are two or more people who each provide day-to-day care for the child, it is paid only to one. The person who receives child support could decide on an informal basis to pass some of the money to the other person with care, but that cannot be enforced.

In some situations where the day-to-day care of a child is shared, a parent who provides some care may nonetheless be treated as a non-resident parent (see p14).

## Day-to-day care

'**Day-to-day care**' is not specifically defined in the rules. The ordinary meaning of the phrase should be used when deciding who is a person with care and who can, therefore, receive child support. In most cases, it is clear who has day-to-day care.

Two or more people living in different households may each provide day-to-day care for the same child.

In deciding whether a person has day-to-day care of a qualifying child, the CMS should consider the overall care arrangements. The number of nights a year for which a person provides care may be a guide, but should not be the only consideration. If a mother provides care during the day but her children sleep at their father's home, both may be regarded as providing day-to-day care.[39]

A person who is responsible for a child's daily routine may be providing day-to-day care, even if some things are done by another person – eg, a childminder. It may not be necessary for someone to be *with* the child if s/he is nevertheless the person responsible for her/his overall care during that time. What matters is the degree to which a person continues to have control over the child and to be responsible for her/his behaviour and protection.[40]

If a child is placed with her/his parent by a local authority in England and Wales, even though the local authority is legally responsible, the parent is treated as providing day-to-day care.[41]

If a child is a boarding school boarder or a hospital patient, the person who would otherwise provide day-to-day care is treated as still doing so.[42] The person who is treated as having day-to-day care while a child is at boarding school need not be the person who pays the school fees.[43]

Although it is not explicitly stated in the rules, if a child is temporarily in someone else's care, whoever would otherwise have day-to-day care is treated as providing care.[44]

If a change in the pattern of care occurs, the CMS should be informed, as this may affect the amount of child support payable and may be grounds for a supersession (see p204). The CMS is likely to take an overall view of the care arrangements rather than make separate decisions for different periods of time.

## Who is a non-resident parent

A 'non-resident parent' is a parent (see p9) who is not living in the same household (see p13) as her/his child, and the child has her/his home with a person with care (see p11) – eg, where the parents of a child have separated.[45] Only a non-resident parent can be required to pay child support. **Note:** the CMS uses the term **'paying parent'**, rather than 'non-resident parent', in its leaflets and letters.

Both parents can be non-resident parents, in which case they can both be required to pay child support to the person with care – eg, to a grandparent who provides day-to-day care for a child.[46]

If a step-parent adopts a child and, therefore, legally replaces a biological parent, there may be no non-resident parent.[47]

If separated parents reconcile and live together, the non-resident parent is no longer non-resident and the child support calculation ceases to have effect. How soon this happens depends on the circumstances – eg, the nature of the reconciliation and the intentions of the couple. It may mean that the calculation ceases to have effect immediately.

If people share the care of a child, a parent who provides some care for the child may nonetheless be treated as a non-resident parent (see p14).[48]

## Household

'Household' is not defined in the child support legislation. A household is something abstract, not something physical like a home (see p11). It is either a single person or a group of people held together by social ties.[49] In many cases, whether or not people are members of the same household is obvious. If it is not obvious, the CMS considers other factors. No one factor on its own should be conclusive. There does not need to be any settled intention about future arrangements for a household to exist.[50]

The meaning of household has been considered in family law and social security cases as well as child support cases, and this caselaw may be used to help make child support decisions.

Caselaw has established the following.
- There can be two or more separate households in one house.[51]
- One or more members of a household can be temporarily absent from the home without ending their membership of the household.[52]
- There does not need to be a relationship like marriage for people to share a household – eg, two sisters can form a household.[53]

If there is a polygamous marriage, the CMS decides whether the qualifying child lives in a different household from at least one of the parents when establishing whether there is a non-resident parent. There can only ever be two legal parents, regardless of the number of partners either parent may have.

A couple may become members of the same household even if they get back together only briefly, assuming that they are hoping the relationship and their domestic arrangements will be indefinite.[54] In this case, a new household could be formed immediately, whether or not it then ceases to exist a few weeks or months later. A household can be formed as soon as people live together intending to form a household, and before they have arranged joint domestic and financial matters.

**Note:** a decision by the CMS or First-tier Tribunal that the couple share a household for child support purposes is likely to mean that they share a household for benefit or tax credit purposes. For more information about cohabitation decisions for benefits and tax credits, see CPAG's *Welfare Benefits and Tax Credits Handbook*.

## When a parent with care is treated as a non-resident parent

If both parents share the care of a child for whom a child support application has been made and the CMS accepts that they both have 'day-to-day care' (see p11), there can only be a liability to pay child support if one of the parents is treated as the non-resident parent [55]

If one parent is treated as a non-resident parent (see p12), s/he is liable to pay child support, and the entire amount is paid to the other parent (or person with care).

If one or both parents share the child's care with a person with care who is not the child's parent (eg, a grandparent), at least one of the parents must be treated as a non-resident parent in order for there to be a liability to pay child support. Both parents may be treated as non-resident and liable to pay child support to the person with care.

A parent with care who applies to the CMS for child support from the non-resident parent but ends up being deemed the non-resident parent and being required to pay child support can request that the application be withdrawn (see p28).

If a parent with care is treated as a non-resident parent, the amount of child support s/he must pay is worked out as usual. However, see p80 for how the amount of care s/he provides affects her/his liability.

If both parents share the care of a qualifying child equally, no one is liable to pay child support (see below).

### Example

Susan and her partner Geoff are separated. Their daughter Katherine lives with Susan three nights each week. Susan works some night shifts, so Katherine stays with her grandmother two nights each week. Katherine stays with Geoff for two nights each weekend.

Susan applies for child support. Although Geoff also provides day-to-day care of Katherine, he provides care to a lesser extent than Susan. He is treated as the non-resident parent (see below) and is liable to pay child support (the amount is adjusted for the care he provides). All the child support is paid to Susan. She decides to pay two-fifths of it to Katherine's grandmother to reflect the regular care she provides.

### Who is treated as the non-resident parent

A parent with care is treated as the non-resident parent if s/he provides care to a lesser extent than another person with care.[56] A 'lesser extent' could mean either fewer nights a week on average or fewer hours a week overall, but the overall pattern of care arrangements should be considered.

The CMS usually assumes that the parent who does not receive child benefit is providing the lesser amount of care, and s/he is therefore treated as the non-resident parent.[57] This may lead to competing claims for child benefit. If more than one person who is entitled makes a claim for child benefit, an order of priority is used to decide who receives it.[58] For example, the person with whom the child is living has priority over other claimants. If the priority rules do not decide the matter and the claimants cannot come to an agreement, HM Revenue and Customs makes the decision. Priority can be conceded by a higher priority claimant to someone else, in writing.

**Note:** if someone has elected not to receive child benefit because s/he would be liable for the 'high-income child benefit charge' in income tax, child benefit is still treated as payable in respect of the child.[59]

See CPAG's *Welfare Benefits and Tax Credits Handbook* for full details of the rules on child benefit.

If you think a decision that you are a non-resident parent is wrong, get advice. You may need to provide the CMS with evidence (eg, a diary), showing the pattern of care.

If the evidence shows that day-to-day care is shared equally between a qualifying child's parents, neither parent is treated as non-resident and there is no liability for child support. This is the case even if the two parents have significantly different levels of income. Receipt of child benefit should not be used as a 'tie-break' to decide who is a non-resident parent if the evidence does not otherwise make it clear.[60] The CMS must consider the *overall* care arrangements when deciding whether day-to-day care is shared on an equal basis. It should not focus solely on whether or not the number of nights of care provided by each is equal.[61] So a child being cared for by one parent for a few days more or less than an absolutely equal pattern does not necessarily prevent the CMS from deciding that care is shared equally, although this conclusion is likely to be reached in relatively few cases.[62]

### Example

Marcia and Nathan are divorced. They have two children, Oscar (7) and Patrick (5). Every fortnight the children spend five nights with Nathan. The rest of the time they live with Marcia.

Marcia has the children nine out of every 14 nights = approximately 234 nights a year.

Nathan has the children five out of every 14 nights = approximately 130 nights a year.

Both parents have day-to-day care.

Because Nathan looks after the boys to a lesser extent, he is treated as a non-resident parent and a calculation is carried out to decide how much child support he should pay to Marcia.

Marcia remains the parent with care and has no liability to pay child support.

A year later, Nathan has moved onto shift work. One week he has the children four nights, the second week three nights. Marcia cares for the children the rest of the time. They now share care equally. As Marcia receives child benefit, Nathan is still treated as the non-resident parent.

However, the CMS accepts that care is now shared equally and cancels the calculation.

There may be cases where each child of a family spends a different amount of time with the two parents – ie, the mother may be treated as the non-resident parent for one child, and the father for the other. If this is the case, the situation is similar to that of a divided family in which different children live full time with different parents (also known as **'split care'** – see p67). Two separate calculations are carried out.

---

**Example**

In the example above, Marcia and Nathan's work patterns change, and they agree new arrangements for caring for the children. Marcia now looks after Oscar for nine nights out of every 14 nights. Nathan now looks after Patrick for eight nights out of every 14 nights. As Marcia looks after Oscar for the greater amount of time, Nathan is treated as the non-resident parent for Oscar and is liable to pay child support to Marcia. As Nathan looks after Patrick for the greater amount of time, Marcia is treated as the non-resident parent for Patrick and is liable to pay child support to Nathan.

---

The child support due is calculated separately for each parent based on her/his income. The amount due is reduced to take account of the care she/he provides for the child for whom she/he is the non-resident parent (see p80). The amounts due to be paid by each non-resident parent are offset so that only the parent with the higher liability actually makes a payment.

---

## 2. **When an application can be accepted**

The Child Maintenance Service (CMS) can accept an application for child support if it has jurisdiction. The CMS has jurisdiction if a child is a 'qualifying child' and all the relevant parties (qualifying child, person with care and non-resident parent) are habitually resident in the UK (see p17).[63]

If the CMS decides that it no longer has jurisdiction because one of the parties is no longer habitually resident in the UK, the decision on child support liability should be superseded and the calculation cancelled (see p133).

The child support scheme has priority over the court system. See p19 for the role of the courts if the CMS has jurisdiction for child support.

The CMS cannot accept an application for child support if there are certain maintenance orders made by a court or certain written maintenance agreements for the child(ren) concerned (see p18).

A CMS decision on whether it has jurisdiction can be revised (see Chapter 9) and subsequently appealed to the First-tier Tribunal (see Chapter 10).[64]

## Habitual residence

The CMS cannot make a child support calculation unless the qualifying child, person with care and non-resident parent are all 'habitually resident' in the UK.[65]

Other children who affect the child support calcualtion (known as 'relevant other children' – see p64) do not have to be habitually resident in the UK.[66] The person with care does not have to be habitually resident if that 'person' is an organisation.[67]

The UK means England, Scotland, Wales and Northern Ireland (including coastal islands like the Isle of Wight). It does not include the Isle of Man or the Channel Islands.[68]

If a person is not habitually resident in the UK, see p23.

### What is habitual residence

A person is habitually resident if s/he is ordinarily resident in the UK and has been for an appreciable period of time.[69] 'Ordinary residence' means 'residence for a settled purpose'.[70]

There is no set definition of what is an appreciable period of time and no comprehensive list of factors that are relevant when deciding whether a person is habitually resident in the UK. A decision must take into account all her/his circumstances and intentions. Some of the most important factors that are considered include:

- the person's usual centre of interest or connections to a particular place;
- the length, continuity and purpose of residence in the UK;
- the length and purpose of any absence from the UK; *and*
- the nature of the person's work.

The following principles have been established by caselaw. Cases that do not relate directly to child support are 'persuasive', but do not necessarily have to be followed.[71]

- A person can habitually reside in more than one country, or in none.[72]
- A person may continue to be habitually resident in the UK even though s/he is absent from the UK for some time – eg, because s/he has employment and accommodation elsewhere.[73]
- A person cannot be habitually resident in the UK if s/he has never been here. S/he must actually be resident, not just intend to reside here in the future.
- There is no minimum period of time required to have been living in another country before a new habitual residence can be established, but you must have a 'settled intention' to make the relevant area your home.[74] You must provide evidence of your intention.
- A person who leaves the UK intending never to return to reside stops being habitually resident in the UK on the day s/he leaves.[75] The intention never to return must be a settled intention and not to see how things will work out in another country.[76]

- A person held in a country against her/his will may not be habitually resident there, even after long residence (but see below).[77]
- A person who is in the UK unlawfully may be habitually resident.

If a non-resident parent is not habitually resident in the UK, the CMS can still make a calculation if s/he is employed by the civil service, the armed forces, a UK-based company (ie, a company which employs a person to work outside the UK but which makes payment arrangements in the UK), a local authority or the NHS.[78]

A person returning to the UK after an absence may have remained habitually resident in the UK during her/his absence.[79] A temporary absence abroad, such as for a holiday or to visit relatives, does not mean that a person ceases to be habitually resident. When deciding whether someone has ceased to be habitually resident for child support purposes, the emphasis should be on the nature and degree of her/his connections with the UK, and any future intentions.[80] If the non-resident parent requests a supersession of the calculation because s/he is no longer habitually resident in the UK, the onus is on her/him to prove that this is the case.[81]

## Children

Whether or not a child is habitually resident is a question of fact that depends on her/his age and circumstances. The assessment of habitual residence should be centred on the child. The habitual residence of the parent or person with whom a child lives, and the intentions of that person for the child, are relevant but they do not necessarily determine the habitual residence of the child. Her/his place of habitual residence should reflect a degree of integration in a social and family environment.[82] A new habitual residence may still, however, be established quickly – eg, depending on the degree to which a move is planned and the child disengaged from the social and family environment in the previous country of residence.[83]

If there are two people with parental responsibility (see p10) who live in different countries, the habitual residence of the child depends on the circumstances. Any existing residence order, or order for custody or care and control, is an important factor. A young child will usually have the same habitual residence as the person who cares for her/him. This may not necessarily be the case for a child of school age or an adolescent.[84]

## Court orders and written maintenance agreements

If the CMS has jurisdiction to make a calculation (see p16), regardless of whether or not an application is actually made, the child support scheme has priority over the court system in terms of determining regular maintenance payments for qualifying children. This section explains the role of the courts in these circumstances and its relationship with the statutory child support scheme.

**Note:** it is advisable to obtain legal advice about any court proceedings. The following is not intended to be a comprehensive guide to the law.

## The role of the courts if the Child Maintenance Service has jurisdiction

If the CMS has jurisdiction to make a child support calculation, the courts do not normally deal with child maintenance. In general, the courts cannot make, vary or revive an order for periodic payments of child maintenance if the CMS has jurisdiction. The courts can still, however, make orders in certain circumstances – ie, for situations not covered by the child support scheme (see below). The courts can also formalise written maintenance agreements made by the parties (see p20), revoke an existing maintenance order, and enforce payment of any arrears arising from a period before the CMS had jurisdiction.[85]

The child support scheme does not change the courts' powers in relation to other aspects of relationship breakdown (eg, contact and residence orders, maintenance for a spouse or civil partner and the division of property) or the courts' jurisdiction to deal with parentage disputes (see p44).

### Orders that can still be made by the courts

If the CMS has jurisdiction, the courts can still make maintenance orders for:[86]
- a young person who is no longer considered by the CMS to be a qualifying child (see p8);
- any stepchildren of the non-resident parent – ie, children who were accepted by that parent as members of her/his family when they used to live with her/him, but who are not qualifying children;[87]
- the expenses of a child's education or training;[88]
- additional expenses relating to a child's disability. A child counts as disabled if s/he is getting disability living allowance (DLA) or personal independence payment (PIP), or does not get DLA/PIP but is blind, deaf, without speech or is substantially and permanently disabled by illness, injury, mental disorder or congenital deformity.[89] The courts can extend payments beyond the age at which the child may no longer be a qualifying child for child support purposes;[90]
- the person with care;[91] *and*
- a qualifying child in excess of the maximum worked out under child support rules. An assessment based on the maximum gross weekly income first needs to be obtained before a court has jurisdiction to consider whether the non-resident parent's circumstances (eg, if her/his gross weekly income is substantially over £3,000) justify its making an order for additional child maintenance.[92]

Some of these types of orders are often referred to as 'top-up' orders.

The courts can backdate these maintenance orders to the 'effective date' (see p131) of a child support calculation, if the application is made within six months of that date.[93] Backdating is at the court's discretion and can ensure that other maintenance is in step with child support.

People with court orders for child maintenance can use the CMS's collection and enforcement service for amounts due under these orders, provided child support is also being collected (see p145).

The courts can also make a lump-sum award for a child. This power should not be used to make awards that are intended to provide regular support for the child in place of child support. It should only be used to meet a need for a particular item of capital expenditure – eg, acquiring a home.[94]

If a court makes an order which affects, or is likely to affect, a child support calculation, the relevant court officer must notify the CMS of this if s/he knows a calculation is in force.[95]

### Written maintenance agreements

Even if an application could be made to the CMS for child support, parents can still choose to make a maintenance agreement.[96] Maintenance agreements can be informal 'family-based' arrangements, which are flexible but cannot be enforced. They can also be converted into a legally enforceable form – ie, endorsed by a court in a consent order (or made as a registered minute of agreement in Scotland).[97] In this case, the courts can enforce the terms of the agreement through enforcement methods similar to those available to the CMS (see p161).

*Maintenance agreements and consent orders*

'**Maintenance agreement**' means an agreement to make (or to secure the making of) periodic payments of maintenance (or aliment in Scotland) to, or for the benefit of, a qualifying child.[98] This does not include any agreement to make a lump-sum payment (a 'capitalised payment'), even if this is intended to be the equivalent of regular child maintenance payments for a future period.[99]

A '**consent order**' is an order made by the court with the written consent of both parties. It is legally binding and can be enforced like any other court order and cannot be changed by one party without the court's permission.

A '**minute of agreement**' is an agreement drawn up between two parties in Scotland in the presence of their solicitors, but without the need for formal court action. If it is registered for preservation and execution in the Books of Council and Session (a public register of formal documents in Scotland), it can be enforced by officers of the courts.

Parents who want a consent order or registered minute of agreement should obtain assistance from a family law solicitor. Consent orders for child maintenance are often made at the same time as other court action – eg, on divorce proceedings. A consent order must be made as part of a formal application to the court and must refer to the family law provisions under which it is made.

## When an existing court order prevents a child support application

If there is an informal maintenance agreement for periodic payments for the benefit of a child which was made on or after 5 April 1993, an application can still be made to the CMS for child support for the same child. Any clause included in the agreement that claims to prevent someone from applying to the CMS is void.[100]

An order for periodic payments of maintenance for a child (see below) made by a court before 3 March 2003 prevents an application for any child to whom it relates – ie, the CMS will refuse to make a calculation.[101]

Any such order made on or after 3 March 2003 that has been in force for less than one year also prevents an application. A consent order or registered minute of agreement made on or after 3 March 2003 also prevents an application.[102]

The wording of the order is important – eg, a consent order containing an order to provide maintenance for the parent with care, and undertakings to provide maintenance for the children, may not prevent a calculation by the CMS.[103]

Therefore, if a new agreement is made and formalised by a consent order or registered minute of agreement, this will be the basis of the child maintenance payable for at least a year. If a child support application is made within a year of an order made after 3 March 2003, the CMS may hold it until after the one-year period expires and then treat it as an application, rather than insist that a new application be made.[104]

An application can be made to the CMS, even if there is one of the court orders listed on p19 (orders a court can still make) or if the court order is a 'Segal order'. This is one that makes specific provision for an award of maintenance to reduce at a later date because a child support calculation is made.[105]

A court order only prevents an application to the CMS in the following circumstances.

- It requires periodic payments of maintenance (or aliment in Scotland) to be made to, or for the benefit of, a qualifying child.[106] However, because an order only prevents an *application* to the CMS, an order made *after* the application (eg, a 'top-up order' – see p19) does not stop the CMS making a calculation, or prevent the CMS from revising or enforcing an existing calculation. A court order directing capital payments (ie, not periodic payments) does not count as an order for these purposes.[107]
- It must be in force. The meaning of 'in force' is not defined in the legislation, and so you may wish to obtain advice, as this can be a complex issue. The fact that parties may have waived their rights under an order, or agreed to make different arrangements, does not affect the status of the order itself.[108] It may be arguable that an order is in force only if it is still relevant – eg, the non-resident parent against whom the order was made is still a non-resident parent.[109] An order is in force if some undertakings or arrangements, such as for residence of the child, are still in effect, even though there is no further

liability for maintenance payments[110] or if the liability for child maintenance under the order has not yet begun.[111] If a court decides that it has no power to vary or enforce an order, an application can be made to the CMS.[112]

- It must be made under one of certain legal provisions (see Appendix 2).[113] The order usually states the legal provision under which it was made.

If you cannot apply to the CMS because of an order, you can ask the court to:
- vary or enforce the amount of maintenance under the order;
- revoke the order.

Although the courts can revoke child maintenance orders, this is not usually done simply to allow an application to be made to the CMS.[114] If you are considering asking for an order to be revoked, get advice on the likely child support calculation.

### How a child support calculation affects a court order or maintenance agreement

If the CMS is aware that an order is in force, it must notify all the parties and the relevant court when it makes a calculation.[115]

When a child support calculation is made any existing court order or maintenance agreement either ceases to have effect or has effect in a modified form in relation to periodic payments from the effective date of the calculation (see p131).[116]

These rules apply even to 'clean break' orders or agreements. There are conflicting court decisions on whether the child support scheme allows the court to reopen the capital or property part of such an order.[117] The arrangement may be self-adjusting to address the effect of a child support calculation. This could mean, for example, a legal charge on the transferred home so that the non-resident parent could recover any child support paid from the transferred property.[118] It could also mean an order that the non-resident parent top up any future child support to a certain total amount of maintenance.[119]

If the order includes provisions for additional maintenance (eg, for a child's education or training expenses or for a disabled child's special needs), only the elements for periodic maintenance payments for a qualifying child should cease to be in force. If the order is made solely for these additional expenses, it remains in force.[120] Parts of the order for matters other than periodic maintenance for the children named in the calculation (eg, other children or spousal maintenance) remain in force.[121]

Maintenance agreements are unenforceable from the effective date of the child support calculation.[122] This only affects the part of the agreement to pay periodic maintenance for the children named in the calculation. The agreement remains unenforceable until the CMS no longer has the power to make a calculation.[123]

If a court order is cancelled because it was made by mistake when a CMS calculation was in force, any payments made under the order are treated as payments of child support.[124]

If a court order ceases to have effect because of a child support calculation, but the CMS revises its decision and decides no child support is, in fact, payable because the previous decision was made in error, the court order revives and any child support already paid counts as maintenance paid under that order.[125]

## The role of the courts if the Child Maintenance Service has no jurisdiction

If the CMS does not have jurisdiction (eg, because one parent or the qualifying child is not habitually resident in the UK), the courts may make, vary or revive a maintenance order.

The courts may use the child support scheme as a guide when setting levels of child maintenance. This may avoid child support applications being made as soon as circumstances change and the CMS has jurisdiction in the case. If you are seeking an order, ask your solicitor to prepare a calculation. An online calculator is available on the gov.uk website.

In England and Wales, applications for maintenance are made to the family court or High Court. In Scotland, they are made to the sheriff court or Court of Session.

If a child support calculation is cancelled because the non-resident parent moves abroad (see p133), an application for maintenance can be made to the court. The person with care can apply for a 'reciprocal enforcement of maintenance order' to recover maintenance from someone living abroad.[126] If the application is made within six months, the order can begin from the date that child support ended.[127]

The courts also have the power to enforce orders and agreements, including those made by courts in other countries.[128]

In Scotland, if the CMS ceases to have jurisdiction to make a calculation in respect of a child, an order previously made revives from the date the CMS ceases to have jurisdiction.[129] The same is not explicitly stated for England and Wales, which means that the original order does not revive when CMS involvement ends. However, it could be argued that it should apply, since the court order has not been revoked but simply ceased to have effect for the duration of a child support calculation. If the original order does not revive, a new order or agreement must be obtained.

# 3. **How to apply**

Before applying to the Child Maintenance Service (CMS), a parent must contact the Child Maintenance Options service (see p2) and take part in a 'gateway' conversation. Child Maintenance Options is normally contacted by telephone or an online chat service. Face-to-face appointments may be arranged if required.

The gateway conversation is intended to encourage parents to consider the range of child maintenance options available before applying to the statutory scheme and, in particular, to consider making a private family-based arrangement. It is also intended to provide details of other support and information services. If you are an applicant and you state that you have experienced domestic violence (see below), you are fast-tracked through the gateway process to apply to the statutory scheme, rather than encouraged to consider an unsuitable family-based arrangement.

## Application fees

There is a fee of £20 for making an application to the CMS.[130] The fee is payable whether or not a child support calculation is actually made as a result of the application. An application is not treated as properly made until the fee is paid or is waived by the CMS.

If an application does not proceed because a qualifying child has died before the calculation is made, the fee must be refunded.[131]

The application fee must be waived if:[132]

- the applicant is aged 18 or under on the date of the application; *or*
- the CMS accepts that the applicant has experienced domestic violence or abuse.

The CMS accepts that an applicant has experienced domestic abuse or violence if s/he:

- has reported the violence or abuse to an 'appropriate person'; *and*
- informed the CMS that s/he has experienced domestic violence or abuse and that s/he has reported this to an appropriate person. The CMS must be informed at the time of making the application or in a written declaration that the CMS may ask the applicant to complete (provided the application fee has not already been paid before the declaration has been returned).

*Domestic violence*

The CMS has published guidance on how it decides whether a person has experienced domestic violence or abuse.[133]

'**Domestic violence**' is defined as 'any incident or pattern of incidents of controlling, coercive or threatening behaviour, violence or abuse towards the applicant which is between persons aged 16 or over who are or have been intimate partners or family members, regardless of gender or sexuality. This can encompass, but is not limited to, the following types of abuse: psychological, physical, sexual, financial, emotional.[1] Abuse can include a person witnessing the abuse of her/his child by a current or previous partner. The CMS has also published guidance on who is accepted as an '**appropriate person**' for these purposes.[134] These are:

– a court;
– the police;
– a medical professional;
– social services;
– a multi-agency risk assessment conference;
– a specialist domestic violence organisation or service, including a refuge;
– an employer;
– educational services;
– a local authority;
– a legal professional;
– specialist support services.

**Note:** an application fee has not been introduced in Northern Ireland.[135]

## Making the application

After the gateway conversation with Child Maintenance Options, if you wish to apply to the statutory scheme, you are given a unique 12-digit reference number that allows an application to be made. Child Maintenance Options does not deal with applications for the statutory scheme, but transfers people to the CMS at the end of the gateway conversation or provides a contact number for making an application to the CMS at a later date. If you do not have a reference number or you have lost or forgotten it, you are usually told to contact Child Maintenance Options first before the CMS proceeds with an application.

The CMS can determine how an application should be made and what information must be provided to process it.[136] In practice, this means that applications usually begin by contacting the CMS by telephone. Applications can also be made in writing. Contact details for the CMS can be found on the gov.uk website and in Appendix 1.

The CMS can require the applicant to provide any evidence or information reasonably needed to process the application (including sufficient information to allow the non-resident parent to be identified).[137] The application is treated as having been properly made when any information required to process it has been provided to the CMS.[138] In most cases, the CMS expects to gather information by telephone and paper application forms are not routinely issued. An application by a child in Scotland is always dealt with by telephone.

The reference number given by Child Maintenance Options is used to verify identity and personal details when contacting the CMS about the application.

## Information required for an application

An applicant is likely to have to provide the following information in order for the CMS to process an application:

- personal details – eg, name, address, national insurance (NI) number, date of birth, phone numbers and the best time to ring, and armed forces service number;
- child(ren) being applied for – eg, name, date of birth, NI number if 16 or over, who gets child benefit for the child, maintenance arrangements and any shared care arrangements (or local authority care);
- if the parent/person with care is applying, whether the non-resident parent knows that s/he is named as the parent and whether s/he knows where the applicant lives;
- the child's education (if aged 16–19) – eg, school/college, course, type of course and hours;
- local authority details (if the child is being cared for);
- the non-resident parent's details – eg, name and other names used, address or last known address and when s/he lived there, NI number, date of birth, employment details, phone numbers and whether the parent is the father or mother of the child;
- payment details – eg, whether child support is to be collected by the CMS, the preferred method and frequency of payment to the person with care and bank/building society details;
- details of any representative – eg, name, address, phone numbers and the best time to ring. If the representative is a solicitor, an attorney under a power of attorney, Scottish mental health guardian, mental health appointee or receiver, the representative can apply on behalf of the applicant.

The CMS may wish to see original documents to confirm certain details – eg, any relevant court order or a power of attorney document.

There are penalties for knowingly providing false information (see p39). See Chapter 3 for full details of the information requirements.

## Applications with more than one non-resident parent

An applicant can choose from which non-resident parent s/he wishes to apply for child support. So, if someone is a person with care of qualifying children of more than one non-resident parent, s/he could apply for child support from one (or more), but not necessarily all, of them.

## When to apply

There are no time limits for applying to the CMS. An application can be made as soon as someone becomes a person with care or a non-resident parent, or at any later date.[139] Liability to pay child support usually starts from two days after the date the non-resident parent was sent notification of the application. The CMS cannot do this until it receives an effective application (see below). This means that delaying the application may delay the start of liability. This is the case even if the reason for the delay is that the person with care has been in touch with the Child Maintenance Options service and is considering alternatives, such as setting up voluntary maintenance arrangements. You cannot apply in advance – eg, before the birth of a baby.

## If an application is refused

The CMS may refuse to accept an application – eg, because it believes an existing maintenance order prevents an application or because it does not have jurisdiction (see p16). If this happens, you should explain to the CMS why you believe you are entitled to apply and ask for a written decision. If a written decision is issued, you can try to challenge this by requesting a revision (see Chapter 9) and then appealing to the First-tier Tribunal (see Chapter 10). If this is not successful, or if the CMS refuses to respond in writing, a complaint (see Chapter 11) and/or judicial review (see p198) could be considered.

## Effective applications

The CMS can only make a child support calculation if the application is 'effective'.[140] This means that all applicants must provide information to enable the non-resident parent to be identified and traced and the amount of child support payable to be calculated and recovered (see Chapter 3).[141] If an applicant does not supply this information, the CMS may refuse to process the application (see p28).

The CMS cannot refuse to deal with an effective application, even if it considers that processing it would be against the welfare of the children concerned.[142] If the CMS refuses to accept an application, see above.

Once an effective application has been made, the address of the non-resident parent has been verified and any application fee due has been paid, the CMS must notify the non-resident parent in writing as soon as possible and ask her/him for any information required to determine her/his child support liability. (This applies even if the non-resident parent is the applicant.) S/he is informed of the 'effective date' of the application (see p131), that the CMS can estimate income in certain circumstances and of the rules on 'default maintenance decisions' (see p129).[143]

For delays in dealing with applications, including if the non-resident parent is not co-operating, see p127.

## Amending the application

An application can be amended at any time before a child support calculation is made, but not to take into account a change which occurs after the effective date. For details of this and of changes after the effective date, see p128.

# 4. **Withdrawing or cancelling an application**

## The applicant no longer wants to proceed

An applicant can request that the Child Maintenance Service (CMS) cancel her/his application for child support. The request can be made at any time, whether or not a calculation has been made. The CMS cannot refuse this request.[144] For more information on when an application is cancelled or a calculation ceases to have effect, see p132. Requests can be made by telephone or in writing to the CMS office processing the application.

## The Child Maintenance Service cancels an application

The CMS may cancel an application before a calculation is made if the applicant does not provide information (see below).

The rules are different if the qualifying child dies before the calculation decision is made (see below).

### An applicant does not provide information

The CMS can only cancel a case if no effective application has been made (see p27). If a person with care does not provide sufficient information, the CMS can close the case and s/he will not receive child support.

If there *is* an effective application, a decision must be made and notified to the parties, even if it is a decision not to make a calculation (see p128). If an effective application is cancelled against your wishes, get advice.

### The qualifying child dies

If a qualifying child dies before a calculation has been made, a decision on liability is still made for the period up to the date of her/his death. If the child was the only child named in the application, the decision is then cancelled with effect from the date of death; otherwise, it is changed (superseded) with effect from that date.[145]

# 5. **Multiple applications**

If more than one person applies for child support in respect of the same qualifying child before the decision on how much child support is payable is made, only one application can go ahead (see below).[146]

If one application is given priority, information provided in the other application may still be taken into account to help make a decision.

**Note:** once a calculation is in force, any subsequent application for child support made in the same circumstances in respect of the same person with care, non-resident parent and qualifying child(ren) may be treated as a request for a supersession (see p204) or, depending on the circumstances and information contained in the application, as a request for a variation (see Chapter 5).[147]

## Which application goes ahead

The Child Maintenance Service (CMS) decides which application goes ahead, using the following order of priority.[148]
- In Scotland, an application from a person with care or a non-resident parent has priority over an application from a child.
- In other circumstances, an earlier application has priority over a later one.

In the following circumstances, the CMS treats the applications as a single application in relation to the qualifying child.[149]
- An application is made and both parents of a qualifying child are non-resident – eg, an application made by a person with care who is not the parent of the qualifying child, or by a child in Scotland whose parents are both non-resident.
- Both parents of a qualifying child are non-resident and both apply for child support.

Although the law does not state this explicitly, if more than one application is made by the same person in the same circumstances, they are likely to be treated as if they were a single application if the calculation decision has not been made.

## Applications for additional children

If there is an existing child support calculation and an application is made for an additional child of the same non-resident parent cared for by the same person with care, this is a relevant change of circumstances. A new calculation is made which supersedes the existing one (see p204).

---

# 6. **Communicating with the Child Maintenance Service**

Most contact with the Child Maintenance Service (CMS) is by telephone. This is the CMS's preferred method of communication. You must make a request if you wish to be contacted by letter instead. Details of the relevant office handling the case are on any letters received from the CMS.

The CMS should answer telephone calls promptly. It should reply to letters, resolving the issue or agreeing what will happen next, within three weeks. If you have difficulty in contacting the CMS, or obtaining a response within a reasonable time, complain (see Chapter 11).

The CMS does not normally offer face-to-face interviews, but these may be arranged if the CMS considers that the case involves complex issues and an interview may help to resolve them more quickly. An interview may also be considered if someone has communication difficulties which make other methods problematic. A request for a face-to-face interview by anyone involved in a case should be considered seriously if the CMS agrees that it is the most effective way to make contact or if all other ways of progressing the case have been exhausted.

The CMS should also meet any accessibility or language needs of the applicant – eg, if English is not her/his first language or if s/he has difficulty using the telephone.

Once an application is made, applicants can register with the government 'gateway' to manage their case through an online account.[150] This allows applicants to check the progress of an application, opt in or out of a text messaging service, report changes in their circumstances, upload documents and personal details, make one-off payments and view calculation details and payment history.

It is always advisable to keep copies of letters and make a note of the date, time and content of telephone calls.

## Dates of postage

A document sent to the CMS is treated as being sent on the day the CMS receives it.[151] If the CMS posts a document to a person's last known address (or the address the person last notified to the CMS), it is treated as being received two days after the day it was posted.[152] It is understood that this is intended to exclude Sundays and bank holidays. A document is likely to be treated as having been 'sent' by the CMS if it was properly addressed, pre-paid and posted. Evidence that it was not received does not show that it was not sent.[153]

These rules are important when determining whether something has been done within a time limit.

**Note:** if no statutory timescale applies for a particular action to be done or for information to be provided, the CMS generally allows 14 days to provide information, and extends this to 16 days to allow for the time taken for information to reach the CMS by post.

## Representatives

Anyone dealing with the CMS can appoint a representative to act on her/his behalf.[154] If the person is not legally qualified, authorisation for her/him to act needs to be confirmed in writing, although if you are with the representative during a telephone call, you can authorise the representative verbally for the duration of the call. An authorised or legally qualified representative can complete forms, receive documents and supply information. A person with care may also choose to have payments of child support made to a representative.

A representative who understands the law and/or is experienced in dealing with the CMS may find it easier to get a quick response and clearer information from the CMS, and can advise about rights and options. For information about how to find independent advice, see Appendix 3.

A representative with legal authority to act for a CMS client (eg, someone with power of attorney, a receiver or a mental health appointee or Scottish mental health guardian) can act for her/him in every respect, as if s/he were the client.

The legal advice and assistance scheme in Scotland may help to cover costs in child support cases.

# Notes

**1. Who can apply for child support**
1   s1 CSA 1991
2   s7(1) CSA 1991
3   ss5(1) and 54 CSA 1991
4   s3(1) CSA 1991
5   s55(2) and (3) CSA 1991
6   Reg 76 CSMC Regs; s142(2) SSCBA 1992; reg 1(3) CB Regs; CCS/12604/1996
7   Reg 76 CSMC Regs; s142(2) SSCBA 1992; reg 3 CB Regs
8   CCS/1181/2005
9   Reg 76 CSMC Regs; s142(2) SSCBA 1992; reg 1(3) CB Regs; *CF v CMEC (CSM)* [2010] UKUT 39 (AAC); CCS/1181/2005
10  Reg 76 CSMC Regs; s142(2) SSCBA 1992; reg 6 CB Regs
11  s54 CSA 1991
12  s39 AA 1976; s39 A(S)A 1978; s26(2) CSA 1991, Case A
13  ss54 and 54A HF&EA 2008; s26(2) CSA 1991, Case B
14  ss27(2) and (3) and 29(1) HF&EA 1990
15  s28(2) HF&EA 1990; *Re CH (Contact: Parentage)* [1996] 1 FCR 768, [1996] 1 FLR 569, [1996] Fam Law 274
16  s28(6) HF&EA 1990
17  s28(3) HF&EA 1990
18  See *Re D (A Child Appearing by her Guardian Ad Litem)* [2005] UKHL 33
19  Because such a clinic would not have a UK licence: *U v W (A-G intervening)* [1997] 3 WLR 739, [1997] 2 CMLR 431, [1997] 2 FLR 282
20  ss35-37 HF&EA 2008
21  s42 HF&EA 2008
22  ss43 and 44 HF&EA 2008
23  ss40 and 46 HF&EA 2008
24  **EW** s67 A&CA 2002
    **S** s40 A&C(S)A 2007
    **All** s54 CSA 1991, definition of 'parent'
25  **EW** CA 1989
    **S** C(S)A 1995
26  **EW** s3(4) CA 1989
    **S** s3(3) C(S)A 1995
27  R(CS) 6/03
28  s2(1) CA 1989; s3(1) C(S)A 1995
29  ss4(1)(b) and 4ZA(1)(b) CA 1989; s4(1) and 4A(1) C(S)A 1995
30  s4A CA 1989, as amended by s75 CPA 2004
31  ss4(1)(c), 4ZA(1)(c), 4A(1)(b) and 5(6) CA 1989; s11 C(S)A 1995
32  s4(1)(a) CA 1989
33  Civil Partnership (Scotland) Bill (SP Bill 57, Session 5 (2019))
34  s4ZA(1)(a) CA 1989; s3(1)(c) and (d) C(S)A 1995
35  s3(3) CSA 1991
36  s54 CSA 1991
37  s3(3)(c) CSA 1991; reg 78(1) CSMC Regs
38  Reg 78(1)(b) and (d) CSMC Regs

39  *GR v CMEC (CSM)* [2011] UKUT 101
    (AAC)
40  R(CS) 11/02; *GR v CMEC (CSM)* [2011]
    UKUT 101 (AAC)
41  Reg 78(1)(b) and (d) CSMC Regs. This
    applies if a child is placed under s22C(2)
    CA 1989 or s81(2) Social Services and
    Well-being (Wales) Act 2014.
42  Reg 55 CSMC Regs
43  R(CS) 8/98
44  This principle was explicitly stated for
    the '2003 rules': reg 1(2)(b)(i),
    definition of 'day-to-day care',
    CS(MCSC) Regs
45  s3(2) CSA 1991
46  s1(3) CSA 1991
47  *RW v SSWP (CSM)* [2013] UKUT 576
    (AAC)
48  Reg 50 CSMC Regs
49  *Santos v Santos* [1972] 2 WLR 889,
    [1972] All ER 246 (CA)
50  CCS/2318/1997
51  CSB/463/1986
52  R(SB) 4/83
53  R(SB) 35/85
54  CCS/2332/2006
55  Reg 50 CSMC Regs
56  Reg 50(2) CSMC Regs
57  Reg 50(3) CSMC Regs
58  s144(3) and Sch 10 SSCBA 1992
59  Reg 50(4) CSMC Regs
60  *CF v SSWP and CG (CSM)* [2018] UKUT
    276 (AAC)
61  *JS v SSWP and another (CSM)* [2017]
    UKUT 296 (AAC); *MR v SSWP and LM
    (CSM)* [2018] UKUT 340 (AAC)
62  *CF v SSWP and CG (CSM)* [2018] UKUT
    276 (AAC)

**2. When an application can be accepted**
63  s8 CSA 1991
64  R(CS) 3/97
65  s44(1) CSA 1991
66  CCS/2314/2008; *AF v SSWP* [2009]
    UKUT 3 (AAC)
67  s44(2) CSA 1991
68  Sch 1 Interpretation Act 1978
69  *Nessa v Chief Adjudication Officer* [1998]
    2 All ER 728, [1998] 2 FCR 461, [1998] 1
    FLR 879, [1998] Fam Law 329 (CA),
    applying *Re J (A Minor) (Abduction:
    Custody Rights)* [1990] 2 AC 562, [1990]
    3 WLR 492, [1990] 2 All ER 961, [1991]
    FCR 129, [1990] 2 FLR 442, [1991] Fam
    Law 57 (HL); *Cruse v Chittum* [1974] 2 All
    ER 940; *Brokelmann v Barr* [1971] 3 All ER
    29; *Langford Property Co v Athanassoglou*
    [1948] 2 All ER 722

70  *Shah v Barnet LBC* [1983] 2 AC 309,
    [1983] 2 WLR 16, [1983] 1 All ER 226
    (HL)
71  *R (on the application of Nahar) v Social
    Security Commissioners* [2002] 1 FLR 670
72  CCS/2314/2008; *AF v SSWP (CSM)*
    [2009] UKUT 3 (AAC); *Armstrong v
    Armstrong* [2003] EWHC 777 (Fam),
    [2003] 2 FLR 375
73  *CJ v SSWP and VW (CSM)* [2017] UKUT
    498 (AAC); *Arthur v HMRC* [2017] EWCA
    Civ 1756
74  *AB v CD* [2018] EWHC 1021 (Fam)
75  *Re J (A Minor) (Abduction: Custody Rights)*
    [1990] 2 AC 562, [1990] 3 WLR 492,
    [1990] 2 All ER 961, [1991] FCR 129,
    [1990] 2 FLR 442, [1991] Fam Law 57
    (HL)
76  CCS/3574/2008; *H v CMEC* [2009]
    UKUT 84 (AAC)
77  *Shah v Barnet LBC* [1983] 2 AC 309,
    [1983] 2 WLR 16, [1983] 1 All ER 226
    (HL); *Re Mackenzie* [1940] 4 All ER 310
78  s44(2A) CSA 1991; reg 7A CS(MAJ) Regs
79  R(CS) 5/96
80  R(CS) 5/96
81  CSCS/6/2006
82  *B (A Minor: Habitual Residence)* [2016]
    EWHC 2174 (Fam) and *SR (A Child:
    Habitual Residence)* [2015] EWHC 742
    (Fam), citing and summarising the
    following UK Supreme Court
    judgments: *A v A (Children: Habitual
    Residence)* [2013] UKSC 60; in *Re L (A
    Child) (Custody: Habitual Residence)
    (Reunite International Child Abduction
    Centre intervening)* [2013] UKSC 75; in
    *Re LC (Children) (Reunite International
    Child Abduction Centre intervening)*
    [2014] UKSC 1; in *Re R (Children)
    (Reunite International Child Abduction
    Centre and others intervening)* [2015]
    UKSC 35; *Re B (A Child) (Habitual
    Residence: Inherent Jurisdiction)* [2016]
    UKSC 4.
83  *AB v CD* [2018] EWHC 1021 (Fam)
84  *AB v CD* [2018] EWHC 1021 (Fam)
85  s8(1), (3) and (4) CSA 1991. It has been
    decided that this lack of access to the
    courts is not inconsistent with Art 6(1)
    European Convention on Human Rights.
    See *R v SSWP ex parte Kehoe* [2005]
    UKHL 48.
86  s8(6)-(10) CSA 1991
87  **EW** MCA 1973
    **S** FL(S)A 1985
88  s8(7) CSA 1991
89  s8(8) and (9) CSA 1991

90  Sch 1 para 3(2)(b) CA 1989. In *C v F* [1997] 3 FCR 405 the court held that where s8(1) CSA 1991 applies, s8(8) CSA 1991 limits this power to children aged under 19. However, this seems to be wrong because the fact that CSA 1991 only applied at the time of the judgment to those aged under 19 cannot prevent an order being made under CA 1989 for a person aged 19 or over.

91  s8(10) CSA 1991

92  s8(6) CSA 1991; *Dickson v Rennie* [2014] EWHC 4306 (Fam)

93  s29(7) MCA 1973; s5(7) DPMCA 1978; Sch 1 para 3(57) and (6) CA 1989, as amended by Sch 3 paras 3, 5 and 10 CSPSSA 2000 respectively

94  Sch 1 para 1(2)(c) CA 1989; *Phillips v Pearce* [1996] 2 FLR 230

95  Reg 6 CS(MAJ) Regs

96  s9(2) CSA 1991

97  **EW** Child Maintenance (Written Agreements) Order 1993, No.620
**S** Child Support (Written Agreements) (Scotland) Order 1997, No.2943
**All** s8(5) CSA 1991

98  s9(1) CSA 1991

99  *SJ v SSWP (CSM)* [2014] UKUT 82 (AAC), reported as [2014] AACR 32

000  CCS/316/1998; CCS/8328/1995

100  s9(3) and (4) CSA 1991

101  ss4(10)(a) and 7(10)(a) CSA 1991; reg 2 CS(APD) Regs

102  ss4(10) and 7(10) CSA 1991; reg 2 CS(APD) Regs

103  CCS/316/1998; CCS/8328/1995

104  *YW v CMEC (CSM)* [2011] UKUT 176 (AAC)

105  CCS/4047/2007, citing *Dorney-Kingdom v Dorney-Kingdom* [2000] 2 FLR 855

106  s8(11) CSA 1991

107  CCS/4741/1995, upheld by the Court of Appeal in *AMS v CSO* [1998] 1 FLR 955

108  CCS/4049/2007

109  CCS/4049/2007. This and other cases have disagreed with the conclusions reached in R(CS) 4/96. The Court of Appeal in *Kirkley v Secretary of State for Social Security and the Child Support Officer* (unreported, December 15, 1995) ruling on an application for leave to appeal against R(CS) 4/96 also disagreed with the reasoning. Authorities differ as to whether changes in a child(ren)'s residence (eg, from the parent with care to the non-resident parent) mean that an order ceases to have effect (CCS/3127/1995) or not (CCS/2567/1998). In the latter case, the commissioner suggested that it would instead be grounds to seek to vary the court order.

110  CCS/4741/1995

111  CCS/11364/1995

112  Reg 9 CS(MAJ) Regs

113  s8(11) CSA 1991; reg 2 CS(MAJ) Regs. Provisions repealed before 1 April 1980 are not listed.

114  s8(4) CSA 1991; *B v M (Child Support: Revocation of Order)* [1994] 1 FLR 342, [1994] 1 FCR 769, [1994] Fam Law 370

115  Reg 5(1) CS(MAJ) Regs

116  s10(1) and (2) CSA 1991; reg 3(2) CS(MAJ) Regs

117  *Crozier v Crozier* [1994] 1 FLR 126; *Mawson v Mawson* [1994] 2 FLR 985

118  *Smith v McInerney* [1994] 2 FLR 1077. However, an arrangement like this might be void under s9(4) CSA 1991 because it would 'restrict the right to apply for a maintenance assessment', though the commissioner in CCS/2318/1997 thought not.

119  See the arrangement in CCS/2318/1997.

120  Reg 3(3) CS(MAJ) Regs

121  Reg 3(2) CS(MAJ) Regs

122  Reg 4 CS(MAJ) Regs

123  Reg 4(3) CS(MAJ) Regs

124  Reg 8(2) CS(MAJ) Regs

125  Reg 8(1) CS(MAJ) Regs

126  **EW** HMCTS, *A Guide to Reciprocal Enforcement of Maintenance Orders*, June 2015
**S** scotcourts.gov.uk/taking-action/frequently-asked-questions/reciprocal-enforcement

127  s29(7) MCA 1973; s5(7) DPMCA 1978; Sch 1 para 3(7) CA 1989

128  MO(RE)A 1992

129  Reg 3(4) CS(MAJ) Regs

### 3. How to apply
130  s6 CMOPA 2008; reg 3 CSF Regs 2014
131  Reg 5 CSF Regs 2014
132  Reg 4(1)-(3) CSF Regs 2014
133  DWP, *Guidance on Regulation 4(3) of the Child Support Fees Regulations 2014: how the Secretary of State will determine if an applicant is a victim of domestic violence or abuse,* July 2017, available at gov.uk
134  DWP, *Guidance on Regulation 4(3) of the Child Support Fees Regulations 2014: list of persons to whom an applicant must have reported domestic violence or abuse,* 2 December 2013, available at gov.uk
135  Department for Communities press release, 20 September 2013
136  Reg 9(1) CSMC Regs
137  Reg 9(1) CSMC Regs
138  Reg 9(2) CSMC Regs
139  R(CS) 10/02
140  Reg 9(2) CSMC Regs
141  ss4(4), 6(7) and 7(5) CSA 1991
142  R(CS) 4/96; CCS/14/1994; CCS/17/1994; CCS/16535/1996
143  Reg 11 CSMC Regs

### 4. Withdrawing or cancelling an application
144  ss4(6) and 6(5) CSA 1991
145  Reg 18(3) CSMC Regs

### 5. Multiple applications
146  s5(2) CSA 1991
147  *DB v CMEC* [2010] UKUT 356 (AAC). This decision relates to a '2003 rules' case. However, the same principle should apply to the '2012 rules', although this is not explicitly stated in those rules.
148  Reg 10(2) CSMC Regs
149  Reg 10(3) CSMC Regs

### 6. Communicating with the Child Maintenance Service
150  childmaintenanceservice.direct.gov.uk/onlinerevive/public/landing-screen
151  Reg 7(1) CSMC Regs
152  Reg 7(2) CSMC Regs
153  R(CS) 1/99
154  Reg 8 CSMC Regs

# Chapter 3

· · · · · · · · · · · · · · · · · · · · · · · · · · · · · · · · · · · · · · · · · · ·

# Information

**This chapter covers:**
1. Information-seeking powers (below)
2. Contacting the non-resident parent (p39)
3. Parentage investigations (p42)
4. Further investigations (p51)
5. Change of circumstances (p53)
6. Disclosure of information (p53)

## 1. Information-seeking powers

The Child Maintenance Service (CMS) has wide powers to obtain information from (among others) parents, employers, local authorities and HM Revenue and Customs (HMRC).[1] It can require information to be provided in order to make any child support decision.[2]

In addition, the CMS can appoint inspectors who have extensive powers to obtain information (see below). In general, CMS staff seek information by telephone, but may also carry out face-to-face enquiries.

### When information can be requested

After a child support application has been made, the non-resident parent is notified in writing (see p39). The date this notice is issued sets the 'effective date' for the calculation (see p131). The notice is followed up by a telephone call to the non-resident parent to gather and confirm information.

The CMS can request information in order to:[3]
- determine an application for child support and any issues that arise from it – eg, to establish which parent is the child's main carer if care is shared (see p14);
- make any other decisions – eg, to determine the income of the non-resident parent;
- enable child support to be calculated, collected and enforced.

See p36 for who can be required to give information, and p39 for what happens if someone fails to provide it.

## What information can be requested

The CMS can request information on many issues, including:
- the habitual residence of the person with care, the non-resident parent and any child covered by the application, to determine whether the CMS has jurisdiction;
- the name and address of the person with care and non-resident parent, their marital or civil partnership status, and the relationship of the person with care to any child covered by the application;
- the name, address and date of birth of any child covered by the application, the child's marital or civil partnership status and details of the child's education;
- if there is more than one person with care:
  - who has parental responsibility (or parental rights in Scotland) for any qualifying child; *and*
  - how much time is spent by that child with each person with care;
- who is the parent of a child or, if parentage is disputed, information to determine whether someone can be assumed to be a parent (see p44);
- the name and address of any current or recent employer of a non-resident parent and her/his gross earnings from that employment;
- if the non-resident parent is self-employed, the address, trading name, gross receipts and expenses, other outgoings and taxable profits of the trade or business;
- any other income of the non-resident parent;
- how much is paid or payable under a court maintenance order or maintenance agreement;
- details of anyone who lives in the same household as the non-resident parent, their relationship, and the date of birth of any child(ren);
- details and statements of any account in the name of the non-resident parent, including bank and building society accounts (and including joint accounts);
- whether someone counts as a qualifying child for child support purposes (see p8);
- information to decide whether a calculation should end (see p131).

## Who must provide information

Information can be required from the following, if they have the information or evidence in their possession or can reasonably be expected to acquire and provide it:[4]
- a 'relevant person' – ie, the person with care, non-resident parent or child applicant in Scotland (see below);
- someone who denies parentage of a child (see below);
- court officials (see below);
- the Department for Work and Pensions (DWP – see p38);

- HMRC (see p38);
- others, including employers, local authorities and banks (see p38).

Information or evidence can also be given to the CMS when there is no obligation to provide it – eg, from a relative, neighbour or landlord. For information on disclosure by the CMS, see p53.

## A relevant person

All child support applicants must provide information required by the CMS to:[5]
- identify and trace a non-resident parent; *or*
- calculate, collect or recover child support.

The person with care and non-resident parent (or a parent treated as non-resident – see p14) must provide the information listed on p36, if requested.[6] A child applicant in Scotland must provide the same information, except information enabling the non-resident parent to be identified.[7]

If information is not provided by a person with care (or child applicant in Scotland), the application may be treated as withdrawn (see p28). If a non-resident parent does not supply the requested information, a 'default maintenance decision' may be made (see p129).

## Someone who denies parentage of a child

Someone who denies parentage of a child named in an application is required to give information:[8]
- to identify a non-resident parent; *or*
- to decide whether or not all the relevant people are habitually resident in the UK and, therefore, whether the CMS has jurisdiction.

This means, for example, that if the CMS only wants to identify someone as the non-resident parent, her/his employment details would not normally be necessary and so should not be requested until parentage is established.

## Court officials

Certain court officials can be required to give information for the purposes listed on p36 – eg, to allow the CMS to:[9]
- identify how much is payable under a court maintenance order;
- collect child support or maintenance under a court order;
- identify any proceedings about a court maintenance order;
- decide whether a maintenance order is in force that may affect whether an application can be made (see p18);
- decide who has parental responsibility for the qualifying child if there is more than one person with care (see p10).

## The Department for Work and Pensions

Any DWP agency or anyone providing services to the DWP may give information held for benefit purposes to the CMS.[10]

## HM Revenue and Customs

There are specific arrangements for passing information about the non-resident parent's gross income from HMRC to the CMS (see p68).

In addition, HMRC can be required to disclose information or evidence for the purposes listed on p36.[11] Information provided can be used for any function related to child support. If a parent is self-employed, this also includes details of her/his taxable profits, gross receipts and expenses. It is unlawful for HMRC to give the CMS any other information.[12]

## Others

The CMS can also require the following to provide information for the purposes listed on p36:

- current or previous employers of the non-resident parent;[13]
- people or organisations for whom the non-resident parent provides, or has provided, goods or services under a contract.[14] This could include individuals, a company or partnership, or a government department, and means, for example, that a self-employed consultant could be traced and have her/his income investigated through companies for which s/he has provided services;
- a person who acts, or has acted, as the non-resident parent's accountant;[15]
- credit reference agencies;[16]
- the local authority in whose area either the non-resident parent or person with care lives or has lived.[17] The CMS may require the local authority to provide information, such as address and bank account details, relating to, for example, rent and council tax or a housing benefit claim;[18]
- the Driver and Vehicle Licensing Agency. In particular, it may be asked for information needed to trace the non-resident parent, and to collect and enforce payments;[19]
- prison authorities;[20]
- banks and building societies. See p170 for details of specific information requirements on banks or building societies in relation to enforcement action to deduct funds from an account, particularly joint or business accounts;[21]
- gas and electricity suppliers;[22]
- mortgage lenders (qualifying lenders include banks, building societies, insurers and local authorities);[23]
- trustees, managers or administrators of occupational pension schemes.[24]

## When must the information be provided

A person who has been requested to provide information must do so if that information or evidence is in her/his possession or if s/he can reasonably be expected to acquire and provide it.[25]

The information must be provided as soon as it is reasonably practicable.[26] The CMS can allow information to be provided by a later date if it is satisfied that the delay is unavoidable.

See p30 for when documents are treated as having been sent and received.

## What happens if the correct information is not provided

It is a criminal offence for a person, without reasonable excuse, to fail to provide information, to provide false information or to allow false information to be provided.[27] All requests for information issued by the CMS must state this.[28]

If someone fails to provide information or provides false information, the CMS may decide not to process the application (see p28). If a parent does not give the required information, the CMS may ask another person for the information – eg, her/his employer or accountant. If s/he is a non-resident parent, a default maintenance decision may be made (see p129). A decision based on her/his estimated income could be made in certain circumstances instead (see p73).

The CMS may also go to court, and a fine (currently up to £1,000) can be imposed on anyone who is required to provide information and fails, without reasonable excuse, to do so. Fines are paid to the court, not to the CMS. A non-resident parent who fails to provide information may have both a default maintenance decision and a fine imposed. If a non-resident parent makes an application and the parent with care fails to provide information, the parent with care can be fined, although this would be rare.

### Disputing the information required

A request for information can be challenged (see p198) if:
- it is not relevant to the reason for the request; *or*
- it is of a very different kind from the examples given in the regulations; *or*
- it is made to a person who cannot be required to give it; *or*
- the CMS already has sufficient information to make a full calculation.

If you think this applies to any information the CMS has asked you to provide, explain this, preferably in writing, in order to avoid a penalty. A complaint could also be made (see Chapter 11).

## 2. Contacting the non-resident parent

When a new child support application is made, the applicant must verify the address of the non-resident parent and pay the application fee (see p24). The

Child Maintenance Service (CMS) must then notify the non-resident parent in writing as soon as reasonably practical. The notification asks about any information needed to make the calculation. The non-resident parent may dispute any of the facts relating to the application at this point (see above). The date on which liability for child support usually starts (known as the 'initial effective date' – see p131) is specified in the notice. The CMS may telephone the non-resident parent on or before the initial effective date and then confirm this in writing to the parent's last known address. If the CMS does not telephone the parent, it must send written notice to her/his last known address at least two days before the initial effective date.[29] The initial effective date is usually expected to be two days after the written notice is issued.

If you are the person with care and there is a long delay by the CMS in starting this process, you can complain (see Chapter 11).

## Tracing the non-resident parent

The CMS can use its information-seeking powers (including contacting the people and agencies on pp36–38) to identify and trace the non-resident parent.

### Finding a reliable address

The CMS seeks to confirm the identity and address of the non-resident parent from information given by the person with care, Department for Work and Pensions (DWP) computer records and other methods. The CMS can decide that an address it holds for the non-resident parent can reliably be used as her/his current address, without having to establish it beyond all reasonable doubt.[30] If the DWP computer gives the non-resident parent's address and it is the same as that of the person with care, this is not considered reliable.

### Information from the person with care

When s/he applies for child support, the person with care is asked for the address of the non-resident parent, or for any information that could help trace her/him. This could include:

- her/his middle name(s) and any other names by which s/he may be known;
- other addresses at which s/he may have lived;
- her/his place of work and any previous employers;
- the name and address of her/his accountant;
- any benefit claims made; *and*
- if s/he has a car, the registration or make, model, colour and other details.

The CMS may contact the person with care again if additional information is required – eg, if parentage is disputed. A parent may be asked to provide a recent photograph of the non-resident parent if DNA testing may be involved, and to provide any relevant documents, such as a marriage certificate or expired passport. A person with care could also be asked other detailed questions – eg, whether the non-resident parent has ever lived with her/him. The CMS may contact friends and relatives with whom the non-resident parent may be living. If it does this, it must preserve confidentiality and should not disclose its interest.

The CMS does not normally offer face-to-face interviews (see p29), but these may be arranged if the CMS considers that the case involves complex issues and an interview may help to resolve them more quickly.

## Initial contact with the non-resident parent

The initial notification (see p39) to the non-resident parent that an application has been made includes a provisional child support calculation, based on the details provided by the applicant and information received by the CMS from HM Revenue and Customs (HMRC) or other parts of the DWP.[31] This is not a decision, but an illustration of the non-resident parent's child support liability based on the information the CMS currently has. It takes account of any information about shared care provided by the applicant.

The notification advises the non-resident parent of any information that s/he is required to provide for the child support calculation decision to be made. Details of the non-resident parent's income are normally provided to the CMS automatically by HMRC (see p68), unless HMRC has no income data or is unable to supply it, in which case the non-resident parent is asked for this.

A few days after issuing the notification, the CMS phones the non-resident parent to obtain information for the calculation decision. If the CMS is unable to contact the non-resident parent by telephone, a reminder notice is issued in writing. If there is no response from the parent after 14 days, the CMS may then make a default maintenance decision (see p129) or, in certain circumstances, a calculation based on estimated income (see p73).

**Note:** the CMS intends to obtain all (or most) of the information needed to work out child support by phone. If a non-resident parent prefers to be contacted in writing, s/he must request this.

If the parent is unaware of the child or is not named on the birth certificate, the CMS may try to arrange a face-to-face interview, although this is not expected to be done often.

There are special rules for young non-resident parents (see p42).

During the initial phone call, the non-resident parent may be asked questions in order to obtain or confirm any information needed to make a calculation. This information can also be provided by the parent in writing if s/he wishes.

For example, the non-resident parent may be asked to confirm:

- personal details – eg, name, address, other names used, phone number(s), national insurance (NI) number, date of birth and best contact times;
- details required to confirm whether the CMS has jurisdiction;
- whether s/he accepts parentage for the named qualifying child(ren);
- any means-tested benefits being claimed by, or for, her/him;

- student details, if appropriate – eg, name of college, course and qualification, and whether it is full or part time (evidence is requested);
- children who live with her/him – eg, date of birth, NI number (if appropriate) and who gets child benefit for the child (evidence is requested);
- details of any shared care or other special arrangements;
- employment details – eg, job title, employer (name, address and phone number), and start and end dates (if appropriate);
- income details – eg, frequency of pay, gross pay, bonuses and expenses (pay slips may be requested);
- self-assessment form or tax calculation notice if the parent is self-employed;
- any other income – eg, pensions;
- payments made to a personal or private pension;
- collection details – eg, when the CMS will collect the child support and bank details, such as account number and sort code;
- representative details – eg, name, address, phone number and best contact times (signed authorisation is needed in certain circumstances).

The non-resident parent should be warned that a default maintenance decision (see p129) or, in certain circumstances, a calculation based on an estimate of income (see p73), may be made if s/he fails to provide sufficient information to make a calculation. At various stages, s/he is given the opportunity to provide more information, and is usually given at least seven days to do so.

S/he must also be informed that failure to provide the information requested, or knowingly to provide false information, is a criminal offence (see p39).

Information given can be amended at any time before a calculation is made. See p204 for what happens if there is a change in circumstances after the effective date.

## Young non-resident parents

A face-to-face interview is likely to be arranged with a young non-resident parent – ie, one under 16 years of age (or aged 16–19 and treated as a child – see p8). No calculation can be made until the non-resident parent ceases to be treated as a child, but s/he is asked to confirm parentage for future reference. An adult must be present at the interview.

# 3. **Parentage investigations**

Disputes about whether someone is the parent (see p9) of a qualifying child can arise both before and after a child support calculation is made. The dispute can be about one or all of the qualifying children. Parentage is most commonly disputed by alleged non-resident fathers.

If the parentage of a qualifying child is denied or is in doubt, a child support application cannot be decided unless the Child Maintenance Service (CMS) can assume parentage (see p44) or parentage is determined.

An alleged non-resident parent may deny parentage during the initial phone contact with the CMS or in writing before a calculation is made.

The CMS can proceed with the calculation for any children for whom parentage is accepted or assumed while investigations are taking place for others.

The CMS carries out investigations to determine whether parentage may be established or assumed. Both the non-resident parent and person with care can submit evidence to resolve the matter, and may be interviewed (see p45). The qualifying child's other parent may also be interviewed if s/he is not the person with care. The CMS may seek a DNA test or court action to establish parentage. The person with care or alleged non-resident parent may also pursue court action at any time.

If an alleged non-resident parent accepts parentage when responding to CMS enquiries, neither the CMS nor the First-tier Tribunal can then cancel the child support calculation, unless a court decides that s/he is not, in fact, the parent.[32]

Once a calculation has been made, a non-resident parent who then disputes parentage can request a revision (see Chapter 9). However, s/he must still pay child support until s/he provides conclusive evidence that s/he is not the parent.[33] At this stage, it is not sufficient to deny parentage: evidence must be provided to raise doubt – eg, if the parent with care was having another relationship when the child was conceived.

If the alleged non-resident parent provides evidence in the form of a previous negative DNA test or a declaration/declarator of parentage, this is sufficient proof that s/he is not the parent.[34] The child support calculation is then cancelled and any payments made may be refunded. Whether or not all payments made are refunded may depend on how long after the calculation was made the parent disputed parentage, and a refund may only be made from the date when parentage was denied.[35]

If evidence provided by the alleged non-resident parent is not conclusive but raises a doubt about parentage, the parent with care is contacted by the CMS for comments on the non-resident parent's evidence.

- If the parent with care accepts that there may be doubt about parentage, a DNA test may be offered.
- If the parent with care disputes the non-resident parent's evidence, the decision is not revised. The non-resident parent is advised to obtain a DNA test or declaration/declarator of non-parentage; the CMS does not offer a DNA test in this case. The alleged non-resident parent is informed of her/his right to appeal to a court.

If a decision is not revised, the alleged non-resident parent may have to apply to the family court (in England and Wales) or the sheriff court (in Scotland) for a declaration/declarator of parentage. A decision to refuse to revise can be challenged (see Chapter 10), but parentage can only ultimately be established by the court.

## When someone is assumed to be a parent

If a person denies being the parent of a child, in certain circumstances the CMS must assume that s/he is the parent. (This does not apply if the child has subsequently been adopted by someone else.) S/he must then co-operate with the CMS, unless the CMS accepts proof that s/he is not, in fact, the parent of the child. The CMS must assume parentage if:[36]

- in England, Wales or Northern Ireland, a declaration of parentage or, in Scotland, a declarator of parentage, is in force for that person, including if the person with care or the CMS has applied to court for a declaration on whether the person is a parent of the child;[37]
- in England and Wales,[38] the person is a man who:
  - was married to, or in a civil partnership with, the mother at any time between the child's conception and birth; or
  - acknowledged his paternity and was acknowledged by the mother and was named as the father on the birth certificate issued in the UK;
- in Scotland, the above also apply, except where the person is a man who was in a civil partnership with the mother.[39] **Note:** equivalent changes to the law relating to civil partnerships between different-sex couples in Scotland are proposed but not yet enacted;[40]
- the person is a man who was found to be the father by a court in England or Wales in proceedings under certain legal provisions (see Appendix 2). The court decision usually states the legal provision under which it was made;[41]
- the person is a man who was found by a court in Northern Ireland to be a father in proceedings under similar legal provisions to those in Appendix 2;[42]
- the person is a man who was found by a court in Scotland to be the father in any action for affiliation or aliment;[43]
- the person is a man who refuses to take a DNA test, or if the result of a test shows that he is the father (even if he refuses to accept it);[44]
- a parental order has been made in favour of that person following an application made within six months of a birth which is the result of a surrogacy arrangement;[45]
- certain types of fertility treatment have been carried out by a licensed clinic and the person is treated as a parent of the child under the Human Fertilisation and Embryology Acts 1990 and 2008.[46]

If none of the above applies, the CMS cannot make a calculation until parentage is admitted by a person or decided by a court.

If no one can be assumed to be a parent, the CMS usually attempts to arrange voluntary DNA testing or applies to court for a declaration/declarator of parentage.

If the alleged non-resident parent disputes that the rules apply (eg, s/he says the person named in a court order is someone else), s/he can appeal against the CMS decision. This appeal is dealt with by the family/sheriff court rather than by the First-tier Tribunal.[47]

If the alleged non-resident parent accepts that the rules apply, but disputes the correctness of the court order referred to by the CMS (eg, the court declaration/ declarator of parentage was wrong), s/he should consider applying to the court to set aside its order and/or making a late appeal against it. It is not possible to challenge a decision about parentage through the revision and appeals process outlined in this *Handbook*.

## Interviews if parentage is disputed

If parentage is denied after the CMS's initial contact, the parent with care may be interviewed in order to establish the case to be put to the alleged non-resident parent. In other cases, sufficient information may already be available to contact the non-resident parent. However, both parties are interviewed before offering DNA tests (see p50) and, even if the parent with care has already been interviewed or parentage is assumed, s/he may be reinterviewed to see how s/he responds to the alleged non-resident parent's version of events. If the parent with care has already completed a parentage statement, s/he is only reinterviewed if the alleged non-resident parent has new evidence.

Interviews are usually conducted by phone. If someone does not want to be interviewed in this way, an interview may be conducted in the CMS office or at her/his home. It is not compulsory to take part in any interview, but see p36 for who can be required to provide certain information.

If the parent with care or alleged non-resident parent is under 16 (or 16–19 and treated as a child – see p8), her/his parent or guardian must consent to the application progressing. The young person must have a face-to-face interview in the presence of a parent or guardian. A child support calculation is not made for a young person in these circumstances, but a parentage statement is required for future use. Additional information may be sought about a young alleged non-resident parent to determine whether or not s/he should be treated as a child – eg, details of her/his current education or training.

### Interviewing the alleged non-resident parent

If the alleged non-resident parent denies parentage, s/he is asked whether s/he has evidence that s/he is not the parent. S/he may ask for further time to obtain documentary evidence: seven days is usually allowed.

If documentary evidence cannot be supplied, the person with care may be interviewed to gather her/his evidence. If no evidence can be provided to establish or assume parentage (see p44), the case may progress to DNA testing.

In an interview with an alleged father, the CMS could ask:

- whether he was in the country at any time between the date of conception and the child's birth;
- whether he had sex with the mother and, if so, over what period of time;
- if conception was assisted, whether he agreed to the treatment;
- how long the relationship lasted and whether he lived with the woman as husband and wife;
- whether or not he has had any contact with the child(ren);
- his reasons for thinking that he is not the father; *and*
- whether there is any other information that might support his view.

This is not an exhaustive list. The alleged non-resident parent need only answer such questions if he denies parentage and the information is needed to decide the issue.

The alleged non-resident parent is sent information about disputing parentage and the reduced-cost DNA test (see p47) before the interview. At the interview, the possibility of DNA testing is explained and his agreement sought.[48]

Interviewing officers should take notes, and details of the interview (including any statement made by the non-resident parent) should be recorded.

If the alleged non-resident parent does not comply with requests to be interviewed, the CMS may consider a home visit or court action.

If the alleged non-resident parent accepts parentage, the CMS proceeds to make a child support calculation.

## Interviewing the parent with care

If someone has been named as the parent of a qualifying child and denies it, the CMS informs the parent with care of this and explains the procedures that follow.

The parent with care is asked for any documentary evidence from which the CMS could assume parentage – eg, a birth or marriage certificate.[49] S/he is also questioned about her/his relationship with the alleged non-resident parent.

If no evidence can be provided to establish or assume parentage, the parent with care is asked whether s/he is willing to take a DNA test (see p47).

The CMS asks about the alleged relationship and the circumstances of conception and birth. A mother who is the parent with care is likely to be asked personal questions including:

- the place the child was born and whether the pregnancy was full term;
- who are named as the child's parents on the birth certificate;
- the man's reaction to the pregnancy;
- whether she and the alleged non-resident parent ever lived together and, if so, when and where;

- whether she considered them to be a couple at the time the child was conceived;
- whether the alleged non-resident parent has ever acknowledged the child;
- whether the alleged non-resident parent has ever paid any maintenance;
- whether there is, or has been, any contact with his family;
- whether she has any letters or cards acknowledging the child, or witnesses to her association with the alleged non-resident parent;
- whether the child's conception was assisted and, if so, whether the man agreed to the treatment and gave notice of this;
- whether she has any photographs of him; *and*
- whether she is willing to give evidence in court.

If you are a parent with care and consider the question(s) inappropriate, you should question their relevance. If the interviewer insists, you could ask to end the interview to consider whether or not to provide the information. You can ask the interviewer to write down the questions and the reason for them. If, at the interview or later, you refuse to answer any of the questions, you should indicate that you have given all the information that is necessary to trace and identify the father.

A parent with care may also be asked to make a parentage statement. You can refuse to sign this and the refusal forms part of the evidence, along with any reasons given. You may ask for a copy of the parentage statement and your reasons for not signing it. The statement is added to the report of the interview and can be used in court proceedings (see p50).

### Interviewing a person with care who is not the parent

If both parents are non-resident and an alleged non-resident parent continues to deny parentage after an interview, the person with care may be interviewed. The questions depend on the person with care's relationship with the alleged parents – eg, a grandparent may know the length of the relationship between the parents. S/he is asked for the addresses of both parents, and any letters or cards from them. S/he is also asked why s/he is looking after the child(ren), whether there is any documentation about the care arrangements and whether s/he gives her/his consent for the child(ren) in her/his care to undergo a DNA test (see below) if s/he has parental responsibility.

## DNA testing

DNA testing involves taking a cell sample from the parent with care, alleged non-resident parent and qualifying child. The test establishes the genetic fingerprint of the individual and is virtually conclusive. The test is usually done by taking a cheek cell sample from the inside of the mouth using a swab. It is possible for blood to be taken for the DNA test instead, but all parties must use the same method. If young children are involved, a cheek cell sample is usually preferred.

DNA testing is used when parentage cannot be assumed and the parties involved give their consent. If the CMS has applied to a court for a declaration/declarator of parentage, the court may order DNA testing.

The CMS arranges the DNA test. An alleged non-resident parent can also choose to arrange his own test (see p49).[50]

## Consent

If there is a dispute about parentage, both the parent with care and the alleged non-resident parent are asked to agree to a DNA test. Written consent must be obtained before a test can be carried out. If the qualifying child is under 16, her/his parent or guardian must give consent.

There are consequences if someone refuses to take the test.

- If the parent with care accepts DNA testing, but refuses consent for the child, a court can direct DNA testing if it is in the best interests of the child, but it cannot force the child to take the test.
- An alleged non-resident parent may be assumed to be the parent (see p44).[51]
- If a non-resident parent already assumed to be the parent refuses to take a test, the CMS will not revise the calculation.
- If a child support applicant refuses consent for her/himself and/or a qualifying child, the case may be closed.
- There is no guidance on what happens when a parent or guardian of a child applicant in Scotland refuses consent, but Department for Work and Pensions policy indicates that action may be taken to get a declarator of parentage.

The reason for any refusal must be explored. As the DNA test usually involves taking a cheek cell sample, any objections (eg, to blood tests on medical or religious grounds) may not be regarded as reasonable.

If the alleged non-resident parent agrees to the test, but fails to attend the appointment, parentage is assumed unless there are good reasons – eg, he was in hospital, did not receive the test notification or was ill.

If a qualifying child aged 16 or over refuses consent, the non-resident parent must apply to the court for a declaration/declarator of non-parentage.

## Paying for a DNA test arranged by the Child Maintenance Service

If an alleged non-resident parent is found to be the father, he is responsible for the costs of tests arranged by the CMS. He is responsible for the costs for himself, the parent with care and the child(ren). If he is found not to be the father, a full refund of the cost of the test is made.[52]

At the time this *Handbook* was written, the fee for a test arranged by the CMS was £239.40. The fee is higher if more than one child is tested.[53]

If the alleged non-resident parent says he cannot afford to pay for the test before a calculation is made, the CMS may pay for it, provided he agrees to accept the results and to repay the fee should the test show that he is the father. If he still refuses to take the DNA test, parentage may be assumed (see p44).

The CMS can recover the costs of the test from the alleged non-resident parent if the test does not exclude him from being the father and:[54]
- he does not now deny that he is the father; *or*
- a court has now made a declaration/declarator of parentage.

## Private testing

An alleged non-resident parent may choose to arrange the test himself. In the meantime, the CMS may still assume parentage if the CMS test has been refused.[55] Prices vary depending on which company is used, but are likely to be higher than for a test arranged by the CMS. If the alleged parent has arranged a test himself, the fee is not refunded if the test proves negative.

The test must be carried out by an approved agency and proper security measures must be in place; otherwise, even if the test is negative, the CMS and court may not accept the result.[56]

Tests must involve the parent with care; a test with only the alleged non-resident parent and the qualifying child is not accepted. No action can be taken against a parent with care who does not consent to a private test. If the alleged non-resident parent cannot arrange a private test because he does not know the address of the parent with care, the CMS does not provide contact details.

## DNA test results

Once the DNA-testing company has received all the samples, the test usually takes 10 days. The results are sent by post to the parent with care, the alleged non-resident parent and the CMS. The results are confidential and are not given by phone.[57]

If the alleged non-resident parent is shown to be the parent, he is also sent notification by the CMS. The CMS also asks for any additional information needed. (The 'effective date' of liability for child support remains the date two days after the original notification of the application was sent – see p131.) If the alleged non-resident parent still does not accept parentage, he must take court action to obtain a declaration/declarator of non-parentage. The CMS may make a calculation (or, if already made, refuse to revise one) because a positive DNA test is grounds to assume parentage.

If the DNA tests confirm that the person who took the test as the alleged non-resident parent is not the parent, action is taken to confirm the identity of the person tested. If the alleged non-resident parent sent someone else to take the test, the CMS passes the case to the fraud team. If the wrong person has been traced, the CMS pursues further tracing. If the identity is confirmed, the parent with care may be reinterviewed about any other possible non-resident parent.[58]

## Court proceedings

When all possible action and investigations have been completed, the CMS may decide to apply to a court for a declaration/declarator of parentage.[59] Court action is rare, as there are other ways of being able to assume parentage (see p44). Examples of situations where court action may be taken include:

- if a DNA test is inconclusive;
- cases involving fertility treatment where an alleged non-resident father denies he consented to the treatment;
- if the parent with care disputes the non-resident parent's inconclusive evidence after a child support calculation has been made. In this case, the non-resident parent must apply to court (the CMS may not be involved in this action, but may be informed of the outcome).

If the CMS decides not to take court action, the person with care may initiate proceedings her/himself.[60] The person with care or non-resident parent may start court proceedings at any time.

The CMS or the person with care can apply to court for a declaration/declarator of parentage. If the CMS is willing to do so, usually the person with care should not also apply, because s/he will probably have to pay her/his own legal costs (and those of the alleged non-resident parent) if s/he loses (see below). If the CMS suspends the case, but the person with care wants to go to court her/himself, s/he should obtain legal advice.

Only the courts have the power to order blood tests (including DNA tests – see p47) in any civil proceedings in which parentage is an issue.[61] If convinced that blood testing would be against the child's interests, the court should not order it.[62] A court can direct that blood tests be used to establish whether or not someone is a parent of the child, but cannot force anyone to give a blood sample. It can, however, overrule a child's lack of consent if it believes it is in the child's interests.[63] However, the court may draw its own adverse conclusions if a person fails to comply, depending on the circumstances of the case.[64] The costs of testing ordered by the court are treated as the costs of the party who applied for the testing.[65] However, if that person wins the case, the court usually orders the losing party to pay costs, which can include the costs of any test. In Scotland, if an alleged non-resident parent applies for a declarator of non-parentage and the CMS does not defend the action, no expenses can be awarded against the CMS.[66]

### Outcome of the court proceedings

If no child support calculation has been made, once a declaration/declarator of parentage is issued, the CMS contacts the non-resident parent to gather the information needed to make it.[67]

If the court finds that the person is not the parent, the parent with care is approached to establish whether a different alleged non-resident parent can be named.[68] Unless the parent can name an alternate alleged non-resident parent, the case may be closed.

The court can order any party to pay some, or all, of the legal costs of another party – eg, solicitors' fees. Usually, the losing party is ordered to pay the other party's costs.

# 4. Further investigations

The Child Maintenance Service (CMS) may make further enquiries when considering an application. In practice, the CMS usually makes no further investigations if:

- parentage is accepted; *and*
- information is provided to make a calculation; *and*
- any documents requested are provided – eg, a copy of a maintenance agreement, pay slips or a tax calculation notice.

Even if one parent challenges the details provided by the other, the CMS may be reluctant to make any further enquiries unless the parent can provide sufficient evidence to give the CMS reasonable grounds to investigate – ie, to persuade the CMS that there are grounds for a revision or supersession to be considered.

The CMS should not request any corroboration of evidence (ie, other evidence to support what the CMS already has), unless the evidence the CMS has is self-contradictory, improbable or contradicted by other evidence.[69]

## Asking the Child Maintenance Service to investigate

If you are not satisfied with the way the CMS has investigated the case, you can ask it to make further enquiries. Phone the CMS and explain all the information, ask what enquiries have already been made and suggest further ones. Refer to the CMS's power to request information (see p35) and to use an inspector to conduct investigations (see below). If the CMS refuses to say what steps have been taken or to make further enquiries, a complaint can be made (see Chapter 11) and judicial review may be possible (see p198).

If an appeal has been made, the First-tier Tribunal can also make enquiries (see Chapter 10). It has more powers than the CMS and it may be easier to persuade it to use them.

If you are dissatisfied with the CMS's enquiries, you can also make your own and pass the information to the CMS.

## Inspectors

The CMS can appoint inspectors to obtain the information it requires.[70] The inspector must have a certificate of appointment, which must be produced when entering premises.[71]

Inspectors can enter premises (except those used only as a home) to make enquiries and to inspect documents. They can do so at any reasonable time, and can do so either alone or accompanied by anyone they consider appropriate. An inspector must obtain a warrant from the magistrates' court (in England and Wales) or sheriff court (in Scotland) to enter premises if they are occupied and the occupant(s) have refused to allow her/him entry, or are likely to refuse entry without a warrant.[72]

'Premises' can include vehicles, aircraft, moveable structures and offshore installations. Inspectors cannot enter premises by force. The premises that can be entered include ones where:[73]

- the non-resident parent is, or has been, employed;
- the non-resident parent carries out, or has carried out, a trade;
- there is information held by someone whom the inspector has reasonable grounds for suspecting has information about the non-resident parent acquired in the course of her/his own trade, profession, vocation or business.

Inspectors usually contact the occupier of the premises by phone or letter to arrange a mutually suitable time for the entry and inspection. They will also advise the occupier of the duty to provide information and the penalties if s/he fails to do so or if s/he obstructs an inspector. Where an inspector intends to apply for a warrant, s/he must give the occupier at least 21 days' notice of her/his intention to do so. A warrant expires one month after being issued.[74]

An inspector can question any person aged 18 or over found on the premises and request information and documents s/he might reasonably require from:[75]

- an occupier of the premises;
- an employer or employee working there;
- anyone else whose work or business is based there;
- an employee or agent of any of the above.

No one is required to give any evidence or answer any question that might incriminate her/him or her/his spouse or civil partner. Deliberately delaying or obstructing an inspector from carrying out her/his duties is an offence. Where the premises are occupied, delaying or obstructing an inspector is an offence only if the inspector has a warrant authorising entry. Failing or refusing to answer a question or to provide the evidence requested is also an offence, unless there is a good reason for not doing so. The maximum fine is currently £1,000.[76]

A solicitor is entitled to claim 'privilege' concerning information about a client's confidential affairs and can refuse to give information. The CMS has also given assurances that the powers of inspectors will not be used to investigate other representatives – eg, an adviser. This does not apply to information required from an employer about an employee.

# 5. **Change of circumstances**

There is no general duty to give information about any change of circumstances to the Child Maintenance Service (CMS).

However, in some circumstances, there is a duty to disclose information to the CMS if the CMS has the right to request the information.

- The non-resident parent must notify the CMS within seven days if s/he changes address.[77] If s/he does not do so, s/he may have committed a criminal offence and a fine (currently up to £1,000) may be imposed.[78] The non-resident parent must also inform the CMS of certain changes when a deduction from earnings order is in force (see p162). In certain circumstances, the CMS may also require the non-resident parent to notify it of increases in her/his gross income (see p78).

- A person with care has a duty to tell the CMS if s/he believes that a calculation has ceased to have effect.[79] This may be because:
  - a relevant person (ie, the person with care, non-resident parent or qualifying child) has died;
  - a relevant person is no longer within CMS jurisdiction – ie, s/he is not habitually resident in the UK (see p17);
  - the non-resident parent is no longer a non-resident parent of the child(ren) named in the calculation – eg, because the child has been adopted;
  - a child no longer counts as a child, or as a qualifying child (see p8); *or*
  - the person with care has stopped being a person with care in relation to the child(ren) named in the calculation.

  The person with care must give the reasons for her/his belief in writing, and may be required to give further information to allow a decision to be made.

  The person with care is not required to inform the CMS until the change has taken place.

For the consequences of failing to disclose information when required, see p39.

In practice, any party may want to tell the CMS of changes or new information that may affect the amount of child support payable. See Chapter 9 for details of when a calculation may be changed.

# 6. **Disclosure of information**

In the course of its investigations, the Child Maintenance Service (CMS) collects information and evidence about people affected by child support applications. The non-resident parent and person with care (and a child applicant in Scotland) must be given details of how the amount of child support has been worked out (see p130). The CMS must also give certain other information it has to the courts, the First-tier Tribunal, other parts of the Department for Work and Pensions (DWP) and local authorities.

The CMS cannot give information to third parties without the written permission of the person to whom the information relates. Any unauthorised disclosure of information is a criminal offence.

However, the CMS *can* disclose information given to it by one party (see below) to a child support calculation to another party to explain:[80]

- why an application for child support, or for revision or supersession of a decision, has been rejected;
- why an application cannot proceed or why a calculation will not be made;
- why a calculation has been cancelled or ceases to have effect;
- how the amount of child support has been worked out;
- why a decision has been made not to collect child support, or to stop collection;
- why a particular method of enforcement has been used;
- why enforcement methods have not been used or enforcement has ceased;
- why a decision has been made not to accept part payment of arrears;
- why a decision has been made not to write off arrears in certain circumstances.

### Parties

For the purposes of the CMS's disclosure of information, the **'parties'** are the person who made the application for child support, the person with care, the non-resident parent and a qualifying child.[81] If one of these people has died, and a revision, supersession, appeal or variation request is pending but not decided at the date of death, a representative who was dealing with the request on her/his behalf is also a party.[82]

Any request for the above information must be made in writing to the CMS, giving reasons.[83] However, the CMS can provide the information without a request.

The CMS must only disclose a person's address (or other information which could reasonably be expected to lead to that person being located) if s/he has given her/his written permission.[84] (If you are appealing, you should notify the First-tier Tribunal if you do not want your address or other information disclosed – see p216.[85]) Also, the CMS must not disclose information which could reasonably be expected to lead to the identification of any person other than a person with care, non-resident parent or a qualifying child.[86]

The CMS can disclose any information to the First-tier Tribunal, court and anyone with a right of appeal, if it is for proceedings under the child support or benefits legislation.[87]

In practice, in a child support appeal, CMS papers are included in the CMS submission sent to each party (see p211). The CMS can also disclose information to a court which has made, varied or revived a maintenance order or agreement, if that information is required in relation to those proceedings or other matters arising from them.[88] The CMS can also disclose information to local authorities for their use in administering housing benefit.[89]

In certain circumstances, the CMS can disclose information about the non-resident parent to a credit reference agency (see below). See also p170 for details of information about a non-resident parent that can be disclosed to joint account holders when the CMS is considering enforcement action by deductions from bank accounts.

If you want to see a copy of information about you held by the CMS, you can apply in writing. This information must be supplied without delay, and normally within one month of the request at the latest.[90] It should be provided free of charge (but a reasonable fee based on the administrative costs of providing the information may be charged if a request is unfounded or excessive, particularly if it is repetitive). If you have concerns about the collection, retention, accuracy or use of this information, contact the Information Commissioner's Office (ICO).[91]

## Disclosure to other government departments

The CMS can disclose information to government departments dealing with benefits, including DWP agencies.[92] This includes information obtained using its powers and information disclosed to the CMS voluntarily.

As the DWP has close links with the Home Office, disclosure may create problems for people from abroad and those prohibited from having recourse to public funds. If you have doubts about whether information should be disclosed to the CMS, get advice first from a law centre or independent advice centre dealing with immigration issues (see Appendix 3). You can only be prosecuted for refusing to give information if it has been requested by the CMS or an inspector (see p51).

CMS staff can exchange information with their counterparts in Northern Ireland and vice versa.

## Disclosure to credit reference agencies

In certain circumstances, the CMS can disclose information about a non-resident parent to credit reference agencies. This means that any arrears of child support are likely to have the same effect on a parent's credit assessment as other debts s/he may have.

The parent must normally consent to the information being passed to the agency. If a liability order (see p180) is in force against her/him, the parent's consent is not required.[93]

The following information can be passed to a credit reference agency:[94]
- the parent's name, last known or notified address and date of birth;
- the CMS reference number for the parent's case;
- the date any liability order in force against the parent was made;
- the amount covered by the liability order;
- the address stated in the liability order, if different from the last known or notified address.

Before passing any information to an agency, the CMS must notify the parent in writing by post to her/his last known or notified address (if s/he can be traced) that it intends to do so. The notification must be sent at least 21 days before the information is given to an agency.[95]

The CMS can also tell a credit reference agency without first notifying the non-resident parent:[96]

• that the amount covered by the liability order has been paid, and the date it was paid;
• that a liability order against the parent has been 'set aside' or quashed.

# Notes

1. **Information-seeking powers**
1  s14 and Sch 2 CSA 1991
2  s12 CSPSSA 2000
3  Regs 3 and 4(1) CSI Regs
4  Reg 7(1) CSI Regs
5  ss4(4) and 7(5) CSA 1991; reg 3 CSI Regs
6  Regs 3 and 4 CSI Regs
7  Reg 3(2) CSI Regs
8  Reg 5 CSI Regs
9  Reg 6 CSI Regs
10  See s3 SSA 1998
11  Sch 2 para 1 CSA 1991; Sch 6 para 2 CMOPA 2008
12  s6 and Sch 1 Taxes Management Act 1970; s182 Finance Act 1989
13  Reg 4(2)(b) and (3) CSI Regs
14  Reg 4(2)(c) and (3) CSI Regs
15  Reg 4(2)(d) CSI Regs
16  Reg 4(2)(f) CSI Regs – credit reference agencies are as defined by s145(8) Consumer Credit Act 1974 and Art 89B Financial Services and Markets Act 2000 (Regulated Activities) Order 2001, No.544
17  Reg 4(2)(g) CSI Regs
18  s122D SSAA 1992
19  Reg 4(2)(h)(i) CSI Regs
20  Reg 4(2)(h)(ii) CSI Regs
21  Reg 4(2)(i) CSI Regs
22  Reg 4(2)(j) and (k) CSI Regs
23  Reg 4(2)(l) CSI Regs
24  Reg 4(2)(m) CSI Regs
25  Reg 7(1) CSI Regs

26  Reg 7(2) CSI Regs
27  s14A CSA 1991
28  Reg 8 CSI Regs

2. **Contacting the non-resident parent**
29  Regs 7, 11 and 12 CSMC Regs
30  CCS/2288/2005
31  Child Maintenance and Enforcement Commission, *The Child Support Maintenance Calculation Regulations 2012: a technical consultation on the draft regulations*, December 2011

3. **Parentage investigations**
32  R(CS) 13/98
33  CMS leaflet CMSB010GB, *What Happens When Someone Denies They Are the Parent of a Child?*, October 2013
34  CMS leaflet CMSB010GB, *What Happens When Someone Denies They Are the Parent of a Child?*, October 2013
35  CMS leaflet CMSB010GB, *What Happens When Someone Denies They Are the Parent of a Child?*, October 2013
36  s26 CSA 1991
37  Under ss55A or 56 Family Law Act 1986, Art 32 Matrimonial and Family Proceedings (Northern Ireland) Order 1989, No.677 or s7 LR(PC)(S)A 1986
38  s26(2) CSA 1991, Cases A1 and A2
39  s26(2) CSA 1991, Case E; s5(1) LR(PC)(S)A 1986
40  Civil Partnership (Scotland) Bill (Scottish Parliament Bill 57, Session 5 (2019))

41 s26(2) CSA 1991, Case F(a)(i) in 'relevant proceedings' under s12(5) Civil Evidence Act 1968 or affiliation proceedings

42 s26(2) CSA 1991, Case F(a)(i) in 'relevant proceedings' under s8(5) Civil Evidence Act (Northern Ireland) 1971 or affiliation proceedings

43 s26(2) CSA 1991, Case F(a)(ii) in affiliation proceedings

44 s26(2) CSA 1991, Case A3

45 s26(2) CSA 1991, Case B

46 s26(2) CSA 1991, Case B1

47 **EW** Arts 3 and 4 CSA(JC)O
**S** Arts 2 and 3 CSA(JC)(S)O

48 CMS leaflet CMSB010GB, *What Happens When Someone Denies They Are the Parent of a Child?*, October 2013

49 CMS leaflet CMSB010GB, *What Happens When Someone Denies They Are the Parent of a Child?*, October 2013

50 CMS leaflet CMSB010GB, *What Happens When Someone Denies They Are the Parent of a Child?*, October 2013

51 s26 CSA 1991, Case A3(b)

52 CMS leaflet CMSB010GB, *What Happens When Someone Denies They Are the Parent of a Child?*, October 2013

53 gov.uk/get-a-dna-test

54 s27A CSA 1991

55 CMS leaflet CMSB010GB, *What Happens When Someone Denies They Are the Parent of a Child?*, October 2013

56 For a current list of accredited agencies, see gov.uk/get-a-dna-test.

57 CMS leaflet CMSB010GB, *What Happens When Someone Denies They Are the Parent of a Child?*, October 2013

58 CMS leaflet CMSB010GB, *What Happens When Someone Denies They Are the Parent of a Child?*, October 2013

59 ss27 and 28 CSA 1991

60 **EW** s27(2) CSA 1991
**S** s7 LR(PC)(S)A 1986

61 s20 FLRA 1969; *Re H (Paternity: Blood Test)* [1996] 2 FLR 65

62 *W v Official Solicitor* [1972] AC 24

63 s21 FLRA 1969

64 s23 FLRA 1969; *Re A (Paternity: Refusal of Blood Test)* [1994] 2 FLR 463

65 s20(6) FLRA 1969

66 s28(2) CSA 1991; s7 LR(PC)(S)A 1986; r152 AS(CSA)(AOCSCR), inserting Act of Sederunt (Sheriff Court Ordinary Cause Rules) 1993, No.1956, Chapter 33.89

67 CMS leaflet CMSB010GB, *What Happens When Someone Denies They Are the Parent of a Child?*, October 2013

68 CMS leaflet CMSB010GB, *What Happens When Someone Denies They Are the Parent of a Child?*, October 2013

4. **Further investigations**

69 *DB v CMEC* [2010] UKUT 356 (AAC)

70 s15(1) CSA 1991

71 s15(8) CSA 1991

72 ss15(4ZA) and 15A CSA 1991

73 s15(4), (4A) and (11) CSA 1991

74 s15A(3)(d) and (8) CSA 1991

75 s15(5) and (6) CSA 1991

76 s15(7),and (9) and (9A) CSA 1991

5. **Change of circumstances**

77 s14A(3A) CSA 1991; reg 9 CSI Regs

78 s14A CSA 1991

79 Reg 10 CSI Regs

6. **Disclosure of information**

80 Reg 13 CSI Regs; R(CS) 1/00

81 Reg 13(2)(a) and (b) CSI Regs

82 Reg 13(2)(d) CSI Regs

83 Reg 13(3) CSI Regs

84 Reg 13(4) CSI Regs

85 r19(3) TP(FT) Rules

86 Reg 13(4) CSI Regs

87 Reg 12 CSI Regs

88 Reg 12(3) CSI Regs

89 s122C(2)(a) SSAA 1992

90 EU Reg 2016/679, with effect from 25 May 2018

91 ico.org.uk

92 s3 SSA 1998

93 s49D(3) CSA 1991

94 Reg 14A(1)(a)-(e) CSI Regs

95 Reg 14A(2) and (3) CSI Regs

96 Reg 14A(1)(f) and (g) and (2) CSI Regs

# Chapter 4

......................................................

# Calculating the amount of child support

**This chapter covers:**
1. The rates of child support (below)
2. The non-resident parent's income (p67)
3. Shared care (p80)

## 1. The rates of child support

There are four rates of child support:
- nil rate (see p59);
- flat rate (see p60);
- reduced rate (see p61);
- basic rate, including 'basic rate plus' (see p62).

The amount of child support calculated is a weekly amount. In all cases, fractions of a penny are disregarded if they are less than a half, or rounded up to the next penny if a half or over.[1]

If there is more than one non-resident parent in relation to a qualifying child, child support is calculated for each parent separately. This means that a person with care could receive different rates from each – eg, the flat rate from one non-resident parent and an amount worked out using the basic rate from the other. If there is more than one person with care, see below.

**Note:** the child support calculation can be varied in certain circumstances – eg, if the non-resident parent has certain special expenses or additional income. See Chapter 5 for details.

### If there is more than one person with care

If there is more than one person with care, each caring for a different qualifying child in relation to a non-resident parent, the amount of child support may be apportioned between them in relation to the number of qualifying children each person cares for.[2]

Apportionment occurs after child support has been calculated at the appropriate rate, but before any decrease for shared care (see p80).[3]

In basic- and reduced-rate cases, if an adjustment is made that reduces the non-resident parent's liability to less than £7 (eg, because of shared care or a variation), the amount payable is £7 apportioned between the people with care.[4]

Child support liability is calculated for only one person with care in respect of each qualifying child. If, in practice, another person who is not the non-resident parent provides care for a qualifying child, the Child Maintenance Service (CMS) does not apportion the child support between them. The person with care who receives the child support could agree to pass some of it on to any other person who also provides care for the child. However, this would be an informal agreement and would not be monitored or enforced by the CMS.

## Nil rate

Some non-resident parents do not need to pay any child support. This 'nil rate' applies if the non-resident parent:[5]
- is a child (see p8 for the meaning of 'child'); *or*
- is a prisoner (including if serving a prison sentence and detained in hospital); *or*
- is 16 or 17 years old and receiving universal credit (UC) calculated on the basis that s/he has no earned income (or s/he is a member of a couple and her/his partner is receiving UC calculated on this basis); *or*
- is 16 or 17 years old and receiving income support (IS), income-based jobseeker's allowance (JSA) or income-related employment and support allowance (ESA) (or s/he is a member of a couple and her/his partner is receiving one of these benefits for her/him); *or*
- receives an allowance for work-based training for young people. Young people may receive a training allowance or (in Scotland and Wales) an education maintenance allowance; *or*
- is resident in a care home or independent hospital, or being provided with a care home service or/and independent healthcare service, and receives one of the prescribed benefits for the flat rate (see below) or has all or part of the cost of her/his accommodation met by a local authority; *or*
- has a gross income (including income from any of the prescribed benefits for the flat rate) of less than £7 a week.

*Example*
Kerry is a parent with care of two children, Mia and Lewis. Her ex-partner, Craig, is in prison. In this case, the nil rate applies. When he comes out of prison, Kerry could ask for a supersession as their circumstances have changed.

## Flat rate

A 'flat rate' of £7 a week applies if the non-resident parent does not qualify for the nil rate and:[6]
- her/his weekly income is £100 or less; *or*
- s/he receives one of the following benefits:[7]
  - category A, B, C or D retirement pension;
  - state pension;
  - incapacity benefit;
  - contributory ESA;
  - carer's allowance;
  - maternity allowance;
  - severe disablement allowance;
  - industrial injuries benefit;
  - widowed mother's or widowed parent's allowance;
  - widow's pension;
  - contribution-based JSA;
  - a training allowance (other than for work-based learning for young people);
  - war disablement pension;
  - war widow's, war widower's or surviving civil partner's war pension;
  - payments under the Armed Forces Compensation Scheme;
  - a social security benefit paid by a country other than the UK; *or*
- s/he, or her/his partner, receives one of the following means-tested benefits:[8]
  - UC calculated on the basis that s/he does not have any earned income;
  - IS;
  - income-based JSA;
  - income-related ESA;
  - pension credit.

The flat rate can be halved if the non-resident parent has a partner who is also a non-resident parent with a child support calculation in force, and the non-resident parent or her/his partner receives one of the means-tested benefits above. Each pays £3.50.[9] If the non-resident parent is in a polygamous relationship and there is more than one partner who is also a non-resident parent and the non-resident parent or her/his partner receives one of these means-tested benefits, each is liable to pay £3.50 a week.

If there is more than one person with care caring for different qualifying children, the flat rate is apportioned between them (see p58).

**Note:** the flat rate is not reduced to take account of any relevant other children (see p64) or relevant non-resident children (see p65).

There are special rules about shared care (see p83).

If the flat rate is paid by deductions being made directly from the non-resident parent's benefit (see p141), a collection fee of 20 per cent is added and the deduction is £8.40 a week.

*Example*

The situation is as in the previous example on p59. Craig has now come out of prison and gets UC. Kerry requests a supersession and Craig pays the flat rate of £7 child support each week. (A monthly amount of £36.40 would be deducted from his benefit if he pays that way).

If Craig moved in with his new partner, Joan, and claimed UC as a couple, the flat rate of £7 would still apply and Kerry would receive £7 a week. However, if Joan were also a non-resident parent with a child support application in force, the flat rate would be halved. In this case, Kerry would receive £3.50 a week.

## Reduced rate

The reduced rate applies if the non-resident parent does not qualify for the flat rate or the nil rate and her/his weekly gross income is more than £100 but less than £200. The flat rate of £7 is added to a percentage of the parent's income between £100 and £200[10] – eg, if gross income is £150, the percentage is applied to £50. The percentage depends on the number of qualifying children (see p8), including any relevant non-resident children (see p65) the non-resident parent has, as well as the number of other children who live with her/him ('relevant other children' – see p64).[11]

*Reduced rate percentages*

| Number of relevant other children | Number of qualifying children (including relevant non-resident children) | | |
| --- | --- | --- | --- |
| | One | Two | Three or more |
| None | 17% | 25% | 31% |
| One | 14.1% | 21.2% | 26.4% |
| Two | 13.2% | 19.9% | 24.9% |
| Three or more | 12.4% | 18.9% | 23.8% |

### Step one

Work out the gross weekly income between £100 and £200.

### Step two

Work out the relevant percentage. Apply this percentage to the income worked out in Step one and add this to £7.

### Step three

If different qualifying children are cared for by different people with care, apportion the amount worked out in Step two between them, depending on the number of qualifying children each cares for.

*Example*

Simon is due to pay child support to Fiona for two qualifying children, Harry and Lily. Simon lives with his new partner, Julie, and their baby, Paul. Paul is a relevant other child. Simon's gross income is £180 a week. The reduced rate of child support applies.

**Step one:**    Gross weekly income = £180
                Income between £100 and £200 = £80

**Step two:**    Relevant percentage for one relevant other child and two qualifying children is 21.2 per cent.
                £7 + (21.2% x £80) = £7 + £16.96 = £23.96

Simon is due to pay £23.96 child support a week to Fiona.

If Lily was being cared for by Fiona and Harry stayed with his grandmother, there would still be two qualifying children, each cared for by a different person with care. The child support calculated would need to be apportioned between them.

**Step three:**    Each person cares for one qualifying child, so the child support is divided by two.
                £23.96 ÷ 2 = £11.98

Simon now pays Fiona £11.98 a week and the grandmother £11.98 a week.

If the non-resident parent shares the care of any qualifying children, the reduced rate may be decreased by applying the shared care rules (see p83).

## Basic rate

The basic rate applies if none of the other rates (nil, flat or reduced) apply.[12]

If the non-resident parent has a gross weekly income of £200 or more, child support is calculated using the basic rate. If her/his gross weekly income is over £800, the 'basic rate plus' applies. The maximum amount of gross weekly income that can be included in the child support calculation is £3,000. Even if a variation for additional income is being applied (see Chapter 5), the amount of gross income taken into account cannot be more than this.[13]

The basic rate is a percentage of the non-resident parent's gross weekly income, depending on the number of qualifying children (see p8), including the number of any relevant non-resident children (see p65), s/he has.

If the non-resident parent has other children living with her/him (relevant other children – see p64), her/his gross income is reduced by a certain percentage before the basic rate is calculated. The basic rate is therefore worked out in two steps.

## Step one

Work out the gross weekly income of the non-resident parent. Reduce this by the appropriate percentage, depending on the number of relevant other children s/he has.

*Basic rate: reduction in gross income for relevant other children*[14]

| Number of relevant other children | Percentage by which gross income is reduced |
|---|---|
| One | 11% |
| Two | 14% |
| Three or more | 16% |

## Step two

Work out the amount of child support as a proportion of the gross income calculated in Step one, depending on the number of qualifying children (including any relevant non-resident children).
- If gross weekly income is £800 a week or less, the basic rate of child support is 12 per cent, 16 per cent or 19 per cent of this gross income.
- If gross income is over £800 a week, the 'basic rate plus' of child support is 12 per cent, 16 per cent or 19 per cent of £800 plus 9 per cent, 12 per cent or 15 per cent of the amount over £800.

*Basic rate percentages*[15]

| Number of qualifying children (including relevant non-resident children) | Percentage of gross income up to £800 | Percentage of gross income above £800 |
|---|---|---|
| One | 12% | 9% |
| Two | 16% | 12% |
| Three or more | 19% | 15% |

*Example*

Alfie and Susan have separated and their three children, Tracey, Sara and Jon, live with Susan. Alfie lives with his new partner and her daughter, Donna. Alfie's gross weekly income is £450 a week. Tracey, Sara and Jon are the qualifying children, and Donna is a relevant other child.

**Step one:**   Alfie's gross weekly income is £450. There is one relevant other child, so this is reduced by 11 per cent.

11% x £450 = £49.50

£450 – £49.50 = £400.50

**Step two:** There are three qualifying children, so child support is 19 per cent of the remaining gross income.

$19\% \times £400.50 = £76.10$

Alfie therefore pays £76.10 a week in child support to Susan.

Alfie's gross weekly income increases to £979.85, so the 'basic rate plus' applies.

**Step one:** Alfie's gross weekly income is £979.85. There is one relevant other child, so this is reduced by 11 per cent.

$11\% \times £979.85 = £107.78$

$£979.85 - £107.78 = £872.07$

**Step two:** This amount is over £800 and there are three qualifying children. So child support is 19 per cent of £800 plus 15 per cent of the 'excess' above £800 – ie, 15 per cent of £72.07.

$19\% \times £800 = £152$

$15\% \times £72.07 = £10.81$

Alfie, therefore, now pays £162.81 (£152 + £10.81) a week in child support to Susan.

## Step three

If there is more than one person with care caring for different qualifying children, apportion the amount worked out at Step two between the people with care depending on the number of qualifying children each cares for.

*Example*

Alfie currently pays £162.81 a week in child support to his ex-wife, Susan, for his three children, Tracey, Sara and Jon. When Jon goes to live with his grandmother, the £162.81 child support is split between Susan and the grandmother.

**Step three:** £162.81 is apportioned between two people with care.

Susan cares for two children and so she receives two-thirds of the child support due. Alfie pays her £108.54 a week.

The grandmother cares for one child and so she receives one-third of the child support due. Alfie pays her £54.27 a week.

If the non-resident parent shares the care of any of the qualifying children, the child support calculated may be decreased by applying the shared care rules (see p83).

## Relevant other children

The number of relevant other children affects the calculation of child support. A 'relevant other child' (or 'relevant child') is the term used by the CMS for a child, other than a qualifying child, for whom the non-resident parent or her/his partner receives child benefit.[16] This can include a child who does not live with the parent all the time – eg, because s/he is at boarding school or there is a shared care arrangement for her/him. It can also include a child for whom the non-resident parent or her/his partner would get child benefit, but for the fact that:[17]

- the rules about presence in Great Britain are not met; *or*
- the non-resident parent or her/his partner has elected not to receive child benefit because s/he would be liable to the 'high-income child benefit charge' in income tax.

If a relevant other child is cared for by a local authority for some or all of the time, s/he continues to count as a relevant other child if the non-resident parent or her/his partner receives child benefit for her/him.[18]

See CPAG's *Welfare Benefits and Tax Credits Handbook* for full details of the rules on child benefit.

## Relevant non-resident children

The number of relevant non-resident children affects the calculation of child support. **'Relevant non-resident child'** is a term used by the CMS to refer to a child of the non-resident parent for whom an application for child support cannot be made because the non-resident parent is liable to pay maintenance for her/him under a maintenance order (or, in Scotland, registered maintenance agreement), an order of a non-British court or under the legislation of a country outside the UK.[19] This is a child who would be considered a qualifying child if an application for child support could be made for her/him. It includes a child who does not live with the non-resident parent and a child whose care is shared between the non-resident parent and someone else. See p18 for more information about when a court order prevents an application for child support being made.

A child who is not a qualifying child and who is habitually resident in the UK (see p17) can also count as a relevant non-resident child if the non-resident parent is paying maintenance for her/him under another 'informal' maintenance arrangement – eg, a family-based arrangement. There is a wide definition of the other arrangements that can qualify, including verbal agreements. The arrangement must be between the non-resident parent and person with care of the relevant child, and must be for regular payments for the benefit of the child. Payments made to third parties can count, as well as those made to the parent with care.[20]

Where a child is not habitually resident in the UK, informal maintenance arrangements can be treated the same way. A child abroad can still be treated as a relevant non-resident child if the non-resident parent has a liability to pay child maintenance under the legislative system of another country and is making such payments. A formal court order to that effect is not required. An informal family-based arrangement to support a child abroad may be sufficient.[21]

When working out the basic and reduced rate of child support (including if payable after a variation), a relevant non-resident child counts as a qualifying child, even though no amount of child support is paid for her/him.[22]

The amount of child support calculated is divided by the total number of qualifying children, including any relevant non-resident children. This amount is then multiplied by the number of qualifying children, excluding any relevant non-resident children. This gives the amount of child support the non-resident parent must pay.

If there is more than one person with care, each caring for a different qualifying child, the child support is apportioned between them in relation to the number of qualifying children they care for, including any adjustment for shared care.[23] If the total amount payable by the non-resident parent is less than £7, s/he pays £7 instead, apportioned between the persons with care as appropriate.[24]

The amount being paid by the non-resident parent for the relevant non-resident child (eg, under a maintenance order) is not affected by the child support calculation.

There is no adjustment of the notional amount for a relevant non-resident child because the non-resident parent shares care or because the child is being looked after by the local authority for part of the time.

### Example

James lives with his new partner, Amanda, and her son, Liam. James has three other children. Two (Emma and Joshua) are cared for by Elizabeth; one (Rachel) is cared for by Hilary. James has a court order for child maintenance for Rachel and pays £45 a week maintenance to Hilary. Hilary cannot apply for child support as the court order is in force. In this case:

Emma and Joshua are qualifying children.

Liam is a relevant other child (even though he is not James's child, James's new partner, Amanda, gets child benefit for him).

Rachel is a relevant non-resident child.

James's gross income is £675 a week. His child support is worked out using the basic rate as follows.

| | |
|---|---|
| **Step one:** | James' gross income is £675. There is one relevant other child, so this is reduced by 11 per cent. |
| | 11% x £675 = £74.25 |
| | £675 – £74.25 = £600.75 |
| **Step two:** | There are two qualifying children and one relevant non-resident child. So child support is 19 per cent of £600.75. |
| | 19% x £600.75 = £114.14 |

| Step three: | Divide the child support by the number of qualifying children, including the relevant non-resident child – ie, divide £114.14 by 3 = £38.05. Multiply £38.05 by the number of qualifying children, excluding the relevant non-resident child – ie, £38.05 x 2 = £76.10. |
|---|---|

James is due to pay £76.10 a week child support to Elizabeth.

Hilary receives her usual court order maintenance of £45 a week.

**Note:** if Hilary could apply for child support, she would receive £38.04 (£114.14 – £76.10).

If the situation changes and Emma is now cared for by her grandmother and Joshua is still cared for by Elizabeth, apportionment applies between Elizabeth and the grandmother. As each cares for one qualifying child, each would receive £38.05 a week child support.

## Divided families

If a couple has more than one child together and at least one child is living with each parent, child support liability is still calculated for both parents. However, the amounts are offset so that only the parent with the higher liability makes a balancing payment, while the other parent does not pay anything.[25] The CMS may use the term 'split care' when referring to this situation.

---

# 2. The non-resident parent's income

The amount of child support payable is based on the non-resident parent's gross weekly income.

'Gross weekly income' is calculated by using either the non-resident parent's 'historic income' (see p68) or 'current income' (see p72) at the 'effective date' of the application (see p131) and converting this into a weekly amount.[26] The rules on the type of income taken into account are complex and are based on how income is treated for income tax purposes. It is not the total income on which tax is due which counts, but the total income on which the parent is 'charged to tax'.[27]

Both historic income and current income are composite figures of all income from relevant sources. The non-resident parent's income is assessed on one or the other. There is no scope for income from employment to be based on current income and income from self-employment to be based on historic income or vice versa.[28]

Income from sources other than those described in this section is not counted. Taxable social security benefits are not included, except that incapacity benefit (IB), contributory employment and support allowance (ESA), jobseeker's allowance (JSA) and income support (IS) are included in the historic income figure provided by HM Revenue and Customs (HMRC). Working tax credit is *not* counted as part of the non-resident parent's income.

In some cases, income that is not counted in gross income for the calculation can be taken into account by a variation, as can notional income from assets (see Chapter 5). For example, if a non-resident parent has unearned income from property or investments, or has valuable assets that do not generate a declared income, a person with care could ask for a variation on the grounds that s/he has additional income. However, in many cases, an application for a variation is only likely to be made if a person with care is aware that the non-resident parent has other sources of income or assets.

**Note:** the government has announced plans to allow unearned income to be included in the initial calculation, rather than only be taken into account after an application for a variation (see p101).[29] No date has yet been set for these changes to take effect.

Contributions to an approved personal or occupational pension scheme (ie, a scheme registered with HMRC) by the non-resident parent in the relevant tax year are deducted when calculating gross weekly income. No other deductions are taken into account.

There is no limit on the amount of pension contributions that can be deducted. If a person with care is aware of the amount of contributions and considers them to be excessive, or considers that arrangements have been set up deliberately to reduce liability for child support (eg, if the non-resident parent has made a salary sacrifice arrangement in return for increased employer contributions), s/he can apply for a variation on the grounds of diversion of income (see p95).

All the parties (ie, the person with care, the non-resident parent and, in Scotland, any child applicant) are notified of the income figure used in the child support calculation. This applies whether the calculation is based on historic income or current income (including if current income is estimated). This does not include a breakdown of the types of income included.[30] See p130 for further details on the notification of decisions.

**Note:** if the Child Maintenance Service (CMS) does not have sufficient information to make a calculation, it may make a default maintenance decision (see p129).

There are special rules for annual reviews of income (see p75), periodic checks if current income is being used (see p77) and for reporting changes to current income (see p78).

## Historic income

In most cases, the child support calculation uses a non-resident parent's 'historic' income. The CMS aims to avoid having to obtain information on income from the parent or her/his employer, and so information on historic income is provided by HMRC using an automated system. This is intended to reduce the possibility of delay, the supply of inaccurate information and demands on employers.

The historic income figure takes into account the non-resident parent's taxable income from:[31]
- employment – ie, her/his income from earnings (see p71);
- pensions (see p71);
- the taxable amount of the following social security benefits – IB, contributory ESA, JSA and IS (**Note:** a parent currently receiving one of these benefits usually pays the flat rate – see p60); *and*
- her/his profits from self-employment (see p71).

The CMS requests a historic income figure for the latest available tax year from HMRC no more than 30 days before the initial 'effective date' (see p131). The 'latest available tax year' is the most recent tax year for which HMRC has received information on the non-resident parent under either:[32]
- the pay as you earn (PAYE) scheme, for which employers complete end-of-year returns on the taxable earnings of their employees; *or*
- the annual self-assessment returns completed by individual taxpayers on various sources of income.

The latest available tax year must be one of the six tax years before the date the information is sought.[33]

The CMS does not have any discretion to use different income figures[34] – eg, if there is evidence that the non-resident parent has under-reported her/his income on the self-assessment (but see p72 for when 'current' income is used for the calculation instead of 'historic' income).

The CMS does not automatically receive a breakdown of the historic income figure, but may request a breakdown from HMRC if one party queries the figure. It does not normally provide the breakdown to the parties, but may give it to the non-resident parent.

If HMRC supplies a figure that is not from the most recent tax year for which it has received information, this is not a valid historic income figure. The CMS can make a further request to HMRC for an up-to-date historic income figure. It should consider doing so particularly carefully where it is not suitable to use current income, as the automated system can normally only request a historic income figure once each year. However, if there is good reason to doubt the validity of the figure provided by HMRC (including reason to doubt whether it is, in fact, for the latest available tax year), the CMS should make a further request.[35] The First-tier Tribunal considering an appeal may direct the CMS to do so.[36]

Self-assessment information is usually available to the CMS by February or March in the year following the end of the tax year on 5 April. Information from PAYE returns is available earlier. If HMRC has information from both the PAYE scheme and a self-assessment for the latest available tax year, information from the self-assessment is used, as it is expected to be more comprehensive.[37]

Information about all forms of a person's taxable income must relate to the same tax year. If an application is made in June 2020, PAYE information may be available for 2019/20, but the most recent self-assessment information is likely to be for 2018/19. What matters is not the availability of one form of information for a tax year, but HMRC's identification of the total amount that was charged to tax for the year. For a person who has to complete a self-assessment, HMRC cannot determine total income until the self-assessment is received, even if it appears that the PAYE information is complete. So, in this example, the latest available tax year for which HMRC can supply inforrmation in June 2020 is 2018/19.[38]

Contributions to an approved personal or occupational pension scheme (ie, a scheme registered with HMRC) by the non-resident parent in the relevant tax year are deducted by HMRC when providing the historic income figure. If the non-resident parent has made pension contributions during the relevant tax year that have not been deducted under net pay arrangements (eg, payments made directly to a personal pension scheme), s/he can request that the weekly average amount of these be deducted from the gross income figure.[39] The CMS may require her/him to provide further information. Because tax relief is given on pension contributions, actual contributions are less than the gross amount included in the pension plan. The higher gross amount should be deducted from gross income. If a gross amount including higher rate tax relief is being claimed, the CMS is likely to require evidence in the form of an HMRC calculation notice.

The rules on the type of income included are intended to ensure that parents are treated consistently, whether the information held on them by HMRC comes from the PAYE scheme or from self-assessment.

The use of historic income information from HMRC means that taxable payments to those in the following occupations or offices are *not* disregarded:
- auxiliary coastguards;
- part-time firefighters and lifeboat crew members;
- reserve or territorial force members;
- local authority councillors.

Maintaining consistency, however, means that some types of income captured by self-assessment are not counted as gross weekly income for the calculation, even though HMRC may hold reliable information about them. This includes some taxable social security benefits and some allowances claimed by employees against taxable earnings.[40]

If a parent is both employed and self-employed, it is possible that at the time the calculation is made PAYE details are available for the most recently completed tax year, but self-assessment only for the year before this. Information on employment income is, therefore, likely to reflect the parent's current circumstances more accurately.

## Income from employment

When HMRC provides information on historic income from employment, gross pay is used. **'Gross pay'** is all payments, such as salary, wages, fees, bonuses, commission, tips and overtime, before any income tax or national insurance contributions are deducted. HMRC deducts contributions to an approved personal or occupational pension scheme. Deductions should also be made for any other allowable deductions (eg, expenses) that will not be taxed.[41] Payments from an employer to reimburse an employee for legitimate work-related expenses should not be counted in gross pay.[42]

Statutory sick pay, statutory maternity pay, statutory adoption pay, statutory parental bereavement pay, statutory paternity pay and statutory shared parental pay are treated as employment income.

Anything of direct monetary value to the employee that derives from the employment or office is also treated as earnings.[43] There are certain exemptions.[44]

A lump-sum redundancy payment is not earnings but a compensation for lost employment. It is not taxed as earnings. To the extent that it exceeds the £30,000 tax-free threshold, it is taxed as other employment income and so may be included in the historic income figure.[45]

## Income from self-employment

Historic income from self-employment is based on the taxable profits from any 'trade, profession or vocation' in the latest available tax year for which a self-assessment has been completed – ie, the profits in the accounting period that ended in the tax year.[46] For example, if a self-employed parent's accounting year ends in June 2018, which is in tax year 2018/19, the self-assessment for that period will not be returned until 19 months later in January 2020.[47]

If a business is run on a commercial basis and has made a loss, gross income is nil for that tax year. In certain circumstances, a loss in a previous year can be carried forward and deducted from profits in the next and later tax years. HMRC deducts such losses when determining the historic income figure for self-employment.[48]

## Pension income

Income (before tax) from a personal or occupational pension, or an annuity or other kind of taxable pension income, counts towards gross weekly income.[49]

The full details of pension income that is taxable are complex.[50] Tax-free lump sums paid under an approved personal pension scheme, retirement annuity contract or tax-exempt pension scheme are ignored completely. A lump sum counts if it is for cashing in a small pension, if the fund is too small to pay a pension (within the 'trivial commutation' limit) or if an occupational pension scheme winds up.[51] If a pension is paid because of a work-related illness or disability caused by an injury on duty, only the amount that would have been paid had the parent retired on non-work-related ill-health grounds counts. Any extra amount paid is ignored.[52] Various war disablement pensions are also not counted.[53]

Pension income for these purposes does not include UK social security pensions, even though they are taxable and appear on a self-assessment return.[54] This means that the following are not counted:[55]

- retirement pension;
- graduated retirement benefit;
- industrial death benefit;
- widowed mother's allowance;
- widowed parent's allowance;
- widow's pension.

## Current income

In certain cases, historic income information may not be available or may differ significantly from the non-resident parent's current circumstances. In this case, the calculation is based on the non-resident parent's current income. Unlike for historic income, the source of the current income figure is not limited to HMRC.[56] The CMS approaches the parent to verify her/his employment or self-employment details and, in some cases, may contact her/his employer or accountant for information.

The CMS can seek information on current income if:[57]

- no historic income figure is available – ie, HMRC does not have information for any one of the six tax years before the date of the CMS's request;[58] *or*
- the CMS is unable, for whatever reason, to request or obtain the required information from HMRC – eg, because of problems with the automatic data-sharing system; *or*
- there is at least a 25 per cent difference between the amount of current income and historic income.

If HMRC supplies a historic income figure of 'nil', the CMS accepts this and does not use current income in this case. If the CMS then becomes aware that the non-resident parent has *any* current income, it is automatically treated as at least 25 per cent different from the nil historic income figure and a new calculation decision can be made.[59]

The 25 per cent threshold for change applies to the total income figures. Both historic income and current income are composite figures of all income from relevant sources. The 25 per cent threshold cannot be applied to income from employment and income from self-employment separately, but to the total. Once the threshold is reached, the parent's gross weekly income is calculated on current income as a whole.[60]

If a person with care believes a non-resident parent with nil historic income has current earnings, s/he can request a revision or supersession (see Chapter 9).

If you are a person with care, you are most likely to want to dispute the accuracy of the historic income figure used and ask for current income to be considered once you have applied for child support and the CMS has started to gather information.

'Current income' is the total (calculated or estimated) income from:[61]

- employment;
- self-employment; *and*
- pensions.

Income from the taxable benefits included in historic income (see p68) is not counted in current income. **Note:** a parent currently receiving one of those benefits usually pays the flat rate (see p60).

Contributions to an approved personal or occupational pension scheme (ie, a scheme registered with HMRC) by the non-resident parent in the relevant tax year are deducted. In many cases, these will already have been deducted by her/his employer when s/he is paid. In this case, the deductions are not included in gross income.[62]

If the non-resident parent has income from employment or self-employment and has made pension contributions during the relevant tax year that have not been deducted by her/his employer (eg, they were made directly to a personal pension scheme), the weekly average amount of these can be deducted from the gross income figure.[63] Because tax relief is given on personal pension contributions, actual contributions are less than the gross amount included in the pension plan. It is the higher gross amount that should be deducted from current income. The CMS does not deduct a higher gross amount to reflect higher rate tax relief, as granting this relief requires a decision by HMRC that it will not yet have been able to make at the time that current income is being assessed.

If any payment is made in a currency other than sterling, charges for converting it to sterling are deducted from the current income figure.[64]

## Estimating current income

The CMS can estimate a parent's current income if the information about it is insufficient or unreliable and:[65]

- the historic income is nil and there is any amount of current income – ie, current income is automatically treated as being 25 per cent different from historic income; *or*
- no historic income information is available, or the CMS is unable, for whatever reason, to request or obtain the required information from HMRC.

The CMS is likely to use this power to encourage non-resident parents to co-operate with providing details of their current income. It can base an estimate on any assumptions about any facts. Assumptions may be based on any information already held about the non-resident parent's circumstances. If the CMS is satisfied that s/he works in a particular occupation, it can assume that s/he has the average weekly income of a person engaged in that occupation in a particular area of the UK.[66] It may use information such as the Office for National Statistics' *Annual Survey of Hours and Earnings*, which gives average earnings for occupations and regions. This can apply to income from employment or self-employment. A parent who works part time or has lower than average wages for any reason should make sure the CMS is aware of this.

If there is no historic income information available, the CMS has not been able to gather information about current income and it does not have enough information to estimate current income, it may make a 'default maintenance decision' (see p129).

## Income from employment

Income from employment is defined for current income purposes in broadly the same way as for historic income (see p71). Gross earnings are taken into account, not including approved pension contributions.

Current income is intended to be assessed in a way that, wherever possible, results in a stable amount of child support liability being set. If the non-resident parent receives any income from a salary, wages or other periodic payments and the CMS considers that this is a settled regular amount likely to continue for the foreseeable future, it converts this into a weekly amount.[67]

If earnings are less frequent, fluctuate or are not a regular settled amount for some other reason, the CMS averages the amounts over an appropriate period before the effective date of the decision and converts this to a weekly amount. Averaging is likely to be used if, for example, the parent is a seasonal worker or has an irregular pattern of hours, shifts or overtime.[68]

Some taxable amounts may be paid at different intervals from regular pay. The total of any bonus or commission payments in the last 12 months that have been paid separately or for a different period than other income is also converted to a weekly amount.[69]

The detailed rules on what income from employment is taxable are complex. Anything of direct monetary value to an employee that derives from her/his employment or office is also treated as earnings, and the amount received in the past 12 months converted into a weekly amount.[70] There are certain exemptions that are not treated as earnings.[71]

A lump-sum redundancy payment is not earnings but compensation for lost employment. It is not taxed as earnings and so is not included in current income.[72]

## Income from self-employment

Income from self-employment is defined for current income purposes in the same way as for historic income – ie, as the taxable profits from any 'trade, profession or vocation' (see p71).

Profits are determined for the most recently completed tax year or accounting period that a parent would normally report in a self-assessment. If no full tax year or accounting period has been completed, the profits are estimated for the current period. The total profit for the period is converted into a weekly amount.[73] The current income of an established business is normally expected to relate to an annual period equal to that covered by most self-assessments. A shorter period is only expected to be used for a new business. In this case, the CMS tries to identify estimated or projected annual profits – eg, using any completed profit and loss accounts to date and business plans.

It is the profits from the self-employment in which the non-resident parent is engaged on the effective date that are determined. If the CMS accepts that the parent had ceased trading on the effective date, s/he is assessed as having no profits, so her/his current income is nil if s/he has no other source of income. If the parent is a partner in a business, the profits are apportioned according to her/his share.[74]

### Pension income

Pension income is defined for current income purposes in the same way as for historic income (see p71). If current income is being used, the CMS averages pension income over an appropriate period to give a weekly amount.[75]

## Income from outside the UK

Income from outside the UK is included in gross income if it falls into one of the categories of taxable income from employment, self-employment or pensions. The detailed rules on what income is taxable are complex. The following are some types of income that are disregarded:

- social security payments from outside the UK, equivalent to non-taxable UK benefits;[76]
- one-tenth of the amount of any overseas pension or of a pension payable in the UK by the governments of certain other countries;[77]
- tax-free lump-sum payments under an overseas pension scheme;[78]
- income the parent is prevented from transferring to the UK by law or by the government of the country where the income arises or because foreign currency cannot be obtained in that country.[79]

## Annual reviews

The CMS must conduct an annual review of gross weekly income. This is done whether gross income is based on historic income or current income.[80]

The review date is normally on the anniversary of the initial effective date (see p131), but the CMS can use a different date for a particular case or type of case.[81]

If a child support calculation is already in force and a new application is made in relation to the same non-resident parent for a different qualifying child, the review dates for the two cases are aligned. This allows the non-resident parent's income to be assessed at the same time for all cases in which s/he is involved. The first review date for the new case is on the next review date for the calculation already in force.[82] If both parents are non-resident and applications for child support from both have been treated as one application (see p28), the CMS can use different review dates for each non-resident parent.[83]

In order to conduct the review, the CMS requests an updated historic income figure for the latest available tax year from HMRC.[84] It can request this no earlier than 30 days before the review date.[85]

If the gross weekly income shown by the updated figure is different from the historic income figure previously used, the CMS supersedes the calculation decision. The supersession decision takes effect from the review date.[86]

If gross weekly income is based on current income, the current income is compared with the updated historic income figure. If current income is still at least 25 per cent different from the updated historic income, the current income figure is still used. If it is within 25 per cent, the updated historic income figure is used and the calculation is superseded, with effect from the review date.

If a variation to the calculation on the grounds of additional income (see p100) is in force, the CMS may also request updated information on unearned income in the latest available tax year when it asks HMRC for the updated historic income figure. If unearned income has changed, a supersession decision can be made. This takes effect from the review date.[87]

When the CMS gets the updated historic income figure, it writes to the person with care and non-resident parent (and child applicant in Scotland) giving details of the income figure to be used for the coming year. This includes a breakdown of the calculation, including details such as qualifying children, relevant other children, other maintenance arrangements taken into account and shared care. This notification is not a formal decision that can be challenged, but a notification that the calculation is expected to be based on this information. The parties have 30 days to notify the CMS of any changes and provide any additional information or evidence.[88]

The formal decision on the child support calculation for the coming year is then issued to the parties on the effective date of the annual review. This formal decision can be challenged by the parties.

Any changes reported by any of the parties during this 30-day period may also result in a supersession of the current child support calculation from the date the change is reported.

- - - - - - - - - - - - - - - - - - - - - - - - - - - - - - - - - - - - - - - - - - - - -

*Example*
Alfie is paying £76.10 a week child support to Susan for their three children. This is based on historic income information, showing his gross weekly income to be £450. The annual review date is 8 March.

On 6 February (30 days before the annual review), the CMS receives updated historic income information, showing a gross weekly income of £500, and notifies Alfie and Susan. The CMS receives evidence from Alfie on 12 February, showing that he has changed his working pattern and that his current gross weekly income is now £320.

This current income figure varies by more than 25 per cent from the updated historic income figure of £500, so Alfie's new child support liability from 8 March is based on the current income figure of £320 gross weekly income.

| | |
|---|---|
| **Step one:** | Alfie's gross weekly income is £320. There is one relevant other child, which means this is reduced by 11 per cent. |
| | 11% x £320 = £35.20 |
| | £320 – £35.20 = £284.80 |
| **Step two:** | There are three qualifying children, so child support is 19 per cent of the remaining gross income. |
| | 19% x £284.80 = £54.11 |

Alfie will, therefore, pay £54.11 a week in child support to Susan from the review date.

The CMS also compares the new current income figure of £320 with the historic income figure used in Alfie's existing child support liability (£450). This is also more than 25 per cent different, so there are grounds for a supersession of the existing liability (see p206). Alfie's liability from the date he reported the change (12 February) until the review date (8 March) is also changed to £54.11 a week.

## Periodic checks of current income

The CMS can undertake a 'periodic check' of a parent's current income if:[89]
- her/his gross weekly income has been based on current income; *and*
- no supersession decision changing the amount has been made for at least 11 months.

A periodic check is likely to happen if the current income figure has not been updated at the annual review and is still at least 25 per cent different from the updated historic income figure obtained at the review.

This periodic check is separate from the annual review process and is not normally done at the same time. If current income is used to determine gross weekly income, in some cases this may only have been in place for a short time at the annual review date. Once it has been in place for 11 months, a periodic current income check takes place.

If current income has previously been used, but the annual review results in historic income now being used, a periodic check of current income is not undertaken. Therefore, if a periodic check is due to take place around the same time as the annual review, the annual review is done first.

The non-resident parent must provide updated evidence of her/his current income for the periodic check.[90] Any updated evidence on current income is compared against the updated historic income figure for the latest available tax year that was provided at the most recent annual review. Any information provided by a person with care can also be considered.

If the person with care requests a supersession while the periodic check is being conducted and provides any relevant information, this is considered as part of the periodic check.[91]

If the evidence provided by the non-resident parent is sufficient to make a new decision on current income, a supersession of the calculation decision is made.[92] If the evidence shows that the up-to-date current income figure varies by at least 25 per cent from the most recently updated historic income figure, the calculation continues to be based on the current income. If the current income is no longer at least 25 per cent different, a supersession decision is made with gross weekly income based on the updated historic income figure. If the non-resident parent fails to provide evidence for the periodic check, the CMS may decide to supersede the calculation decision and use the updated historic income figure for gross weekly income.[93]

The effective date of a supersession decision arising from a periodic check of current income is the day the decision is made.[94] This is usually expected to be 30 days after the CMS writes to the non-resident parent to request her/his updated income details.[95]

If there has been a change in current income that should have been reported by the non-resident parent (ie, a change of 25 per cent or more that s/he should reasonably have understood to be likely to lead to increased liability for child support – see below), the effective date for the supersession decision is the date the income changed.[96]

## Change of circumstances

The CMS intends calculations to remain in place for a reasonable period. In many cases, a calculation based on historic income is likely to remain in force for the year ahead.

If gross weekly income is based on current income, a change of circumstances does not result in a supersession decision unless a parent's current income has changed by at least 25 per cent.[97] Calculations are not adjusted for smaller or short-term changes in income – eg, due to temporary sickness, temporary promotion and seasonal work.

If current income has changed by at least 25 per cent, a supersession decision is made, even if the change means that current income is now less than 25 per cent different from the historic income figure for the latest available tax year.[98]

*Example*

Alfie is paying £76.10 a week child support to Susan for their three children. This is based on current income information, showing his gross weekly income to be £450. Alfie's current income was used at the time the calculation was made as it was more than 25 per cent different from the historic income data provided by HMRC, which showed his gross weekly income to be £300.

After the calculation has been in force for a few months, Alfie provides the CMS with new evidence, showing that he has changed his working pattern and his current gross weekly income is now £320.

This new current income figure is more than 25 per cent different from the current income figure used to make the calculation decision. The CMS makes a supersession decision and calculates his child support liability based on a gross weekly income of £320. This takes effect from the date it received the new evidence. This can be done even though £320 is less than 25 per cent different from the most recent historic income figure.

Even if current income has not changed by 25 per cent, a supersession decision can still be made if:[99]

- the supersession results from changes that are considered by the CMS at an annual review or periodic check; *or*
- the supersession is made on the grounds that the original decision was based on an error of law (see p205); *or*
- the CMS supersedes a calculation that was based on an estimate of current income.

Certain changes to historic income (eg, if the historic income information is changed by HMRC, or if the non-resident parent amends a self-assessment) are grounds for the calculation to be revised.[100] However, HMRC does not routinely inform the CMS of minor changes, and so a revision is only likely to be done if the non-resident parent or person with care queries the accuracy of the historic income figure.

For full details of revisions and supersessions of decisions, see Chapter 9.

## Reporting changes in income

Parents are not required to report changes in their circumstances on a routine basis, except in specific instances – eg, if a qualifying child dies. See p53 for the changes that must be reported. However, there are specific duties on non-resident parents to report certain changes in their income.

If a parent's gross weekly income is based on her/his current income, s/he may be informed by the CMS that s/he must report relevant changes of circumstances. S/he is informed of this in the written notification of the child support calculation decision. S/he must report any such change in writing within 14 days of its occurring. The CMS may specify a longer period.[101] Failure to provide the required information may be an offence (see p39).[102]

If the non-resident parent is paying child support at the basic rate (including 'basic rate plus'), reduced rate or flat rate and gross weekly income is based on her/his current income from employment, s/he must tell the CMS if s/he:[103]

- starts a new job; *or*
- receives a new rate of pay for her/his existing job; *or*
- changes her/his working pattern in her/his existing job.

These changes must be reported if the parent could reasonably be expected to know that they may lead to an increased amount of child support being due. This duty does not apply to those who are self-employed.

Fluctuations in wages from week to week or month to month may not necessarily need to be reported. However, the parent must tell the CMS if her/his wages increase so that over a longer period (ie, five payments if paid weekly, three if paid fortnightly, and two if paid four-weekly or monthly) the average weekly amount is at least 25 per cent more than the gross weekly income that was taken into account in the calculation.[104]

If the non-resident parent is liable for the nil rate and gross weekly income is based on current income, s/he must tell the CMS if her/his gross weekly income increases to £7 or more. This duty applies to income from employment, self-employment and pensions (including income from any of the benefits that qualify for the flat rate).[105]

If gross weekly income is based on historic income, there is no duty on the non-resident parent to notify the CMS if her/his current income becomes (at some point during the year after the calculation decision is made) more than 25 per cent different from the most recent historic income figure. However, if this does happen, the person with care or the non-resident parent could apply for the calculation to be superseded. If the person with care alleges that the current income is at least 25 per cent more than the historic income figure used in the calculation, the CMS is only likely to investigate this if s/he provides information that gives reasonable grounds to do so.

**Note:** if a non-resident parent's income changes significantly due to the outbreak of coronavirus (COVID-19) (eg, due to the need to self-isolate or 'shield', or if s/he has lost her/his job or had to claim statutory sick pay) s/he should report this to the CMS as soon as possible.

## 3. **Shared care**

A number of people may be involved in caring for a qualifying child. The term 'shared care' is used in this *Handbook* to describe a situation where there is more than one person looking after a particular child and those people live in different households. If the people providing care live in the same household (see p13), this is not shared care.[106]

If parents share the care of a qualifying child equally, there is no liability for child support (see p15).[107] However, if one parent provides day-to-day care for a child *to a lesser extent* than the other parent (or person with care), s/he may be treated as a non-resident parent and be liable to pay child support (see p14).

If a parent who is (or who is treated as) non-resident provides sufficient care (see below) for a qualifying child, the amount of child support s/he has to pay may be reduced to reflect the care s/he provides.

If a qualifying child is looked after by a local authority for part of the time, see p88.[108]

**Note:** 'shared care' is different from the situation where different children of the same family have different homes. If the children of a family are divided between two households (eg, if one child lives with one parent and another child with the other parent), two separate child support calculations are carried out. In one, the first parent is the parent with care and the second parent is the non-resident parent. In the second, the roles are reversed. This situation is referred to as 'divided families' in this *Handbook*. The Child Maintenance Service (CMS) may refer to this as **'split care'** (see p67).

## If a non-resident parent shares care

In order for the shared care to affect the child support calculation, a non-resident parent must look after, or be expected to look after, a qualifying child for at least 52 nights a year (ie, one night a week) on average. The care must be provided overnight, and the non-resident parent and the child must stay at the same address.[109] The care could be provided away from the non-resident parent's normal home – eg, while on holiday or at a relative's home. The non-resident parent could also look after the child overnight in the person with care's home while the person with care is away from home during the relevant nights.[110]

The CMS determines the number of nights that count for shared care, based on the number of nights the non-resident parent is expected to provide overnight care for the qualifying child(ren) during the 12 months starting with the effective date of the calculation.[111]

The CMS can use a shorter period than this if it considers it is appropriate to do so – eg, if both parents have agreed a pattern of shared care for a shorter period.[112] If a shorter period is used, the number of nights of care in that period must be in the same ratio as 52 nights is to 12 months in order to amount to shared care.

In determining the number of nights of shared care, the CMS looks at all the evidence. Usually, this information is obtained at the time of the child support application – ie, from telephone contact with the person with care and non-resident parent or from written material provided by them. The CMS must consider:[113]

- the terms of any agreement between the person with care and the non-resident parent, or the terms of any court order providing for contact between the non-resident parent and the qualifying child;
- if there is no such agreement or order, any pattern of care that has been established over the previous 12 months (or a shorter period that the CMS thinks is appropriate to use).

Contact arrangements ordered by a court or agreed in writing, or a past pattern of care, are only evidence that must be considered and not decisive proof of the care situation. The CMS can decide the weight to be given to the contact arrangements in a court order. It is required to consider such arrangements not give effect to them and so will consider the reality of what is happening. If the CMS has good reason (eg, evidence that the arrangements had not been followed in practice), the CMS may decide that the arrangements or pattern should not be the basis for determining the nights of care.[114]

If the evidence of the person with care and of the non-resident parent conflicts, further evidence may be required to resolve the issue. Parents should keep a note of the nights the child spends with them and, in case of a dispute, be willing to supply further evidence – eg, a diary. The CMS (and, in any subsequent appeal, the First-tier Tribunal) must then determine the number of nights spent in each person's care over the period.[115]

The CMS does not routinely review whether agreed shared care arrangements are being kept to. If it is reported that an agreement about shared care is not being complied with, the CMS may seek further evidence from the parties to allow the calculation to be revised or superseded.

If the CMS accepts that the person with care and non-resident parent have agreed to share care, but there is not enough evidence to determine the number of nights of shared care, it can assume that the non-resident parent provides care for one night a week. This assumption can be made if the parties provide conflicting evidence and the number of nights of shared care cannot be determined, even if both parties agree that shared care is provided on more than one night a week. The assumption is applied until a supersession is requested and there is sufficient evidence to determine the actual number of nights of shared care.[116]

If the qualifying child is a boarder at a boarding school or a hospital patient, any night spent there counts as a night with the person who would normally have been looking after the child on that night (see p87).[117]

**Note:** if a non-resident parent is providing some care but not as much as 52 nights a year on average, the child support calculation is not adjusted to take account of the level of care s/he provides, and s/he is expected to pay the same amount of child support as if s/he were not looking after the child at all. This means, for example, that a parent who provides some regular care for her/his children may pay the same amount of child support as one who does not.

However, a non-resident parent in this situation can apply for the calculation to be varied on the grounds that the contact costs are 'special expenses'. A variation for contact costs may also be considered, even if the contact *is* enough to count as shared care and so affect the calculation. See Chapter 5 for details on variations.

## The effect of shared care on the flat rate

If a non-resident parent has been assessed as liable for the flat rate of child support because her/his gross weekly income is less than £100, this is not adjusted to take into account any care s/he provides. However, the amount of child support due is reduced to nil if s/he:[118]

- is liable to pay the flat rate because s/he is in receipt of a relevant benefit or s/he or her/his partner receives one of the relevant means-tested benefits (see p60), including if a reduced flat rate of £3.50 applies; *and*
- cares for the qualifying child for at least 52 nights a year.

The flat rate of £7 is apportioned in relation to the number of qualifying children before any adjustment for shared care is made (see p58). This may mean that a non-resident parent's liability reduces to nil for one person with care because of shared care. However, s/he is still liable for the remaining amounts to the other person(s) with care, in which case s/he pays an amount which is less than £7.

*Example*

Alistair is the non-resident parent of Ben, who lives with his older brother Neil, and Katie, who lives with her mother, Rachel. Alistair looks after Katie one or two nights a week. Both Neil and Rachel apply for child support. Alistair receives income-related employment and support allowance (ESA).

**Step one:** Alistair is due to pay child support at the flat rate of £7, as he receives income-related ESA.

**Step two:** Apportion the flat rate of £7 between the people with care in relation to the qualifying children each cares for – ie, the amount is halved.
To Neil for Ben = £3.50
To Rachel for Katie = £3.50

**Step three:** Alistair cares for Katie over 52 nights a year, so the amount due to Rachel reduces to nil.
Alistair remains liable to pay £3.50 in child support to Neil for Ben.

## The effect of shared care on the basic and reduced rate

If a non-resident parent shares the care of a qualifying child for 52 or more nights a year, the amount of child support s/he is due to pay at the basic rate (including 'basic rate plus') or reduced rate is reduced by an appropriate fraction, depending on the number of nights of shared care.[119] If there is more than one qualifying child, see below.

| Number of nights | Fraction to subtract |
|---|---|
| 52 to 103 | One-seventh |
| 104 to 155 | Two-sevenths |
| 156 to 174 | Three-sevenths |
| 175 or more | One-half |

If a non-resident parent shares the care of a qualifying child for a sufficient number of nights for the one-half fraction to apply, an additional £7 decrease in her/his child support liability is applied in respect of that child.[120] This is known as **'abatement'** and is applied for each child for whom at least 175 nights of shared care applies.

If the decrease results in a non-resident parent being liable to pay a person with care less than £7, s/he pays the flat rate of £7 instead.[121] This includes the situation where the total amount of child support due to all the people with care is decreased to less than £7. In this case, the £7 is apportioned between them in relation to the number of qualifying children.

*Example*

Alex shares the care of Mark with Diane, the parent with care. He looks after Mark on average two nights at the weekend and a couple of weeks in the school holidays. Although Alex provides day-to-day care of Mark, he is treated as a non-resident parent as he does so to a lesser extent than Diane. Alex's gross weekly income is £480.

**Step one:**      Basic rate of child support = 12% x £480 = £57.60
**Step two:**      **Apply decrease for shared care**
                  Alex shares care in the 104–155 band (two-sevenths).
                  £57.60 child support must be decreased by two-sevenths – ie,
                  £57.60 – £16.46 = £41.14

Alex pays Diane £41.14 a week.

**Note:** if Alex has costs for keeping in contact with Mark, he may also be able to apply for a variation (see p95).

Alex increases the amount of time he cares for Mark to three nights one week and four nights the next. In this case, Alex shares care for over 175 nights and the one-half fraction is applied. Alex's child support calculated under the basic rate remains £57.60.

**Step two:**      £57.60 decreased by one-half and a further £7 subtracted – ie,
                  £28.80 – £7 = £21.80

Because of the increase in shared care, Alex pays £21.80 to Diane.

Alex's circumstances change again and his gross weekly income is now £160.

| Step one: | Reduced rate of child support = £7 + (17% x £60) = £7 + £10.20 = £17.20 |
|---|---|
| Step two: | **Apply decrease for shared care** |
| | The fraction to apply remains at one-half, with a further £7 subtracted. |
| | (50% x £17.20) – £7 = £8.60 – £7 = £1.60 |
| Step three: | Child support due is below £7, so Alex pays £7 a week to Diane. |

**Note:** if the increased amount of time Alex spends caring for Mark is accepted as meaning that care is shared equally with Diane, the child support calculation may be cancelled (see p15).

## If there is more than one qualifying child

If a person with care and non-resident parent have more than one qualifying child, the fractions that apply for shared care for each qualifying child are added together, then divided by the number of qualifying children.[122] This applies where care is shared for some, but not all, of the qualifying children or if there are shared care arrangements for each qualifying child.

### Example

Pat is the non-resident parent of Lea and Dylan. Both are cared for by their grandmother, Jean. Lea does not like staying with Pat and only does so occasionally. However, Dylan stays with him on Friday and Saturday nights. Both children stay with him for a few days at Christmas and during the school holidays. Pat's gross weekly income is £420.

| Step one: | Basic rate of child support for two children = 16% x £420 = £67.20 |
|---|---|
| Step two: | **Apply decrease for shared care** |
| | Lea does not stay with Pat for sufficient days for it to count as shared care. |
| | Dylan is in the 104–155 band (two-sevenths). |
| | The fractions which apply are added together and divided by two, as there are two qualifying children cared for by Jean. |
| | (0 + 2/7) ÷ 2 = 2/14 |
| | Pat's child support is decreased by 2/14 of £67.20 = £9.60 |

Because of the shared care, Pat must pay £57.60 (£67.20 – £9.60) to Jean.

**Note:** if Pat has costs for keeping in contact with Lea and Dylan, he may also be able to apply for a variation (see p95).

Lea increases the amount of time she spends with her father and now this counts as shared care.

**Step two:** Lea is in the 52–103 band (one-seventh).

Dylan is in the 104–155 band (two-sevenths).

The fractions are added together and divided by two – ie, $3/7 \div 2 = 3/14$

The child support due is, therefore, decreased by 3/14 because of shared care.

Pat's child support is decreased by 3/14 of £67.20 = £14.40

Because of shared care, Pat must now pay £52.80 (£67.20 – £14.40) to Jean.

Dylan stays with his father more often and increases the amount of care, so that:

**Step two:** Lea is in the 52–103 band (one-seventh).

Dylan is in the 175 or more band (one-half).

The decrease is $(1/7 + 1/2) \div 2 = 9/28$

$9/28 \times £67.20 = £21.60$

£67.20 – £21.60 = £45.60. However, because care for Dylan is in the one-half band, the further £7 reduction applies and the amount of child support due is decreased by a further £7.

Pat now pays Jean £38.60 (£45.60 – £7).

**Note:** if the increased amount of time Pat spends caring for Dylan is accepted as meaning that care is shared equally with Jean, no child support may be payable for Dylan (see p15).

## If care is shared for more than one child with different persons with care

A non-resident parent may be liable to pay child support to more than one person with care (eg, if a father has two children who live with two different mothers) and may share the care of the children with them.

Child support liability is calculated for only one person with care in respect of each qualifying child. The child support due is first apportioned between the persons with care, in proportion to the number of qualifying children each cares for. The amount payable to each is then adjusted to take account of any shared care the non-resident parent provides for the child(ren).

If a second person who is not the non-resident parent provides care for a qualifying child, the CMS does not apportion the child support liability between them. The person with care could agree to pass on some of the child support – eg, an amount reflecting the number of days a week the other person has care of the child. However, this would be an informal arrangement and is not monitored or enforced by the CMS.

*Example*

Ewan is the non-resident parent of two children – Holly, whose parent with care is Ellen, and Jamie, whose parent with care is Laura. Ewan looks after Holly when Ellen is on night shifts, which is every other week apart from holidays, and takes her camping with him on the odd weekend. Jamie and Laura live further away, so Ewan only sees Jamie for a long weekend once a month and two weeks in the summer holidays. Ewan's gross weekly income is £387.50.

| | |
|---|---|
| **Step one:** | The basic rate of child support applies for two qualifying children. |
| | 16% x £387.50 = £62 |
| | The child support due is apportioned between each person with care. Ellen and Laura each care for one qualifying child, so the child support is halved between them. |
| | To Ellen for Holly = £31 |
| | To Laura for Jamie = £31 |
| **Step two:** | **Apply decrease for shared care** |
| | *Child support paid to Ellen for Holly* |
| | Holly is in the 156–174 band (three-sevenths). |
| | 3/7 x £31 = £13.29 |
| | £31 – £13.29 = £17.71 |
| | *Child support paid to Laura for Jamie* |
| | Jamie is in the 52–103 band (one-seventh). |
| | 1/7 x £31 = £4.43 |
| | £31 – £4.43 = £26.57 |
| **Step three:** | The total child support due is £17.71 (to Ellen) + £26.57 (to Laura) |
| | = £44.28 |

# A qualifying child is in hospital or at boarding school

If a qualifying child is in hospital or at boarding school, any night spent there counts as a night with the person who would normally provide care at that time.[123] This includes nights normally spent with a non-resident parent,[124] person with care or local authority.[125]

These nights count in determining whether care of the child is shared and when establishing who is a person with care (see p11) or which parent is to be treated as non-resident (see p14).

*Example*

Nick, who has been living with his mother during the week and spending Friday nights with his father, goes to boarding school. The time as a boarder continues to be treated as if he were living with his mother. Even if the care arrangement changes, so that Nick spends alternate weekends with his father, the nights at school still count as having been spent with his mother.

If the parents agree, or the periods involved are infrequent, the case may be straightforward. However, if the arrangements break down, a normal pattern cannot be established or the parents disagree, the CMS must make a decision on shared care.

*Example*

Ella is a qualifying child cared for most of the time by her mother, Sarah, although her father, Stuart, looks after her on Wednesday and Saturday nights. Over the past year Ella has undergone treatment for cancer, which has resulted in her spending periods in hospital. Because of this, Stuart has only looked after Ella for 42 nights in the year. On 16 of the remaining nights that Ella should have stayed with him, she was in hospital. On the other nights that Ella should have stayed with Stuart, she was unwell and wanted to stay with Sarah. The CMS must decide whether to consider Ella as staying with Stuart for 58 nights or accept that the intention was for her to stay with Stuart on 104 nights in the year. Both parents have the right to challenge the CMS's decision.

If a night spent in hospital or at boarding school would not otherwise have been a night spent with a person with care, a non-resident parent who shares care or a local authority who has part-time care, the child is treated as being in the principal provider's care for that night. For example, if a babysitter looks after a child one night a week, then the child goes into hospital, the babysitter is not a person with care, non-resident parent or local authority. Therefore, that night is treated as one normally spent with the principal provider of day-to-day care.

## A local authority provides part-time care

If a local authority has part-time care of a qualifying child for 52 nights or more in the 12-month period ending with the effective date of the calculation decision (see p131), the child support to be paid by the non-resident parent may be decreased.[126] This applies if:

- a non-resident parent is liable to pay the basic rate (including 'basic rate plus') or reduced rate, (including if a variation has been made which results in her/him paying child support at either of these rates);[127] *and*
- the local authority provides care for at least one night a week on average, but not more than five (see below).

Part-time local authority care has no effect on the flat rate of child support.

A local authority cannot be a person with care.[128] If a child is being looked after by a local authority for more than five nights a week, no child support is payable by the non-resident parent.[129] If a child is at a boarding school, even if this is publicly funded education provision, s/he does not count as being looked after by the local authority.[130]

The CMS may use a period other than the 12 months ending with the effective date if it considers it to be more representative of the current arrangements. A future period may also be considered if the qualifying child is to go into local authority care on or after the effective date.[131] If an alternative period is used, the number of nights of care must be at least in the same ratio as 52 nights to 12 months.[132] (Nights spent in hospital or at boarding school that normally would have been spent in care are included – see p87.)

The child support calculation is only affected if a qualifying child is being looked after by a local authority. If a relevant other child (see p64) is being looked after by a local authority (either full or part time), the calculation is not affected, provided the non-resident parent or her/his partner continues to receive child benefit for her/him (or has elected not to receive child benefit because s/he would be liable for the 'high-income child benefit charge' in income tax).[133]

## The decrease for part-time local authority care

The basic or reduced rate of child support is decreased in relation to the number of nights the qualifying child spends in local authority care.[134] This calculation may be carried out either on its own if a non-resident parent does not share care, or alongside one carried out because a non-resident parent shares care (see p81).

*The effect of part-time local authority care*

| Number of nights | Fraction to subtract |
| --- | --- |
| 52 to 103 | One-seventh |
| 104 to 155 | Two-sevenths |
| 156 to 207 | Three-sevenths |
| 208 to 259 | Four-sevenths |
| 260 to 262 | Five-sevenths |

If a person with care and non-resident parent have more than one qualifying child, the fractions that apply for each qualifying child in local authority care are added together and divided by the number of qualifying children for whom child support is calculated.[135] This applies if one child or all the children are being looked after by the local authority.

If the decrease because of part-time local authority care would reduce the amount of child support to less than £7, the amount due is £7.[136]

*Example*

Jake is the non-resident parent of Michael and Leanne. Michael has just been placed under local authority supervision, which means that over the next six months he will spend four nights a week in a residential unit and the rest of the time with his mother, Naomi. Jake has a gross weekly income of £350 and currently pays child support of £56 (basic rate). This must now be superseded because of the local authority care. The CMS supersedes the decision, considering the ratio in the six-month period.

**Step one:**    The basic rate of child support for two qualifying children applies.
16% x £350 = £56

**Step two:**    **Apply the decrease because of part-time local authority care**
Local authority care for Michael is in the 208–259 band (four-sevenths).
The fractions which apply are added together and divided by the number of qualifying children – ie, (0 + 4/7) ÷ 2 = 4/14
Jake's child support is decreased by 4/14 of £56 = £16

Jake now pays Naomi £40 (£56 – £16).

If Leanne were also in care for two nights a week:

**Step one:**    Same as above.

**Step two:**    Local authority care for Leanne is in the 104–155 band (two-sevenths).
Local authority care for Michael is in the 208–259 band (four-sevenths).
The fractions are added together and divided by two:
(2/7 + 4/7 ) = 6/7 ÷ 2 = 6/14
Jake's child support decreases by 6/14 of £56 = £24

Jake now pays Naomi £32 (£56 – £24).

## A non-resident parent shares care and the local authority has part-time care

If a non-resident parent shares the care of a qualifying child and a local authority also has part-time care of a qualifying child in relation to the same person with care, the appropriate fractions are worked out under each provision and are added together.[137] The non-resident parent's child support liability is then decreased by this fraction.

If this decrease would result in a non-resident parent being due to pay less than £7 , s/he pays £7.[138]

This calculation is carried out at Step two.

*Example*

Jake is the non-resident parent of Michael and Leanne. Michael is still under local authority supervision and spends four nights a week in a residential unit and the rest of the time with his mother, Naomi. Jake's child support is £56 a week. Leanne spends one night a week with Jake, but Michael does not.

**Step two:**     Jake cares for Leanne in the 52–103 band (one-seventh).
The fractions which apply are added together and divided by the number of qualifying children – ie,
$(0 + 1/7) ÷ 2 = 1/14$
Jake's child support liability because of shared care is reduced by 1/14.
Because Michael is in local authority care, the child support due is reduced by 4/14.
$1/14 + 4/14 = 5/14$
Jake's child support liability is reduced by £20 (ie, 5/14 x £56).

Jake now pays Naomi £36 (£56 – £20).

If Leanne were also in care two nights a week, but still spends one night a week with Jake:

**Step two:**     Jake's child support liability because of shared care is reduced by 1/14 (as above).
Local authority care for Leanne is in the 104–155 band (two-sevenths).
Local authority care for Michael is in the 208–259 band (four-sevenths).
The fractions are added together and divided by two:
$(2/7 + 4/7) = 6/7 ÷ 2 = 6/14$
$1/14 + 6/14 = 7/14 = 1/2$
Jake's child support liability is reduced by £28 (1/2 x £56).

Jake now pays Naomi £28 (£56 – £28).

# Notes

**1. The rates of child support**
1 Reg 6 CSMC Regs
2 Sch 1 para 6 CSA 1991
3 Sch 1 para 1(2) CSA 1991
4 Sch 1 para 7(7) CSA 1991
5 Sch 1 para 5(b) CSA 1991; reg 45 CSMC Regs
6 Sch 1 para 4 CSA 1991
7 Sch 1 para 4(1)(b) CSA 1991; reg 44(1) CSMC Regs
8 Sch 1 para 4(1)(c) CSA 1991; reg 44(2) CSMC Regs
9 Sch 1 para 4(2) CSA 1991; reg 44(3) CSMC Regs
10 Sch 1 para 3 CSA 1991
11 Reg 43 CSMC Regs
12 Sch 1 para 1(1) CSA 1991
13 Sch 1 para 10(3) CSA 1991
14 Sch 1 para 2 CSA 1991; reg 2 CSM(CBR) Regs
15 Sch 1 para 2 CSA 1991; reg 2 CSM(CBR) Regs
16 Sch 1 para 10C CSA 1991
17 Sch 1 para 10C(2)(b) CSA 1991; reg 77 CSMC Regs
18 Reg 54 CSMC Regs
19 Reg 52 CSMC Regs
20 Sch 1 para 5A(6)(b) CSA 1991; reg 48 CSMC Regs
21 GC v SSWP & AE (CSM) [2019] UKUT 199 (AAC)
22 Sch 1 para 5A CSA 1991; reg 52 CSMC Regs
23 Sch 1 para 6 CSA 1991
24 Sch 1 paras 5A(2) and 7(7) CSA 1991
25 Reg 5 CS(MPA) Regs

**2. The non-resident parent's income**
26 Reg 34(1) CSMC Regs
27 FQ v SWWP and MM (CSM) [2016] UKUT 446 (AAC), reported as [2017] AACR 24
28 EB v SSWP and CW (CSM) [2019] UKUT 321 (AAC)
29 DWP, The Child Maintenance Compliance and Arrears Strategy: government response to the consultation, July 2018
30 Reg 25(1)(b) CSMC Regs
31 Reg 36(1) CSMC Regs
32 Reg 4(1) CSMC Regs
33 Reg 4(1) CSMC Regs
34 IW v SSWP and DW (CSM) [2016] UKUT 312 (AAC)
35 SB v SSWP and TB (CSM) [2016] UKUT 84 (AAC); IW v SSWP and DW (CSM) [2016] UKUT 312 (AAC); IH v SSWP and EH (CSM) [2018] UKUT 142 (AAC)
36 AR v SSWP and LR (CSM) [2017] UKUT 69 (AAC), reported as [2017] AACR 23
37 Reg 36(5) CSMC Regs
38 AR v SSWP, HMRC & LR (No.2) (CSM) [2019] UKUT 151 (AAC)
39 Reg 35(3) CSMC Regs
40 Reg 36(1)(c) CSMC Regs
41 Reg 36(2) CSMC Regs; in SH v SSWP, CH and HMRC (CSM) [2018] UKUT 157 (AAC) it was decided that reg 36 as originally enacted was internally contradictory and the then para (2)(b) should be disregarded. Para (2) was subsequently substituted – see reg 14 CS(MA) Regs 2019 and Explanatory Memorandum
42 AR v SSWP and LR (CSM) [2017] UKUT 69 (AAC), reported as [2017] AACR 23
43 Part 3 IT(EP)A 2003
44 Part 4 IT(EP)A 2003
45 BB v SSWP and CB (CSM) [2019] UKUT 314 (AAC)
46 Reg 36(1)(d) CSMC Regs; s5 IT(TOI)A 2005
47 s198 IT(TOI)A 2005
48 Reg 36(4) CSMC Regs
49 Reg 36(1)(b) CSMC Regs
50 Part 9 IT(EP)A 2003
51 s637 IT(EP)A 2003
52 s644 IT(EP)A 2003
53 ss638-41 IT(EP)A 2003
54 Reg 36(3) CSMC Regs
55 s577(1) IT(EP)A 2003
56 IW v SSWP and DW (CSM) [2016] UKUT 312 (AAC)
57 Reg 34(2) CSMC Regs
58 Reg 4(2) CSMC Regs
59 Reg 34(2A) CSMC Regs
60 EB v SSWP and CW (CSM) [2019] UKUT 321 (AAC)
61 Reg 37(1) CSMC Regs
62 Reg 38(5) CSMC Regs
63 Reg 40 CSMC Regs
64 Reg 37(2) CSMC Regs

65 Reg 42(1) CSMC Regs
66 Reg 42(2) CSMC Regs
67 Reg 38(2)(a) CSMC Regs
68 Reg 38(2)(b) CSMC Regs
69 Reg 38(3) CSMC Regs
70 Part 3 IT(EP)A 2003; reg 38(4) CSMC Regs
71 Part 4 IT(EP)A 2003
72 *BB v SSWP and CB (CSM)* [2019] UKUT 314 (AAC)
73 Reg 39(2), (3) and (4) CSMC Regs
74 Reg 39(1), (5) and (6) CSMC Regs
75 Reg 41 CSMC Regs
76 s681 IT(EP)A 2003
77 ss567 and 615 IT(EP)A 2003
78 s637 IT(EP)A 2003
79 s575(2)(b) IT(EP)A 2003
80 Reg 19(1) CSMC Regs
81 Reg 19(2) CSMC Regs
82 Reg 19(3) CSMC Regs
83 Reg 19(4) CSMC Regs
84 Reg 20(1) CSMC Regs
85 Reg 35(2)(b) CSMC Regs
86 Reg 20(2) CSMC Regs
87 Reg 21(2) CSMC Regs
88 Child Maintenance and Enforcement Commission, *The Child Support Maintenance Calculation Regulations 2012: a technical consultation on the draft regulations*, December 2011
89 Reg 22(1) CSMC Regs
90 Reg 22(1) CSMC Regs
91 Child Maintenance and Enforcement Commission, *The Child Support Maintenance Calculation Regulations 2012: a technical consultation on the draft regulations*, December 2011
92 Reg 22(3) CSMC Regs
93 Reg 22(2) CSMC Regs
94 Reg 22(4) CSMC Regs
95 Child Maintenance and Enforcement Commission, *The Child Support Maintenance Calculation Regulations 2012: a technical consultation on the draft regulations*, December 2011
96 Reg 22(5) CSMC Regs
97 Reg 23(1) and (2) CSMC Regs
98 Reg 23(4) CSMC Regs
99 Reg 23(3) CSMC Regs
100 Reg 14(1)(f) CSMC Regs; *FQ v SSWP and MM (CSM)* [2016] UKUT 446 (AAC), reported as [2017] AACR 24
101 Reg 9A(1), (4) and (5) CSI Regs
102 s14A(3A) CSA 1991
103 Reg 9A(2) and (6)(a) CSI Regs
104 Reg 9A(2) and (6)(b) CSI Regs
105 Reg 9A(3), (9) and (10) CSI Regs

3. **Shared care**
106 Reg 50(1)(b) CSMC Regs
107 Reg 50(2) CSMC Regs
108 Regs 46, 47 and 50-55 CSMC Regs
109 Sch 1 para 7(4) CSA 1991; reg 46(5)(a) CSMC Regs
110 R(CS) 7/08
111 Reg 46(2) CSMC Regs
112 Reg 46(3) CSMC Regs
113 Reg 46(4) CSMC Regs
114 CCS/2885/2005; *JH v SSWP and LH (CSM)* [2016] UKUT 440 (AAC); *JS v SSWP and ZS (CSM)* [2018] UKUT 181 (AAC); *EA v SSWP and SA (CS)* [2019] UKUT 149 (AAC)
115 CCS/11728/1996
116 Sch 1 para 9(2) CSA 1991; reg 47 CSMC Regs
117 Reg 55 CSMC Regs
118 Sch 1 para 8 CSA 1991
119 Sch 1 para 7 CSA 1991
120 Sch 1 para 7(6) CSA 1991
121 Sch 1 para 7(7) CSA 1991
122 Sch 1 para 7(5) CSA 1991
123 Reg 55 CSMC Regs
124 Reg 46(5)(c) CSMC Regs
125 Reg 53(11) CSMC Regs
126 Reg 53(2) and (4) CSMC Regs
127 Reg 53(1) CSMC Regs
128 Reg 78(1)(a) CSMC Regs
129 Reg 53(10) CSMC Regs
130 R(CS) 1/04; R(CS) 2/04
131 Reg 53(2)(c) CSMC Regs
132 Reg 53(5) CSMC Regs
133 Reg 54 CSMC Regs
134 Reg 53(6) CSMC Regs
135 Reg 53(7) CSMC Regs
136 Reg 53(9) CSMC Regs
137 Reg 53(8) CSMC Regs
138 Reg 53(9) CSMC Regs

# 5

# Chapter 5

# Variations

**This chapter covers:**
1. What is a variation (below)
2. Grounds for a variation (p95)
3. Applying for a variation (p109)
4. What happens after an application is made (p110)
5. Decisions on variations (p114)

## 1. **What is a variation**

A child support calculation (see Chapter 4) can be varied in certain circumstances. A variation allows situations that are not taken into account by the usual calculation to be considered by the Child Maintenance Service (CMS).

A variation can only be made on one of the specified grounds and only if it would be 'just and equitable' to do so (see p95).

You can apply for a calculation to be varied either before it is made or once it is in force.[1]

If an application for a variation is successful, it may result in a child support calculation being made or, if a calculation already exists, its being revised or superseded with the variation incorporated.

If a default maintenance decision (see p129) is in force, an application for it to be varied may contain sufficient information for it to be revised and replaced with a calculation.

Variations are one of the areas of child support law in which disputes frequently arise. There is much caselaw on the issues, and it is best to get advice if you are unsure. Many of the principles established in caselaw were decided on the rules for '2003 rules' cases, but they also apply to variations in '2012 rules' cases.

# 2. Grounds for a variation

A variation can be made for:
- special expenses (see below);
- additional income (see p100).

## Special expenses

A non-resident parent can apply for a variation to have her/his child support liability reduced on the grounds that s/he has the following special expenses:[2]
- costs of maintaining contact with the qualifying child(ren) (see below);
- costs of a long-term illness or disability of a 'relevant other child' (ie, a child who lives with her/him) – see p97;
- previous debts, incurred before the couple separated (see p98);
- boarding school fees paid for a qualifying child(ren) (see p99);
- costs of repaying a mortgage on the home of the person with care and qualifying child(ren) (see p100).

Except for costs associated with an illness or disability of a relevant other child, special expenses can only be considered if they are over £10, regardless of the income of the non-resident parent. If expenses are being considered in more than one category, the £10 threshold applies separately to each. If the expenses in any category are less than £10 a week, a variation is not allowed on that ground. If the expenses in any category are £10 or more a week, the whole amount is counted in full (not just the excess over £10).[3]

The Child Maintenance Service (CMS) can also substitute a lower amount for any special expenses it considers are unreasonably high or have been unreasonably incurred. This may be below the threshold amount or nil. In the case of contact costs, any reduced amount must not be so low that it makes it impossible for the non-resident parent to maintain contact with the child at the level of frequency stated in any court order, provided that contact is actually taking place.[4]

A variation for special expenses reduces the gross weekly income of the non-resident parent that is taken into account in the child support calculation.[5]

## Contact costs

A variation can be considered if the non-resident parent incurs costs, or is reasonably expected to incur costs, in relation to her/his contact with the qualifying child(ren).[6] The costs can be for the non-resident parent or the child. The cost of a travelling companion can also be included – eg, because of disability or long-term illness (of the non-resident parent or the child) or the child's young age. Costs of contact with another child (eg, a child who might have been a qualifying child but for the fact that s/he does not live in the UK) do not count.[7]

Expenses for contact costs may be considered even if they arise for contact that is also being counted as part of a shared care arrangement.

The following count as contact costs:[8]

- public transport fares;
- fuel for a private car. To determine whether the cost for fuel is reasonable, the CMS may compare the amount claimed with an average figure;
- taxi fares, if the illness or disability of the non-resident parent or qualifying child makes it impractical to use another form of transport;
- car hire, if the cost of the journey would be less than by public transport or taxis, or a combination of both;
- accommodation costs for the parent or the child for overnight stays, if a return journey on the same day is impractical, or the pattern of care includes contact over two or more days. The cost of meals does not count;
- minor incidental costs associated with travelling, such as road or bridge tolls or fees. This may include parking fees and ticket reservation fees if it was necessary to incur these to maintain contact with the child. Other costs necessary to maintain contact with the child, such as fees for a contact centre if a court requires contact to be supervised, do not count.[9]

The costs are based on an established pattern of visits, if one exists.[10] If there is no current established pattern, a previous one may be referred to if contact is to begin again. Alternatively, an intended pattern, agreed between the non-resident parent and person with care, may also be used. The pattern set out in a court order may also be used. When contact is set out in a court order, it may only specify an upper limit on visits.

The costs are calculated as an average weekly amount. This is based on a 12-month, or shorter, period that ends immediately before the day the variation would take effect.[11] If it is based on a pattern of contact that has ended before the date of the variation application, the CMS considers the costs incurred between the effective date of the variation and the date on which it would cease – ie, the date on which the circumstances giving rise to the variation end.[12] In other cases, it can be based on anticipated costs.

If a non-resident parent returns from abroad and contact is only one reason for the trip, the CMS may limit costs to those of travel from her/his home in the UK.

Changes in contact may mean the variation is also changed. If contact stops, even through no fault of the non-resident parent, the calculation may be superseded to reflect this.

*Example*

Bronwen has a gross weekly income of £788 and pays the basic rate of child support of £126.08 a week to Ivan for Ursula and Gretchen. She claims a special expenses cost for contact with her children, amounting to £4,100 over a six-month period since the girls attend boarding school. This includes travel from Northern Ireland by ferry, petrol and overnight stays in hotels, amounting to 12 nights over the six-month period.

The amounts included are considered reasonable in the circumstances and the weekly amount is calculated:

£4,100 ÷ 26 = £157.69 a week on average.

This is above the threshold of £10. Therefore, a variation of £157.69 for contact costs may be considered, and Bronwen's gross income reduced by this amount.

Bronwen's gross weekly income is now treated as being £630.31 (£788 – £157.69). The amount of child support due is now £100.85 a week (£630.31 x 16%, as the basic rate applies and there are two qualifying children).

## Costs of a relevant other child's long-term illness or disability

A variation can be considered if the non-resident parent incurs costs for a long-term illness or disability of a relevant other child (see p64).[13]

A long-term illness is one that exists at the date of the variation application or from the date the variation would take effect. It must be likely to last for at least a further 52 weeks or be terminal.[14] A child is considered disabled if:[15]

- the care component of disability living allowance (DLA), the daily living component of personal independence payment (PIP) or armed forces independence payment is paid for her/him; *or*
- s/he would receive DLA care component or PIP daily living component but for the fact that s/he is in hospital; *or*
- s/he is registered blind. (**Note:** in Scotland, the system of registering a person as blind or severely sight impaired no longer applies to children under 16. If that affects your ability to apply for a variation under this rule, seek advice.)

**Note:** receipt of the mobility component of DLA or PIP does *not* count for this purpose.

The reasonable additional costs of any of the following count:[16]

- personal care, attendance or communication needs;
- mobility;
- domestic help;
- medical aids that cannot be provided on the NHS;
- heating, clothing and laundry;
- food essential for a diet recommended by a medical practitioner;
- adaptations to the non-resident parent's home;
- day care, respite care or rehabilitation.

If an aid or appliance can be provided on the NHS, a variation is not normally agreed, even if the item is not available because of a lack of funds at a particular time. However, a variation may be considered if there is likely to be a serious delay in supplying an item which would prevent the child's condition from seriously deteriorating. The CMS may also consider the cost of the aid and whether it can be obtained at a cheaper price.

Any financial help towards these costs from any source, paid to the non-resident parent or a member of her/his household, is deducted if it relates to the expense claimed.[17] Any DLA care component, PIP daily living component or armed forces independence payment being paid for the relevant other child is also deducted from the costs. If DLA, PIP or armed forces independence payment has been applied for, but is not yet in payment, it can be taken into account if it covers the date the variation starts.

### Debts of the relationship

A variation can be considered if the non-resident parent is repaying debts incurred before s/he became a non-resident parent (see p12) of the qualifying child. These costs can count as special expenses, provided the debt arose when that parent and the person with care were a couple.[18] The loan must have been taken out for the benefit of at least one of the following:[19]

- the non-resident parent and person with care, jointly;
- the person with care alone, if the non-resident parent is liable for the repayments;
- a person who is not a child, but at the time the loan was taken:
  - was a child;
  - lived with the non-resident parent and person with care; *and*
  - was the child of the non-resident parent, person with care or both of them;
- the qualifying child;
- any child other than the qualifying child who at the time the debt was incurred:
  - lived with the non-resident parent and person with care; *and*
  - is a child of the person with care.

Loans only count if they are from a qualifying lender, or from a non-resident parent's current or former employer.[20] Qualifying lenders include banks, building societies or other registered lenders – eg, hire purchase.[21]

The following do *not* count as debts for this purpose:[22]

- debts incurred to buy something which the non-resident parent kept for her/his own use after the relationship ended;[23]
- a debt for which the non-resident parent took responsibility under a court order or a financial settlement with her/his ex-partner;
- a debt for which a variation has previously been agreed, but which has not been repaid in the period for which the variation has been applied to the child support calculation;
- debts of a business or trade;
- secured mortgage repayments, except for amounts to buy, repair or improve the home of the person with care and qualifying child;
- endowment or insurance premiums, except those to buy, repair or improve the home of the person with care and qualifying child;

- gambling debts;
- legal costs of the separation, divorce or dissolution of the civil partnership;
- credit card repayments;
- overdrafts, unless taken out for a specified amount repayable over a specified period;
- fines imposed on the non-resident parent;
- any debt incurred to repay one of the above;
- any other debt the CMS considers reasonable to exclude.

Payments on a loan taken out to pay off any negative equity on the former joint home once it has been sold do not count as debts, as the person with care no longer lives there.

A loan taken out to repay a previous debt which would have counted may be included. This means that a debt incurred *after* a person has become a non-resident parent may be grounds for a variation.[24] This can apply whether paying off the previous debt is the sole purpose, or only part of the purpose, of incurring the new debt.[25]

A variation is normally based on the original debt repayment period; any rescheduling of the debt is usually ignored. However, if the person who applied for the variation has been unemployed or ill and the creditors have agreed to extend the repayment period, the CMS can take the extended period into account.

## Boarding school fees

A variation can be considered if the non-resident parent incurs, or reasonably expects to incur, costs for the maintenance element of boarding school fees for the qualifying child.[26] Only term-time costs for non-advanced education at a recognised educational establishment can be included.[27]

If the maintenance element cannot be distinguished from other school fees, the CMS can decide what to include, but this amount should not be more than 35 per cent of the total fees.[28]

If the non-resident parent receives financial help to pay the fees, or pays part of the fees with someone else, a proportion of the costs is included. This is calculated in the same ratio as the maintenance element to overall fees.[29]

In all cases, a variation for boarding school fees must not reduce the amount of income used to calculate child support by more than 50 per cent.[30]

*Example*

Bronwen has a gross weekly income of £788 and pays the basic rate of child support of £126.08 a week to Ivan for Ursula and Gretchen. Bronwen claims special expenses for her contribution to the costs of Ursula and Gretchen's boarding school. She pays the school £1,500 a term – ie, £4,500 a year. Ivan pays the rest of the fees – ie, £4,500 a year.

The fees for each child each term are £1,500 and the maintenance element is £500 a term.

Bronwen's contribution to the maintenance element of the fees is £250 a child each term – ie, £500. Over the three terms this amounts to £1,500, which is converted into a weekly figure (£1,500 ÷ 365 x 7 = £28.77). This is above the threshold of £10, so a variation for a contribution to boarding school fees of £28.77 may be considered. **Note:** if this is accepted, it does not reduce her gross income by more than 50 per cent.

### Payments for mortgages, loans and insurance policies

A variation can be considered if the non-resident parent makes payments to a mortgage lender, insurance company or person with care for a mortgage or loan if:[31]

- it was taken out to buy, or carry out repairs or improvements to, the property by someone other than the non-resident parent; *and*
- the payments are not made because of a debt or other legal liability of the non-resident parent for the period in which the variation is applied; *and*
- the property was the person with care's and non-resident parent's home when they were a couple, and it is still the home of the person with care and qualifying child(ren); *and*
- the non-resident parent has no legal or financial rights in the property – eg, a charge or equitable interest.

Payments may also be considered for an insurance or endowment policy taken out to discharge a mortgage or loan as above, except if the non-resident parent is entitled to any part of the proceeds when the policy matures.[32]

See also p144 for information on when payments made by a non-resident parent to a third party may be offset against child support owed.

### Additional income

A person with care can apply for a variation on the grounds that the non-resident parent has certain additional income that has not been taken into account when calculating her/his child support liability. A variation results in the income being added to her/his gross weekly income used for the calculation, increasing the amount of child support due. **Note:** a variation can only be considered to the extent that it will result in the non-resident parent's gross weekly income not exceeding £3,000. So, if a non-resident parent's gross weekly income is £2,900 and a variation would result in £350 a week additional income, only £100 of that additional income is taken into account.[33]

A variation can be considered if the non-resident parent:
- has unearned income – ie, income that has not been counted in gross weekly income (see p101);
- is on the nil or flat rate in certain circumstances, but has gross weekly income of more than £100 (see p104);

- has 'diverted' income (p105);
- has 'notional income' from assets worth over £31,250 (see p106).

## Unearned income

A variation can be considered if the non-resident parent has taxable unearned income of £2,500 or more a year.[34] Not all taxable income counts. '**Unearned income**' for this purpose is income that is subject to UK income tax from:[35]

- land or property (see p102);
- savings and investments (see p103);
- other miscellaneous sources (see p104).

**Note:** the definitions of the different types of income that are classed as unearned for this purpose are complex and rely on how the sources of the income are treated for income tax purposes. This chapter includes only a summary of some of the main types.

Information on unearned income is collected by HM Revenue and Customs (HMRC) through self-assessment tax returns, and it provides details of the amount in the latest available tax year to the CMS. The CMS only requests this following an application for a variation. **Note:** the government has announced plans to allow unearned income to be included in the initial calculation, rather than only be taken into account after an application for a variation.[36] At the time of writing, no date had been set for this change to take effect.

The CMS can decide the amount of unearned income based on the most recent tax year if:[37]

- the latest available tax year is not the most recent tax year; *or*
- the information for the latest available tax year does not include a self-assessment; *or*
- the CMS is unable, for whatever reason, to request or obtain the information from HMRC – eg, because there has been a failure in the automatic data-sharing system.

The CMS bases the variation decision on actual unearned income figures for a complete tax year. The use of HMRC figures also means that the CMS does not rely on the person with care to provide evidence of the non-resident parent's financial circumstances.

If the CMS agrees to make a variation on this ground, the unearned income is converted into a weekly amount and added to the existing gross weekly income.[38] If the non-resident parent has paid approved pension contributions that have not otherwise been taken into account in the child support calculation, the average weekly amount of these contributions is deducted from the unearned income amount. The pension contributions must have been made in the same tax year to which the unearned income relates.[39]

For a variation based on the value of assets, see p106. If the non-resident parent has sold an asset for a capital gain that would be taxable, this is not, in itself, a ground for a variation. However, the proceeds of the sale could be an asset that is assumed to produce notional income ( see p106).

### Income from land or property

Any taxable income from the use of property or land in the UK or elsewhere counts as additional income. **Note:** if there is no declared income from it, the capital value of property or land may be treated as an asset and a variation considered on the grounds of 'notional income' ( see p106).

In most cases, property income is the rent from tenants or licensees. Certain other payments also count, including:[40]

- ground rent and feu duties;
- if property is let furnished, any payment by the tenant for the use of the furniture;
- premiums and other similar lump sums received for granting certain leases;
- income from caravans or houseboats where these are not moved around various locations;
- service charges from tenants for certain services normally provided by a landlord – eg, cleaning of communal areas, fuel and heating, and arranging repairs;
- deposits/bonds from tenants.

Any expenses incurred wholly and exclusively for the purpose of the property business and that are not of a capital nature (such as the cost of furniture, appliances and improvements to the property) are first deducted from the taxable income.[41] Some of the main categories of allowable expenses include:[42]

- council tax, business rates and water charges, if the agreement specifies that these are the responsibility of the landlord;
- the cost of maintenance and repairs (but not improvements);
- in some cases, the cost of certain energy efficiency measures installed before 6 April 2015;
- for fully furnished properties, certain costs for the wear and tear or renewal of furnishings;
- insurance premiums for contents, building and loss of rent;
- interest on a mortgage or loan taken out to purchase the property;
- the cost of providing services, including the wages of gardeners and cleaners;
- letting agent fees, and certain legal and accountancy fees;
- rent, ground rent and service charges;
- other direct costs – eg, phone calls, stationery and advertising for new tenants.

If only part of a property is let and part is occupied by the non-resident parent, a suitable proportion of the charges can be deducted. Any loss on a property business can usually be set against the property business profits of the following year.[43]

Rent and other income from property outside the UK is treated in the same way. Losses on overseas property cannot be offset against profits on UK property, and vice versa.

If a non-resident parent rents out a room in her/his home under the 'rent-a-room' scheme, the first £7,500 (for the tax year 2020/21) of income a year is not taxable. When calculating the income in this case, expenses cannot be deducted.[44]

Income from property rented as a business (eg, running a hotel, B&B or guest house), or from services not normally offered by a landlord (such as meals, laundry or room cleaning), usually counts as income from self-employment (see p67). Rental income from tied houses and caravan sites, and income from other land-related activity, such as farming and market gardening, are also treated as income from self-employment.[45]

### Income from savings and investments

Any taxable income from savings and investments counts as additional income. **Note:** if there is no declared income from them, the capital value of any savings or investments may be treated as an asset and a variation considered on the grounds of 'notional income' (see p106).

The main types of income that count are:[46]

- interest on invested money, including outside the UK – eg, interest on savings in a bank or building society (including income from selling a right to receive interest);
- dividends and other distributions from UK companies (including the tax credit payable with the dividend), and foreign dividends;
- discounts from securities – ie, the profit from trading in securities such as government stocks and bonds;
- income from government stocks and bonds;
- taxable payments from a life assurance policy, life annuity contract or capital redemption policy;
- payments from a trust;
- payments from the estate of someone who has died;
- interest arising from a debt;
- artificial transactions in futures and options.

Certain types of savings and investment income are exempt from tax and therefore disregarded. These include:[47]

- interest, dividends or bonuses from an individual investment plan, such as an ISA;
- income from certified save as you earn schemes;
- interest under an employee share scheme;
- income from national savings certificates and tax reserve certificates;

- venture capital trust dividends;
- tax-exempt annual payments made by an individual in the UK not for commercial reasons – eg, from a covenant;
- periodic or annuity payments of personal injury damages;
- annuity payments from a Criminal Injuries Compensation Scheme award;
- gains from dealing in certain commodities, financial futures and options;
- the capital element of purchased life annuities;
- tax-free health and employment insurance or immediate-needs annuity payments.

### Miscellaneous income

Any taxable income from other miscellaneous sources may count as additional income. This can include, for example, casual income from one-off jobs, royalties and other income from intellectual property such as sales of patent rights.[48]

Certain types of income that are exempt from tax are not counted, including:[49]
- income from an educational bursary or scholarship;
- payments to adopters;
- certain foreign maintenance payments;
- certain compensation payments to World War Two victims;
- income from domestic electricity microgeneration;
- winnings from premium bonds, lotteries and gambling.

## Income of a non-resident parent liable for the nil or flat rate

In certain circumstances, if a non-resident parent has been assessed as liable for the nil rate (see p59) or flat rate (see p60) of child support and has income which would otherwise be taken into account in a child support calculation, a variation can be considered.

A variation on this ground is possible if the non-resident parent has gross weekly income of more than £100 that would normally be taken into account were it not for the fact that the parent is liable for:[50]
- the nil rate because s/he is:
  - a child; *or*
  - a prisoner; *or*
  - receiving an allowance for work-based training for young people; *or*
  - resident in a care home or independent hospital, or is being provided with a care home service and/or independent healthcare service and receiving one of the qualifying benefits for the flat rate (see p60), or has the whole or part of the cost of her/his accommodation met by a local authority; *or*
- the flat rate because s/he receives a qualifying benefit (see p60). This does not apply if the qualifying benefit is one of the means-tested benefits.

If the CMS agrees to make a variation on this ground, the non-resident parent is treated as having the whole amount of the income for the purpose of calculating a new child support liability. Child support is calculated on this income at the reduced rate (see p61), basic rate or basic rate plus (see p62) as appropriate. The liability calculated in this way is then added to the nil or flat rate.[51]

If a variation has been agreed on this ground, information about the additional income is sought and treated in the same way as for gross weekly income used in the child support calculation. Historic income information from HMRC for the latest available tax year is normally used. If current income is at least 25 per cent different from the historic income, current income can be used for the variation. If current income is used, the non-resident parent must notify the CMS if it changes by 25 per cent or more (see p79).

## Diverted income

A variation can be considered if:[52]
- the non-resident parent can control, whether directly or indirectly, the amount of income s/he receives or the amount that is taken into account as her/his gross income; *and*
- the CMS is satisfied that s/he has unreasonably reduced the amount of income that s/he would have received (and which would have been taken into account in the child support calculation or under a variation) by 'diverting' it to someone else or for some other purpose. The diversion does not have to have been arranged specifically to avoid child support responsibilities. The CMS (or First-tier Tribunal) has a broad discretion to judge what is unreasonable in the circumstances.[53]

This applies to income that would count as gross weekly income and to income that would count as unearned income.

The non-resident parent may have diverted income:
- to a third party – eg, a new partner or close family member;
- to a business (eg, if s/he takes a lower income[54]) or to a pension scheme from which the non-resident parent will benefit later. In this situation, it must be reasonable to make a variation;
- towards other purposes – eg, if s/he uses company assets for private use or business funds for day-to-day expenditure.

Converting earnings from a form that counts as income to one that results in their being excluded in the calculation can be classed as diverting income.[55] The fact that a non-resident parent has failed to take advantage of an opportunity to generate income (eg, s/he chooses to work only part time, or has a second property and chooses not to let it out) does not mean that s/he has diverted her/his income; in order to count as diverted income, the money that might have been generated must be paid to someone else or for another purpose.[56]

The fact that a non-resident parent has disposed of or diverted capital does not mean that s/he has diverted income, even if the capital may have been a source of income.

*Example*

Marcus runs his own import/export business, employing his new partner, Shamira, and his brother. His brother is paid £800 a week and he and Shamira each receive £400. His ex-wife, Helene, gets basic rate child support of £64 for their two children. Helene applies for a variation because she thinks Marcus is diverting income via the company, especially as Shamira does not seem to do any work.

Shamira's salary could be a token payment, and Marcus takes less from the business than he pays his brother. The CMS considers that, on balance, there could be diversion of income via the company and Shamira's wages. Given its contentious nature, the case is referred to the First-tier Tribunal.

Deciding whether a parent has the ability to control the income s/he receives or whether a reduction in income received is unreasonable can be difficult – eg, if a parent is a director, employee or shareholder of a small business. Many cases may require detailed investigation of the circumstances. The way that money is held and distributed in the business is important, particularly whether this follows recognised business and accounting practices and/or is done for justified business reasons.[57] What counts is whether the parent has the ability to control the income in practice (eg, if it is clear that other shareholders involved in a business will agree to her/his proposed distribution of funds) and whether or not this could be legally enforced.[58] The fact that income is moved legitimately within a business (eg, a transfer of all or part of a shareholding in a small business) may still, nonetheless, mean that it is found to have been done to divert income.[59]

The full weekly equivalent amount of any diverted income is added to gross weekly income to calculate the new amount of child support (subject to gross weekly income being capped at £3,000).[60]

## Notional income from assets

A variation can be considered if a non-resident parent has certain high-value assets.[61] A variation on this ground may be appropriate if s/he appears to have an affluent lifestyle, and sources of income that would be taken into account in the calculation cannot be identified. If s/he has significant assets, the CMS can assume a weekly notional income from them.

It is understood that the CMS will not apply a variation on both unearned income grounds and on notional income grounds in respect of the same asset. For example, a non-resident parent owns a second property which is let out. The income from the rent is declared to HMRC and may be grounds for a variation on the basis of having taxable unearned income. The CMS would not also consider a variation on the grounds of having notional income from the property in this case, as it would be unlikely to be considered just and equitable (see p116). Where there is a declared income from the asset, the unearned income ground (see p101) is likely to be the focus. The main aim of the notional income from assets ground is to target parents who appear to be able to support themselves in a way that does not correspond to their declared income.

The CMS must be satisfied that the non-resident parent has a legal or beneficial interest in the asset. This includes any asset which is subject to a trust where the non-resident parent is a beneficiary of the trust.[62]

'Asset' means:[63]
- money – eg, cash, deposits in a bank, building society, post office or credit union account, premium bonds or savings certificates. This also includes any money due to the non-resident parent if the CMS is satisfied that it would be reasonable to require it to be paid to her/him immediately;
- gold, silver or platinum bullion bars or coins;
- a virtual currency which is capable of being exchanged for money – eg, bitcoin;
- land or rights in or over land. A legal or beneficial interest in land is not counted if the land is the primary residence of the non-resident parent or her/his child(ren);
- shares, stocks and unit trusts and gilt-edged securities;
- a claim or right to property which has not been enforced on the date of the application for a variation if the CMS is satisfied that enforcement would be reasonable.

An asset only counts for this purpose if its total value is more than £31,250. A variation on this ground is therefore not possible if a non-resident parent has a large number of low-value assets, even if their combined total value is well over £31,250. The CMS says that if a non-resident parent has a number of items of one class of assets (eg, multiple shares or a number of gold coins), these will be treated as one asset.[64] However, in some cases there may be a dispute about whether a set of rights is to be treated as one asset.[65]

If an asset is subject to a mortgage or charge, its value is established after the amount due on the mortgage or charge is deducted. If an asset is worth less than an outstanding mortgage or charge on it, the 'negative equity' cannot be offset against the value of another asset the non-resident parent has. However, the CMS may consider this when deciding whether it is just and equitable to agree a variation (see p116).[66]

The CMS does not count assets if:[67]
- they have been received by the non-resident parent as compensation for personal injury;
- they are being used in the course of the non-resident parent's trade or business. Shares are not used in the course of a trade or business if the trade or business

is not that of the non-resident parent – eg, if s/he has invested in a company or even owns one, but it is not her/his trade or business;

- it is satisfied that the assets could have been purchased from the non-resident parent's gross weekly income that has already been taken into account in the child support calculation;
- they will need to be sold to meet any extra child support required to be paid as a result of an 'additional income' variation and the CMS is satisfied that the sale would cause hardship to a child of the non-resident parent, or would be unreasonable, taking account of all relevant circumstances. **Note:** it is understood that this is intended to apply only where the asset will need to be sold to meet the extra child support due as a result of a variation on *this* ground, although the wording of the law suggests it applies if an asset would have to be sold to meet the extra due as a result of *any* additional income ground. If you think this applies to your case, get advice.

The income assumed from the assets is determined by using the statutory rate of interest which applies on the date the variation takes effect.[68] This is currently 8 per cent.[69] Eight per cent of the value of the assets is then divided by 52 to give a weekly notional income that is added to the non-resident parent's gross weekly income. This means that a variation on this ground will be considered if the notional income from assets is over £2,500 a year – ie, £31,250 x 8 per cent.

*Example*
Andy pays child support to Rea for their two children. Rea discovers that Andy has recently inherited a property worth £253,500, £40,300 cash and shares worth £17,000. He has also recently bought a second sports car, worth £55,000. Rea applies for a variation on the grounds that Andy should be considered to have notional income from assets.
The shares are an asset, but as their value is not over £31,250, they are not taken into account. The sports car does not fall within the meaning of an 'asset' for this purpose. The property and the cash each count as assets. A weekly notional income of £390 is calculated for the property (ie, £253,500 x 8 per cent ÷ 52). A weekly notional income of £62 is calculated for the cash (ie, £40,300 x 8 per cent ÷ 52). A variation may, therefore, be considered on the basis that Andy has £452 (£390 + £62) a week additional income.
If Andy's gross weekly income for the standard child support calculation is £2,700, only £300 a week additional income is taken into account as this brings his gross weekly income up to the capped amount of £3,000.

## Changes in additional income

Variations on unearned income grounds are based on information provided by HMRC. They are considered by the CMS at the annual review (see p75).

The CMS seeks updated information from HMRC as part of the annual review process and can make a supersession decision on the basis of that information. The supersession decision takes effect from the review date.[70]

If the CMS accepts that the non-resident parent had unearned income in a past tax year but no longer has unearned income in the current tax year (eg, if s/he has sold a property that generated income), it can treat the parent as having no unearned income.[71]

A calculation decision that includes a variation on the ground that the non-resident parent has gross weekly income of more than £100 based on current income can be superseded before the annual review date if her/his current income changes by at least 25 per cent.

There is no obligation on parents who have unearned income included in their gross weekly income to report changes in this.

A variation based on diverted income is not reviewed routinely, as it is not based on information provided by HMRC. A person with care or non-resident parent (or child applicant in Scotland) can apply for a supersession at any time if the circumstances relating to the diversion change.

There is no obligation on parents who have assets that may be assumed to have notional income to report these assets, or changes to them, to the CMS. A variation based on notional income from assets is not reviewed routinely, as it is not based on information provided by HMRC.

# 3. **Applying for a variation**

A person with care, non-resident parent or a child applicant in Scotland can all apply for a variation.[72] An authorised representative can also apply. In certain circumstances, the Child Maintenance Service (CMS) has discretion to reinstate a previous variation without an application having been made (see p121).

An application for a variation can be made either verbally or in writing.[73] You can give details over the phone, although the CMS may ask for a written application – eg, because complicated special expenses are being considered.

The application must state the grounds on which it is made.[74] If it does not, or at least give a reason, it is not accepted as having been properly made.

*Example*
1. Joe applies for a variation because he believes his child support is too high. The CMS does not accept it as a properly made application.
2. Joe applies for a variation because he believes his child support is too high and he cannot afford it because of the high cost of pet food. The CMS accepts the application as properly made, but then rejects it as it is not on one of the specified grounds.
3. Joe applies for a variation because he believes his child support is too high because he cannot now afford the kennel costs he incurs when he travels to see his children. The CMS accepts the application as properly made and it is given a preliminary consideration (see p111). It rejects the application as kennel costs are not one of the specified grounds. Had Joe referred to other contact costs (eg, his travel costs), his application may have proceeded.

An application for a variation can be made before a child support calculation decision has been made.[75] If a calculation is already in force and a new application is made by the same person, the CMS may (but does not have to) treat it as a request for a variation, depending on the circumstances and the information contained in it,[76] even if the application did not expressly ask for a variation.[77] An appeal can also be treated as an application for a variation if it would be more advantageous to the person appealing. The CMS must bear in mind, however, that what is advantageous to the appellant may not be to another party to the calculation.[78]

If an application for a variation is made, but there is insufficient information to decide whether to proceed, the CMS may request further information. This should be provided within 14 days, or a longer period if it is reasonable in the circumstances – eg, if the applicant is in hospital.[79] If the time limit is exceeded without good cause, the effective date of the variation may be affected. If the information is not provided, the CMS has the discretion either to reject the application or to proceed.[80]

There is no specific provision to allow an application for a variation to be amended or withdrawn. In practice, an application could be withdrawn verbally or in writing at any time before a decision is made on it. If a change relates to a period after the effective date of an application, a separate new application for a variation could be made and a separate decision would be made for the period covered by each circumstance.

Two or more applications for a variation may be considered at the same time. In addition, if appropriate, an application made on one ground may be treated as an application on a different ground.[81]

# 4. **What happens after an application is made**

Once an application has been made, the procedure is as follows.
- The Child Maintenance Service (CMS) considers the application (see p111).
- Unless the application is rejected, the other parties are notified and asked to make representations. This is known as 'contesting' (see p112).
- The CMS may make an interim maintenance decision (see p113) or impose a regular payment condition on the non-resident parent (see p113).
- The CMS decides whether or not to vary the amount of child support payable (see p114).

The CMS may also pass a case to the First-tier Tribunal for a determination if the case involves complex or contentious issues (see p114).

The application may not proceed in the above way if the CMS refuses to consider it further – eg, because:[82]
- one of the grounds for rejection is established (see below); *or*
- it is withdrawn; *or*
- the regular payment condition (see p113) has not been met.

## Considering the application

Once an application is properly made, the CMS considers whether it should go ahead (a 'preliminary consideration').[83] At this point, the CMS may reject the application for a variation and decide to:
- revise or supersede the child support calculation, or refuse to revise or supersede it; *or*
- make the calculation, or make a default maintenance decision (see p129).

## Grounds for rejecting an application

The CMS may reject an application for a variation after a preliminary consideration if:[84]
- there are no grounds for a variation; *or*
- it has insufficient information to decide the child support application and so a default maintenance decision is likely to be made; *or*
- the applicant does not state a ground or provide sufficient information to allow a ground to be identified; *or*
- the requirements of the stated ground are not met, or the applicant has not given any information that supports the ground or which is sufficient to allow further enquiries to be made; *or*
- a default maintenance decision is in force; *or*
- the non-resident parent is liable to pay the nil rate, or to pay the flat rate because s/he (or her/his partner) gets universal credit calculated on the basis that s/he does not have any earned income, income support, income-based jobseeker's allowance, income-related employment and support allowance or pension credit (see p60); *or*
- a variation was sought on the grounds that the non-resident parent has additional income, but gross weekly income is already at least £3,000; *or*
- the non-resident parent has applied for a variation on special expenses grounds and:
  - the amount of the expenses is below the £10 threshold (see p95);
  - s/he is already paying £7 or less child support a week;
  - after deducting special expenses, her/his gross weekly income is still above the capped amount of £3,000; *or*
  - gross weekly income has been estimated because insufficient information was available.

## Contesting the application

If it has not rejected an application, the CMS usually then notifies the other relevant parties. This may be done by phone or in writing and must include the grounds on which the application has been made and provide any information or evidence the applicant has given to support it or which has been obtained by the CMS, except information that must not be disclosed (see below).[85]

The CMS may invite the other parties to the child support calculation to make representations within 14 days about anything to do with the application. The 14-day time limit may be extended, if the CMS is satisfied that it is reasonable.[86]

The CMS does not need to notify the other parties if:[87]

- it is satisfied that, on the available information, it will not apply the variation; *or*
- the application is on the grounds of unearned income, the latest available tax year information from HM Revenue and Customs (HMRC) does not show unearned income above the £2,500 threshold and the CMS does not have further information that justifies making further enquiries; *or*
- a previously agreed variation can be reinstated without an application (see p121).

The CMS tends to inform the other parties in writing. If an application has been made by phone, the evidence may be a transcript of the call.

The other parties may respond by phone or in writing, although the CMS may require it in writing. If no contesting information is provided, the CMS may make a decision on the application as it stands.[88]

Any information provided by another party, other than that which must not be disclosed (see below), may be forwarded to the applicant if the CMS considers this reasonable. The applicant is given 14 days to comment on the evidence or information supplied by the other party. This 14-day time limit may also be extended if the CMS is satisfied that it is reasonable. The application must not be decided until this period is over.[89]

It is possible that the applicant may supply further information outside the 14-day time limit and the CMS may already have decided in the meantime to proceed with the application and notify the other parties. In this case, the further information is likely to be passed to the other parties and a further 14 days from the date of this notification (or longer if the CMS is satisfied that it is reasonable) allowed for representations.

## Information that must not be disclosed

In addition to the general rules on disclosing information (see p53), there are additional rules for variations. Supporting evidence or information from one party is not notified to another party if it contains:[90]

- details of an illness or disability of a relevant other child if the non-resident parent has requested that this not be disclosed and the CMS agrees;

- medical evidence that has not been disclosed to the applicant or a relevant person (ie, person with care, non-resident parent or child applicant in Scotland) and which would be harmful to her/him;
- the address of a relevant person or qualifying child, or information that could lead to that individual or child being located, and there is a risk of harm or undue distress to that person or child or any other child(ren) living with that person.

If you request that information is not to be disclosed, this is discussed with you. It may be possible to make an amended application which does not include the relevant details. If you refuse to allow disclosure of information that is relevant for the other party to contest the application, your application could be rejected. However, there may be a good reason for non-disclosure, and each case should be considered on its own merits.

## Interim maintenance decision

If an application for a variation is made before the child support calculation decision has been made, the CMS may make an interim maintenance decision.[91] The amount of the interim maintenance is the child support calculated in the normal way, ignoring the variation. This is to allow the application for a variation to be considered.

An interim maintenance decision can be challenged in the usual way. However, when a calculation is made which replaces this, any appeal against the interim decision may lapse.[92] If the interim maintenance decision is superseded, the usual rule tolerating a change of up to and including 25 per cent in current income (see p78) does not apply.

## Regular payment condition

If a non-resident parent has applied for a variation, the CMS may impose a regular payment condition on her/him if s/he has:[93]
- a poor payment record or arrears; *or*
- failed to make payments while the variation application was being contested and considered; *or*
- special expenses that make it difficult for her/him to meet her/his child support liability.

The amount due under a regular payment condition is either:[94]
- the child support calculated, including that set under an interim maintenance decision; *or*
- the amount that would be due if the variation were agreed.

This means that if the CMS believes that the variation application will be successful, it may set a regular payment condition that adjusts the child support calculated to reflect the variation, reducing the financial burden on the parent. However, if it believes that the application will be unsuccessful and a regular payment condition is imposed, it is set at the calculation rate.

A regular payment condition does not affect the amount of child support the non-resident parent is liable to pay. Therefore, if the amount set is lower than the amount due, there will be arrears if the variation application fails.

The regular payment condition is set independently of any other arrears arrangement the parent may have. It ends either when the CMS makes a final decision on the calculation (whether or not the variation is agreed) or when the variation application is withdrawn.[95]

When a regular payment condition is imposed, the non-resident parent and person with care (and a qualifying child applicant in Scotland) are sent written notification.[96] This makes it clear that if the condition is not met, the application for a variation may lapse.[97]

If a non-resident parent does not meet the regular payment condition within one month of this notification, written notification of this is sent to all the relevant parties.[98] If the regular payment condition has not been met, the CMS may refuse to consider the application for a variation.[99] A refusal to consider the application cannot be appealed.

## Referral to the First-tier Tribunal

Once the application has passed the preliminary consideration and contest stage, it may be passed to the First-tier Tribunal for a determination on whether or not to agree to the variation.[100] This normally only occurs if a particularly contentious or unusual issue is being considered.

If a referral is made, it can only be withdrawn by the CMS. The tribunal can proceed even if the parties come to an agreement.[101] It is also possible for an applicant to add a further ground of variation to an application before it is decided by the tribunal.[102] The tribunal applies the same rules as the CMS and decides whether the variation should be either agreed to or refused.[103] It then passes it back to the CMS to make the child support calculation.[104] This decision by the CMS (ie, to revise or supersede, or to refuse to revise or supersede, the child support calculation) may then be challenged in the normal way (see Chapters 9 and 10).

## 5. **Decisions on variations**

The Child Maintenance Service (CMS) has some discretion when deciding whether to vary the child support calculation. It must bear in mind the general principles of child support law – ie, that:[105]

- a parent is responsible for maintaining her/his children when s/he can afford to do so;
- a parent is responsible for maintaining all her/his children equally;
- the welfare of any child affected by an application for a variation must be taken into account (see p126).

In addition, the CMS must be satisfied that:[106]
- the grounds are met; *and*
- it is just and equitable to agree to the variation (see p116).

The CMS must take into account any representations made by any of the relevant parties to the application.[107]

If the person with care applies for a variation and the CMS needs further information before making a decision, the onus is on the CMS to investigate. There is no onus on the person with care to prove that a variation is justified. The CMS must consider any information that is available to it (eg, information that it can obtain from HM Revenue and Customs), and must take appropriate steps to obtain any such further information.[108]

The CMS must not agree to make a variation if:[109]
- it has insufficient information to make a child support calculation and so would make a default maintenance decision (see p129); *or*
- any of the circumstances apply that would lead to a variation application being rejected after a preliminary consideration (see p111).

A variation is applied by revising or superseding the child support calculation decision. Whether the decision is revised or superseded depends on when the variation application is made. If the grounds for the variation existed at the time the original calculation decision was made, the decision may be revised. If the grounds result from a change of circumstances, the decision may be superseded.

If the CMS agrees to a variation, it can:[110]
- revise or supersede the calculation/replace the interim maintenance decision (see p113); *or*
- make a calculation (this may replace an interim maintenance decision or default maintenance decision – see p129).

In some cases, a variation may be agreed which makes no difference to the amount of child support calculated. A revision or supersession is still carried out, as each decision gives further appeal rights.

Once a variation is made, it is considered each time there is a revision or supersession of the calculation under the usual revision/supersession rules (see Chapter 9). Some changes in circumstances may mean that the variation ceases to have effect, in which case the calculation may be suspended or cancelled in order to remove the variation element. In certain cases, if there is a further change in circumstances, the variation may be reinstated by the CMS without an application (see p121). In other cases, a new request for a variation may need to be made.

## Just and equitable

Even though the grounds are met, a variation is only agreed if it is 'just and equitable' to do so.[111]

There are no specific factors that the CMS must take into account in deciding whether it is just and equitable to make a variation. However, examples of factors that are likely to be considered include:

- the welfare of any child likely to be affected if the variation is agreed (see p126);
- whether agreeing to a variation would lead the non-resident parent or parent with care to give up employment;
- if the applicant is the non-resident parent, whether there is any liability to pay child maintenance under a court order or agreement made before the effective date of the child support calculation;
- if the non-resident parent has applied for a special expenses variation, whether s/he could make financial arrangements to cover those expenses or could pay for them from money currently spent on non-essentials.

This decision is discretionary and the CMS must make it based on the individual circumstances of the case.

The following must *not* be taken into account:[112]

- whether or not the child's conception was planned;
- who was responsible for the breakdown of the relationship between the non-resident parent and the person with care;
- whether the non-resident parent or person with care is in a new relationship with someone who is not the qualifying child's parent;
- any contact arrangements and whether or not they are being kept to;
- the income or assets of anyone other than the non-resident parent;
- any failure of the non-resident parent to pay child support or maintenance under a court order or written agreement;
- the fact that a non-resident parent pays school fees (because the child support legislation leaves the courts to make orders on tuition fees – see p19);[113]
- representations from individuals other than the person with care, non-resident parent or a qualifying child applicant in Scotland.

The CMS must reach a positive conclusion that it is just and equitable to agree to a variation, and not simply that there is no reason not to do so.[114] All factors should be considered, but the CMS (or the First-tier Tribunal on a referral – see p114) decides what weight to give to them.[115] This may mean taking into account circumstances for which either party could have sought a variation, even if s/he did not. For example, since contact costs affect the financial circumstances of a non-resident parent, it may be just and equitable to take these into account when deciding on the variation, even if the application was about something else (and may have been made at the request of the person with care).[116] It may also be just and equitable to take into account voluntary payments by the non-resident parent for expenses that could not have been grounds for a variation.[117] If such wider financial circumstances are taken into account, it must be made clear to all parties on what basis the variation has been decided.

The just and equitable rule cannot be used to increase the amount by which the variation would change the calculation beyond the amount that the ground for variation would suggest.[118] However, the amount may be reduced.[119] For example, the CMS decides that a non-resident parent has notional income from assets of £62 a week. The CMS may decide that it is just and equitable in all the circumstances that only £50 a week additional income is taken into account instead of £62. The CMS cannot decide that it would be just and equitable to take £70 a week into account.

## The effect of the variation

The effect of the variation should not reduce the total amount of child support paid to less than £7, and should not increase the maximum amount of gross income to be taken into account to above the capped amount of £3,000.[120] The following sections examine the effect of a variation on different grounds, including where there is more than one ground. The CMS calls these 'concurrent variations'.

### Special expenses

All special expenses amounts are aggregated (taking account of the threshold rules). The total amount of the non-resident parent's relevant expenses is converted into a weekly amount and deducted from her/his gross weekly income. The calculation is then carried out as normal, using this new total.[121]

If the effect of the variation would be to reduce the child support liability to below the flat rate of £7, the non-resident parent is liable to pay £7.[122]

If the gross weekly income is above the £3,000 capped amount, the special expenses are subtracted from the actual gross weekly income. If this results in a figure that is still above £3,000, the special expenses variation is refused.[123]

*Example*
Bronwen has a gross weekly income of £788 and pays basic rate child support of £126.08 to Ivan for Ursula and Gretchen. She applies for a variation because she has special expenses for the cost of contact with her children, amounting to £4,100 over a six-month period, and she contributes to the maintenance element of their boarding school fees of £500 a term.

Her weekly special expenses are worked out as £157.69 for contact and £28.77 for boarding school costs, totalling £186.46. Both types of special expenses are over the £10 threshold, and so the total amount of £186.46 a week is allowed.

This is deducted from her gross weekly income: £788 – £186.46 = £601.54

Her child support is now worked out in the usual way: 16% x £601.54 = £96.25

The variation for special expenses has reduced her child support liability from £126.08 a week to £96.25.

## Additional income

The amount of any additional income is converted to a weekly amount and added to the non-resident parent's gross weekly income. If this results in a gross income figure above the £3,000 capped amount, the gross income taken into account is restricted to £3,000.[124]

If a variation on additional income grounds is agreed and the child support without the variation would be the flat rate or £7, the amount of child support is £7 plus the amount calculated on the additional income.[125]

*Example*

Helene believes that Marcus is diverting income via his company and applies for a variation. The CMS refers the case to the First-tier Tribunal. The tribunal determines that there should be a variation for additional income on the grounds that Marcus has diverted income, with a weekly value of £360. This amount is added to Marcus's gross weekly income of £400 used in the child support calculation. His gross weekly income is now £760. The amount he is now due to pay Helene is £121.60 a week (£760 x 16%).

If Marcus had been paying the flat rate of child support and the variation for additional income of £360 was agreed, the child support due would now be:

Child support at the basic rate for two qualifying children: 16% x £360 = £57.60

The amount of child support payable: £57.60 + £7 = £64.60

If Marcus's gross weekly income used in the child support calculation had been £2,800, taking account of the diverted income would increase his gross weekly income to the capped amount of £3,000. The remaining £160 of additional income would make no difference to the child support calculation.

## If there is more than one variation

If there is more than one variation element (ie, on both special expenses and additional income grounds, known as a 'concurrent variation'), the results of each variation are added together.[126]

- This aggregate figure is then added to the actual gross weekly income, capping the income at £3,000.

- If the total amount of child support is £7 or less, £7 is payable. The amount payable is apportioned between the people with care, if appropriate.[127]

*Example*

Marcus has a gross income of £400 a week and pays his ex-wife Helene basic rate child support of £64 a week for their two children. The CMS decides that there should be a variation for additional income on the grounds that he has diverted income via his company, with a weekly value of £360. The CMS also decides that there should be a variation on special expenses grounds as Marcus has contact costs of £32 a week for visiting his children and pays £24 a week for debts of the relationship.

The special expenses Marcus pays are deducted from his additional income:

£360 – (£32 + £24) = £304

This amount is added to the gross weekly income: £304 + £400 = £704

Child support at the basic rate for two qualifying children: 16% x £704 = £112.64

The combined effect of the variations is that Marcus now pays Helene an additional £48.64 child support a week.

## When a variation takes effect

If the ground for the variation existed at the initial effective date (see p131) of the child support calculation, the variation takes effect on that date if either:
- the application for a variation is made before the calculation is made;[128] *or*
- the application for a variation is made within 30 days of the date the calculation decision was notified, or within a longer period if the CMS allows a late application for a revision (see p200).[129]

The exception to this is if the non-resident parent applied for a variation on the grounds of previous debts or payments in respect of certain mortgages, loans or insurance policies before the child support calculation was made, and payments towards these are treated as voluntary payments in the initial payment period (see p150). In this case, the variation takes effect from the date on which the non-resident parent was notified of the amount of her/his child support liability.[130]

If the ground did not apply at the initial effective date of the child support calculation, the variation takes effect from:
- the date the ground arose, if this is after the initial effective date but before the calculation is made;[131] *or*
- the date of the variation application;[132] *or*
- the date on which the ground is expected to arise, if the application for variation is made in advance.[133]

If an application for a variation is made before the child support calculation is made and the ground has ceased to exist by the date the calculation is made, the variation is applied for the period the ground existed.[134]

There may be a number of different grounds, agreed over time, and each may have a different date from when it takes effect.

*Example*

Tara applies for child support. The effective date is 27 August 2019. She is notified of her calculation on 19 September 2019. She takes advice and applies for a variation on the basis that an additional income ground applied on 27 August 2019. She makes this application on 8 October 2019 – ie, within 30 days of being notified of the decision on her child support. The variation is agreed and the calculation is revised on 15 November 2019 with effect from 27 August 2019.

Juan, her ex-partner, takes advice and on 3 December 2019 applies for a variation on the grounds that he has been paying off a loan for a car they bought before splitting up and which Tara needs, as she lives in a secluded cottage. He is also just about to start paying boarding school fees for their eldest child in late December. The variation is agreed and a revision is made on 3 January 2020 in which the element for previous debts takes effect from 3 December 2019 and the boarding school fees take effect from 16 December 2019.

Variation for previous debts only applies from December, but Juan could ask that the amounts he paid towards the car before the calculation was made be considered as voluntary payments to offset initial arrears. Had Juan taken advice at the same time as Tara and applied for a variation at the same time as she did, on the grounds of previous debts and that his repayments on the car loan were voluntary payments, there could have been a further variation to the calculation, with the decision taking effect from 27 August 2019.

## When a variation is not applied

A variation is not applied for any period when:[135]
- the non-resident parent is liable for the nil rate, or for the flat rate because s/he is getting a means-tested benefit (see p60); *or*
- a variation was sought on additional income grounds, but the non-resident parent's gross weekly income was already above the capped amount of £3,000; *or*
- the non-resident parent applied for the variation on special expenses grounds and:
  – the amount of the expenses is below the threshold (see p95); *or*
  – the non-resident parent is already paying £7 or less child support; *or*
  – after deducting special expenses, the gross weekly income would still be above the capped amount of £3,000; *or*
  – the gross weekly income has been estimated because insufficient information was available.

When a variation ceases to have effect because of a change of circumstances, a supersession is carried out. This takes effect from the day on which the change occurred. If there is a further later change that means that a variation might apply again, a further application for a variation must be made (unless the CMS has discretion to reinstate the variation – see below).

## Reinstating a variation

The CMS has the discretion to revise or supersede a child support calculation in order to reinstate a variation that has previously been agreed, without the need for a new application. This is most likely to apply to variations on special expenses grounds, as this discretion can be applied if:[136]

- a variation ceases to have effect, because a change of circumstances means that:
  - the non-resident parent's liability is reduced to the nil rate or another rate that means that the variation cannot be taken into account; *or*
  - the child support calculation has been replaced with a default maintenance decision;

*and then:*

- a subsequent change of circumstances means the calculation has been revised or superseded so that the non-resident parent is now liable for a rate which can be adjusted to take the variation into account.

Examples of situations where this could apply include if:

- the non-resident parent is sentenced to a prison term and so becomes liable for the nil rate, but subsequently returns to a basic or reduced rate;
- a variation is agreed and on a subsequent application for a revision or supersession the non-resident parent fails to provide information. Therefore, the child support calculation is replaced by a default decision. Later, the information required is provided and this default maintenance decision is replaced with a calculation. The variation may then be reapplied without a fresh application.

The CMS can reinstate a variation straight away without checking whether the circumstances relating to it have changed. If any party is aware of such changes of circumstances, s/he could apply for a revision or supersession. There is no obligation on the CMS to investigate, so decisions are made based on the information available to it. There is no time limit on the period between the variation ceasing to apply and being reinstated, provided the circumstances that gave rise to the variation remain unchanged.

*Example*

Joe obtains a variation from his basic rate child support on the grounds of his contact costs with his children. He is later convicted of a criminal offence and sentenced to six months in prison. He becomes liable to pay the nil rate. On his release, he becomes liable at the reduced rate. The CMS is not satisfied that the circumstances relating to his eligibility are still the same as it assumes that the pattern of contact with his children may now be different. The CMS does not reinstate the variation. Joe must make a new application for a variation on the grounds of contact costs.

Had a variation been granted on the grounds of previous debts of the relationship, the CMS may have reinstated the variation without Joe having to make a further application, as there is no reason why this ground and its effect should be changed by his imprisonment.

If the calculation ceases, this discretion does not apply. For example, if a parent moves abroad and the CMS ceases to have jurisdiction, but then s/he returns to the UK, a new application for child support and a new application for a variation must be made. However, in some circumstances, the CMS may be able to reinstate the variation without going through the step of its being contested (see p112).

## Challenging a decision

A variation is applied by a decision revising or superseding the child support calculation decision. Once a variation is applied to the calculation, this decision can be challenged by applying for a revision within 30 days (and appealing if necessary). The variation is taken into account in the revision/appeal. Any change of circumstances, whether in relation to the variation or other factors, can result in a revision or supersession of the calculation under the normal rules, depending on the circumstances (see Chapter 9). This also applies to decisions referred by the CMS to the First-tier Tribunal for a decision.[137]

If an application is made for a revision or a supersession of a decision that includes a variation:[138]

- there is no preliminary consideration;
- the usual rules on seeking further information and allowing the application to be contested apply; *and*
- the same factors must not be taken into account when considering whether it would be just and equitable to agree to a variation (see p116).

However, the CMS does not have to notify the other parties and invite representations if:[139]

- the revised or superseded decision would not be advantageous to the applicant; *or*
- it considers that representations from the other parties would not be relevant.

The CMS may decide to revise or supersede, or not to revise or supersede, the decision and notifies the applicant and any relevant parties, as appropriate.

# Notes

### 1. What is a variation
1   ss28A(1) and (3) and 28G(1) and (2)
    CSA 1991; ss28A-28F and Schs 4A and
    4B CSA 1991, as modified by
    CS(V)(MSP) Regs

### 2. Grounds for a variation
2   Sch 4B CSA 1991; regs 63-67 CSMC
    Regs
3   Reg 68 CSMC Regs
4   Reg 68(3) and (4) CSMC Regs
5   Reg 72(1) CSMC Regs
6   Reg 63 CSMC Regs
7   *CMEC v NC (CSM)* [2009] UKUT 106
    (AAC), reported as [2010] AACR 1
8   Reg 63(1) CSMC Regs
9   R(CS) 5/08; *SM v SSWP and FS (CSM)*
    [2013] UKUT 445 (AAC)
10  Reg 63(3)(a) CSMC Regs
11  Reg 63(3)(b) CSMC Regs
12  Reg 63(3)(b)(ii) CSMC Regs
13  Reg 64 CSMC Regs
14  Reg 64(2)(d) CSMC Regs
15  Reg 64(2)(a), (b), (f), (g) and (h) CSMC
    Regs
16  Reg 64(1) CSMC Regs
17  Reg 64(3) CSMC Regs
18  Reg 65(1) CSMC Regs; R(CS) 3/03
19  Reg 65(2) CSMC Regs
20  Reg 65(3)(k) CSMC Regs
21  Reg 2, definition of 'qualifying lender',
    CSMC Regs; see also CCS/3674/2007,
    para 23; s376(4) ICTA 1988
22  Reg 65(3) and (4) CSMC Regs
23  CCS/3674/2007, para 19
24  Reg 65(5) CSMC Regs; R(CS) 3/03;
    R(CS) 5/03; *T v SSWP and A (CSM)*
    [2017] UKUT 492 (AAC)
25  R(CS) 3/03
26  Reg 66 CSMC Regs
27  Reg 66(6) CSMC Regs
28  Reg 66(2) CSMC Regs
29  Reg 66(3) and (4) CSMC Regs
30  Reg 66(5) CSMC Regs
31  Reg 67(2)(a) CSMC Regs
32  Reg 67(2)(b) CSMC Regs
33  Reg 73(1) CSMC Regs
34  Sch 4B para 4(1) CSA 1991; reg 69(1)
    CSMC Regs

35  Reg 69(2) CSMC Regs; Parts 3-5
    IT(TOI)A 2005
36  DWP, *TheChild Maintenance Compliance
    and Arrears Strategy: government
    response to the consultation,* July 2018
37  Reg 69(5) CSMC Regs
38  Reg 69(7) CSMC Regs
39  Reg 69(8) and (9) CSMC Regs
40  Part 3 IT(TOI)A 2005; HMRC, *Property
    Income Manual*
41  ss33 and 272 and IT(TOI)A 2005
42  Part 3 IT(TOI)A 2005; HMRC, *Property
    Income Manual*
43  Reg 69(4) CSMC Regs; s118 ITA 2007
44  ss309, 784, 786, 788(2) and 789(4)
    IT(TOI)A 2005; Income Tax (Limit for
    Rent-a-Room Relief) Order 2015,
    No.1539
45  ss9, 19, 20, 267 and 273 IT(TOI)A 2005
46  Part 4 IT(TOI)A 2005; HMRC, *Savings
    and Investment Manual*
47  Part 6 IT(TOI)A 2005; HMRC, *Savings
    and Investment Manual*
48  ss579, 587, 683 and 687 Part 5 IT(TOI)A
    2005
49  Part 6 IT(TOI)A 2005
50  Reg 70 CSMC Regs
51  Reg 70(2) CSMC Regs
52  Reg 71(1) CSMC Regs
53  *G'OB v CMEC (CSM)* [2010] UKUT 6
    (AAC)
54  *TB v SSWP and SB (CSM)* [2014] UKUT
    301 (AAC); *EH v SSWP (CSM)* [2015]
    UKUT 621 (AAC)
55  R(CS) 6/05; CCS/1769/2007
56  *Green v SSWP and Adams (CSM)* [2018]
    UKUT 240 (AAC), reported as [2019]
    AACR 3
57  See, for example, *RC v CMEC and WC*
    [2009] UKUT 62 (AAC), reported as
    [2011] AACR 38; CCS/1320/2005; CCS/
    409/2005
58  *PS v SSWP and KH (CSM)* [2015] UKUT
    183 (AAC)
59  *AS v SSWP (CSM)* [2018] UKUT 315
    (AAC)
60  Reg 71(2) CSMC Regs
61  Sch 4B para 4(1) CSA 1991; reg 69A
    CSMC Regs
62  Reg 69A(1) and (3) CSMC Regs

63 Reg 69A(2) and (4)(f) CSMC Regs
64 CS(MA) Regs 2018, Explanatory Memorandum, para 7.7(a)
65 CCS 8/2000; *MG v CMEC (CSM)* [2010] UKUT 83 (AAC), reported as [2010] AACR 37
66 *GL v SSWP and EG (CSM)* [2014] UKUT 209 (AAC)
67 Reg 69A(4) CSMC Regs
68 Reg 69A(7) CSMC Regs
69 Reg 69A(8) CSMC Regs; s17 Judgments Act 1838; Judgment Debts (Rate of Interest) Order 1993, No.564; Sch 2 r7.7 Act of Sederunt (Rules of the Court of Session 1994) 1994, No.1443
70 Reg 21 CSMC Regs
71 Reg 69(6) CSMC Regs

**3. Applying for a variation**
72 s28A(1) CSA 1991
73 s28A(4)(a) CSA 1991
74 s28A(4)(b) CSA 1991
75 s28A(3) CSA 1991
76 *DB v CMEC (CSM)* [2010] UKUT 356 (AAC)
77 *DB v CMEC (CSM)* [2010] UKUT 356 (AAC)
78 R(CS) 2/06
79 Reg 58(1) and (2) CSMC Regs
80 Reg 58(3) CSMC Regs
81 Reg 56(3) and (4) CSMC Regs

**4. What happens after an application is made**
82 s28D(2) CSA 1991
83 s28B CSA 1991
84 s28B CSA 1991; reg 57(1) CSMC Regs
85 Reg 59(1)(a) and (5) CSMC Regs
86 Reg 59(1)(b) CSMC Regs
87 Reg 59(2) CSMC Regs
88 Reg 59(4) CSMC Regs
89 Reg 59(3) CSMC Regs
90 Reg 59(5) CSMC Regs
91 ss12 and 28F(5) CSA 1991
92 s28F(5) CSA 1991
93 s28C CSA 1991; reg 62 CSMC Regs
94 s28C(2) CSA 1991; reg 62(1) CSMC Regs
95 s28C(4) CSA 1991
96 s28C(3) CSA 1991
97 s28C(5) CSA 1991
98 s28C(7) CSA 1991
99 Reg 31(2) and (3) CS(V) Regs
100 s28D(1)(b) CSA 1991
101 *Milton v SSWP* [2006] EWCA Civ 1258
102 R(CS) 3/01
103 s28D(3) CSA 1991
104 R(CS) 5/06

**5. Decisions on variations**
105 ss28E(1) and (2) and 28F(2)(a) CSA 1991; *RC v CMEC and WC* [2009] UKUT 62 (AAC), reported as [2011] AACR 38
106 s28F(1) CSA 1991
107 s28E(3) CSA 1991
108 s28D(2A) and (2B) CSA 1991
109 s28F(3) CSA 1991; reg 57(2) CSMC Regs
110 ss28B(2) and 28F(3) and (4) CSA 1991
111 s28F(1) CSA 1991
112 s28F(2)(b) CSA 1991; reg 60 CSMC Regs
113 *DB v CMEC* [2010] UKUT 356 (AAC)
114 R(CS) 3/01
115 CSCS/16/2003
116 CCS/1131/2005
117 *SM v SSWP and BM (CSM)* [2016] UKUT 245 (AAC), reported as [2016] AACR 47
118 R(CS) 5/06
119
120 Regs 72(2) and 74(1A) CSMC Regs
121 Reg 72(1) CSMC Regs
122 Reg 74(1A) CSMC Regs
123 Reg 72(2) CSMC Regs
124 Reg 73(1) CSMC Regs
125 Reg 73(2) CSMC Regs
126 Reg 74(1) CSMC Regs
127 Reg 74(4) CSMC Regs
128 Reg 13(1) CSMC Regs
129 s28G CSA 1991; regs 14(1)(a) and 15 CSMC Regs
130 Reg 13(2) CSMC Regs
131 Reg 13(1)(b) CSMC Regs
132 ss17(4) and 28G CSA 1991
133 Reg 18(2) CSMC Regs
134 Reg 13(3) CSMC Regs
135 Regs 57(1)(d)-(f) and 74(5) CSMC Regs
136 Reg 75 CSMC Regs
137 ss16(1A)(c) and 17(1)(d) CSA 1991; regs 14(1)(a)(ii) and 17(3) CSMC Regs
138 Reg 61(1) CSMC Regs
139 Reg 61(2) CSMC Regs

# Chapter 6

# Decisions

**This chapter covers:**
1. Making decisions about child support (below)
2. The initial child support decision (p126)
3. Default maintenance decisions (p129)
4. Notification of decisions (p130)
5. When liability for child support starts (the 'effective date') (p131)
6. When a calculation ends (p131)

## 1. Making decisions about child support

Child Maintenance Service (CMS) officials are responsible for making decisions about child support. In doing so, they must apply the law to the facts of each case. They have no discretion about how some decisions are made – eg, about the amount of child support due or choosing between alternatives, such as whether a person is habitually resident or not.

Some child support decisions, however, are discretionary decisions – eg, whether a variation would be 'just and equitable' (see p116), or how to collect or enforce payments. The CMS only has discretion if, after deciding on the facts of the case and what the law requires, it still has a choice about what decision to make.

Whenever the CMS makes a discretionary decision, it must take into account the welfare of any child (see p8 for who counts as a child) likely to be affected by the decision.[1] Only the welfare of a child must be taken into account, not that of any adults involved. However, it is not just qualifying children or those named in the application who must be considered; the situation of *any* child likely to be affected by the decision must be looked at – eg, a child of the non-resident parent's new family, or another child of the non-resident parent who does not live with her/him.[2]

This duty to consider the welfare of a child also applies to discretionary decisions made by the First-tier Tribunal and Upper Tribunal.

## The welfare of a child

The duty to consider the welfare of children is a general principle in child support law.[3] The legislation does not make it the paramount consideration, or impose a duty on the CMS or First-tier Tribunal/Upper Tribunal to promote the welfare of any children,[4] but considerable weight should be given to this principle.[5] In general, it should be considered along with the other principles of child support – eg, that each parent of a qualifying child has a duty to maintain her/him.[6]

'Welfare' includes the child's physical, mental and social welfare. For example, if imposing a deduction from earnings order (see p162) would prevent a non-resident parent from visiting a child, that child's emotional welfare may be affected. However, an order may mean the parent with care has more money coming in, which may improve the child's physical and social welfare.

Generally, the welfare of a child must be balanced with the benefits of child support being paid for that child or other children. It is likely to be rare that the welfare of a child will justify a decision or action that is contrary to the principle that parents should support their children. However, if the non-resident parent has a child in her/his household who would be adversely affected by the implications of enforcement action, this might mean that certain enforcement action should not be taken. When deciding on enforcement action, the CMS must not use the welfare of the child principle to avoid the full use of its powers, unless it is genuinely appropriate.[7]

The CMS must record its reasons for any decisions it makes on the welfare of all children who could be affected, and it may be useful to ask to see these records. Give the CMS full details as soon as you can about the effect a discretionary decision may have on a child's welfare. If a decision has been made without considering its effect on a child, supply the information and ask the CMS to reconsider. Some decisions that should involve the welfare of the child principle can be challenged (see Chapters 9 and 10). If the decision cannot be appealed (eg, if it is about enforcement), you could consider making a complaint (see Chapter 11) or applying for a judicial review (see p198).

In addition to the general principle of the welfare of children in child support law, the UK must also comply with international obligations, including a commitment to the welfare of children under the United Nations Convention on the Rights of the Child. This means that in instances where more than one interpretation of the law is possible, the one chosen should be that which more closely complies with protecting the welfare of children.[8]

---

## 2. **The initial child support decision**

Once an effective application has been made (see p27) and the Child Maintenance Service (CMS) has obtained, or tried to obtain, the necessary information, it can:[9]

- make a calculation; *or*
- make a default maintenance decision (see p129); *or*
- refuse to make a calculation (p128).

Details of the case are entered on the CMS computer system and child support is calculated automatically.

The CMS may also make an interim maintenance decision (see p113) if an application for a variation is made before a decision has been made on a child support calculation. The interim maintenance decision will be replaced by the calculation once the application for a variation has been decided.

## Waiting for the calculation decision

If the person with care can provide contact details, the CMS aims to start gathering information from the non-resident parent as soon as possible. It aims to make an accurate decision within a month of an application, but some cases may take up to 26 weeks.[10] If the CMS has to trace the non-resident parent, it is likely to take longer before it can make a decision.

### Delays in dealing with applications

Much of the contact with parents to collect and check information needed to make a calculation and collect payments is done by telephone.

The CMS aims to keep people informed about the progress on their case, and contacts applicants at certain stages – eg, to let them know about negotiations with the non-resident parent about collection or if s/he has made a complaint. However, you can contact the CMS on a regular basis for an update on your application.

A delay after the non-resident parent is contacted about the application does not normally delay the starting date of any calculation (see p131). If the non-resident parent has liability to pay child maintenance under a court order or an agreement, this continues and remains enforceable. Other non-resident parents should consider putting money aside or making voluntary payments (see p150). Parents who are already contributing voluntarily should check whether these payments might be used to offset initial arrears (see p143).

If the non-resident parent is not co-operating, the CMS may make a default maintenance decision (see p129) and may take legal action against her/him (see p39). If you have applied for child support and the CMS does not make a default maintenance decision, request that one be made. If this does not happen, you can complain (see p242). In certain circumstances, the CMS can make a calculation based on an estimate of the non-resident parent's income (see p73).

## Withdrawing the application

If an application is withdrawn or treated as withdrawn (see p28), the CMS cannot make a calculation. If a calculation is made after the application is withdrawn, it can be challenged (see Chapters 9 and 10).

The application cannot be withdrawn after a decision has been made, but the applicant can ask the CMS to cease acting, in which case the calculation is cancelled (see p132).

## Change of circumstances

There is no general requirement to notify the CMS of changes in circumstances. However, both the person with care and the non-resident parent are required to notify the CMS of some changes (see p53).

In practice, any party to a child support calculation (ie, person with care, non-resident person or child applicant in Scotland) may want to tell the CMS of changes or new information that might affect the calculation.

There are also specific rules for when changes of income must be disclosed and which changes result in a calculation being altered (see p78).

When making a decision, the CMS takes into account the information that applied at the date the decision would have effect.[11] Any information about a change after this 'effective date' but before the calculation is made can lead to two or more calculations in respect of different periods. The effective date of each calculation is normally the date the change occurred or is expected to occur.[12]

Changes that occur after a calculation is made may result in a revision or supersession, depending on when the change is notified and its significance (see Chapter 9). Changes resulting in a revision or supersession generally take effect from the day on which an event happens or is expected to happen, or on which a decision is made.

## Refusal to make a calculation

The CMS *must* refuse to make a calculation if:
- the application was made by a person who is not a non-resident parent or a person with care (or, in Scotland, a qualifying child aged 12 or over) (see p7); *or*
- there is a pre-3 March 2003 court order (registered agreement in Scotland) or written agreement (see p20) in force; *or*
- there is a post-3 March 2003 court order (registered agreement in Scotland) that has been in force for less than one year (see p21); *or*
- not all the parties are habitually resident in the UK (see p16); *or*
- there is no non-resident parent, either because both parents live in the same household as the child (see p13) or because the CMS does not accept that the person named is a parent of the child (see p9); *or*
- there is no qualifying child (see p8).

The CMS can also delay making a calculation pending the outcome of a 'test' case (see p236). Otherwise, the CMS must make a calculation.[13]

If there is a change of circumstances so that one of these situations applies for a period beginning after the effective date, the CMS makes a calculation that ends on the date of the change.

If a qualifying child dies before the calculation is made, a decision is still made for the period from the effective date to the date of death (see p28).

The CMS cannot refuse to make a calculation just because it has insufficient information or because it may affect the welfare of a child.[14] The CMS may make a default maintenance decision (see below). If the CMS refuses to make a calculation, the applicant (and, if the applicant is a child in Scotland, any person with care or non-resident parent who had been notified of the application) must be notified in writing of the decision, how to apply for a revision or supersession (see Chapter 9) and the right of appeal (see Chapter 10).[15]

A fresh application may be made after the refusal – eg, if there is a change of circumstances, such as the non-resident parent returning to live in the UK.

# 3. **Default maintenance decisions**

If the Child Maintenance Service (CMS) does not have enough information to make a calculation, or to revise or supersede a decision, it may make a default maintenance decision.[16]

A default maintenance decision is for a set amount. The amount depends on the number of qualifying children applied for:[17]

- £39 a week if there is one qualifying child;
- £51 a week if there are two qualifying children;
- £64 a week if there are three or more qualifying children.

These amounts may be apportioned (see p58) if there is more than one person with care looking after different qualifying children. Any relevant non-resident children (see p65) are ignored.

The 'effective date' of a default maintenance decision is the same as it would have been for a child support calculation decision (see p131).

Notification of a default maintenance decision must state the effective date, the default rate, the number of qualifying children, details of any apportionment and the information needed to make a child support calculation.[18] It should also include details of the right to request a revision, supersession or an appeal.[19]

## When a default maintenance decision ends

A default maintenance decision may be revised at any time – eg, when it is replaced by a calculation.[20] In practice, this only happens when the CMS has sufficient information to determine the case properly (ie, to make a calculation) from the effective date.

# 4. **Notification of decisions**

The Child Maintenance Service (CMS) must notify the person with care and non-resident parent (and child applicant in Scotland) once a child support calculation or interim maintenance decision (see p113) has been made.[21] This also includes default maintenance decisions (but see below). There are similar rules on notifying revision and supersession decisions (see Chapter 9) and decisions to cancel calculations (see p133). A decision does not have full legal effect until the relevant people are notified of it.[22]

There is no requirement for decisions to be notified in writing, although in practice most notifications are. The notification of the calculation or interim maintenance decision, or of a decision to revise or supersede a decision, must include information on:[23]

- the effective date (see p131);
- where relevant, the gross weekly income of the non-resident parent, including:
  – whether it is based on historic or current income; *and*
  – if it is based on current income, whether this has been estimated (see p73);
- the number of qualifying children (see p8);
- the number of relevant other children (see p64);
- the weekly rate of child support and any collection fees;
- any variations;
- any adjustments for apportionment (see p58), for shared care by the non-resident parent or part-time local authority care (see p80), or for maintenance being paid for a relevant non-resident child (see p65); *and*
- the rules for requesting a revision, supersession and appeal.[24]

The CMS does not have to include the information above where it has decided not to supersede a decision. However, it should still notify the parties of the decision where practicable, and should include information on the rules for challenging the decision.[25]

The CMS can correct an accidental error in a decision, or in the record of a decision, at any time (see p196). If it does so, it must also notify the person with care and non-resident parent (and child applicant in Scotland) as soon as practicable. This notification must be in writing.[26]

Unless the people concerned have given written permission, a notification should *not* contain:[27]

- the address of anyone else other than the recipient or information that could lead to her/his being located; *or*
- information on anyone other than people with care, non-resident parents or qualifying children.

If there are errors or someone disagrees with the decision, s/he may challenge it (see Chapter 9).

If there is a court order for maintenance, the court is notified of the calculation.

## 5. When liability for child support starts (the 'effective date')

The date a child support calculation first comes into force and liability begins is called the **'effective date'** or 'initial effective date'.[28] The 'effective date' is specified in the notice issued to the non-resident parent informing her/him that an effective application for child support has been made (see p27). The Child Maintenance Service (CMS) may telephone the non-resident parent on or before the effective date and then confirm this in writing to the parent's last known address. If the CMS does not telephone the parent, it must send written notice to the parent's last known address at least two days before the effective date.[29] The initial effective date is usually two days after the written notice is issued.[30]

An alleged non-resident parent cannot delay the effective date of a calculation by disputing parentage. The CMS does not make a calculation until the issue of parentage is resolved (see p42) but, if it later decides that the person is the non-resident parent, the calculation is backdated to the initial effective date.

When making a decision, the CMS takes into account the information that applied at the date the decision would have effect.[31]

There are different rules for effective dates after a supersession or revision (see Chapter 9) and for calculations replacing default maintenance decisions (see p129).

## 6. When a calculation ends

A calculation continues until the Child Maintenance Service (CMS):

- cancels it at the request of the person who applied for child support (see below); *or*
- supersedes it after a change of circumstances means it has ceased to have effect (see p132); *or*
- supersedes it for another reason (see p204); *or*
- revises it (see p199).

In some circumstances, this means that the calculation is replaced by another; in others, no further calculation is made. When the cancellation takes effect depends on the grounds on which the supersession or revision was made, or the nature of the request (see p133). Any arrears remaining after a calculation ends may still be collected (see Chapter 8). If an application is made for a child of the non-resident parent who is not named in the existing calculation, the calculation is superseded and a new calculation replaces the old one.

## Requesting a cancellation

A calculation must be cancelled when the applicant requests that the CMS cease acting.[32]

The request may be made verbally or in writing. The CMS must then stop all action, including collecting and enforcing arrears, although the person may specifically ask for action on arrears to continue.

### If the parents are living together

When the request to cancel a calculation is made, reasons need not be given. However, if the reason is that the parent with care and non-resident parent are living together, the CMS should be told. Once all the parties share a household, the non-resident parent is no longer non-resident (see p12), so the child is no longer a qualifying child and the calculation ceases to have effect (see below).

## The calculation ceases to have effect

Some changes of circumstances mean that the calculation is automatically terminated. The CMS must cancel a calculation (including a default decision) if the calculation ceases to have effect because:[33]

- the non-resident parent or person with care dies; *or*
- the only, or all, qualifying child(ren) is (are) no longer a qualifying child(ren); *or*
- the non-resident parent ceases to be a parent of the only, or all, qualifying child(ren).

This means that the calculation is cancelled, for example, when:

- a child aged 16 or over leaves non-advanced education or becomes too old to count as a child (see p8); *or*
- the qualifying child, non-resident parent and parent with care start living together (see p12); *or*
- the qualifying child goes to live with someone else and, as a result, the person with care no longer counts as a person with care; *or*
- the qualifying child is adopted, in which case the non-resident parent is no longer a parent; *or*
- the non-resident parent is no longer considered a parent because of the results of a DNA test or a declaration/declarator of parentage.

## Other cancellations

If the event leading to a possible cancellation requires investigation, cancellation of a calculation requires a formal decision by the CMS, either at its own initiative or following a request or application (see p131). The calculation remains in force until cancelled by a CMS decision (or until it ceases for some other reason).[34]

The CMS must cancel the calculation if the person with care, non-resident parent or qualifying child is no longer habitually resident in the UK (see p16).[35]

If a non-resident parent has successfully contested parentage, the calculation is cancelled and s/he may obtain a refund of any child support paid (see p42).

If an applicant fails to provide the CMS with enough information to make a revision or supersession decision, the CMS *may* cancel the calculation.

## When the cancellation takes effect

If a calculation is cancelled because it ceases to have effect or because of another relevant change (including the circumstances above), the cancellation takes effect from the date the change occurred.[36]

If the cancellation is because the non-resident parent is not considered to be the parent because of a DNA test or declaration/declarator of parentage, the cancellation takes effect from the effective date of the original calculation (see p131).[37]

If a person with care requests that a calculation be cancelled, the cancellation normally takes effect from the date the request was received. A different date may apply, depending on the reason for the cancellation.[38] It may be appropriate to end the calculation on a later date if an applicant has asked for this.

## Notification of the cancellation decision

When the CMS cancels a calculation or refuses to cancel one, it must notify the non-resident parent, person with care and child applicant in Scotland, and must also provide information on revisions and supersessions and on the right of appeal.[39]

If the calculation was made following an application from a child in Scotland and that child is no longer a qualifying child, the CMS must notify the person with care, non-resident parent and any other children aged 12 or over who are potential child applicants that the calculation has been cancelled.[40]

# Notes

### 1. Making decisions about child support
1 s2 CSA 1991
2 CCS/1037/1995
3 s2 CSA 1991
4 *Brookes v SSWP* [2010] EWCA Civ 420
5 *R v Secretary of State for Social Security ex parte Biggin* [1995] 2 FCR 595, [1995] 1 FLR 851
6 s1(1) CSA 1991; *Brookes v SSWP* [2010] EWCA Civ 420
7 *Brookes v SSWP* [2010] EWCA Civ 420
8 *Smith v SSWP* [2006] UKHL 35

### 2. The initial child support decision
9 s11 CSA 1991
10 gov.uk/making-child-maintenance-arrangement
11 Reg 5 CSMC Regs
12 Sch 1 para 15 CSA 1991; regs 13 and 18(2)-(4) CSMC Regs
13 s11(2) CSA 1991
14 R(CS) 2/98
15 Reg 24 CSMC Regs

### 3. Default maintenance decisions
16 s12(1) CSA 1991
17 Reg 49 CSMC Regs
18 Reg 25(2) CSMC Regs
19 Reg 24(2) CSMC Regs
20 s16(1B) CSA 1991; reg 14(3) CSMC Regs

### 4. Notification of decisions
21 Regs 24 and 25 CSMC Regs
22 *R (Anufrijeva) v SSHD* [2004] 1 AC 604; *SSWP v AM (IS)* [2010] UKUT 428 (AAC)
23 Regs 24(1), 25(1) and 26 CSMC Regs
24 Reg 24(2) CSMC Regs
25 Regs 24(2) and 26(2) CSMC Regs
26 Reg 27A(3) CSMC Regs
27 Reg 25(3) CSMC Regs

### 5. When liability for child support starts (the 'effective date')
28 Reg 12 CSMC Regs
29 Regs 7, 11 and 12 CSMC Regs
30 Reg 12 CSMC Regs
31 Reg 5 CSMC Regs

### 6. When a calculation ends
32 ss4(5) and (6) and 7(6) and (7) CSA 1991
33 Sch 1 para 16 CSA 1991 Sch 1 para 16 CSA 1991
34 *SM v CMEC* [2010] UKUT 435 (AAC); *GR v CMEC* [2011] UKUT 101 (AAC); *TB v SSWP and RB (CSM)* [2017] UKUT 218 (AAC)
35 s44(1) CSA 1991
36 Reg 18(3) CSMC Regs
37 s16(3) CSA 1991
38 s17(4) CSA 1991
39 Regs 24 and 27 CSMC Regs
40 Reg 27(2) CSMC Regs

# Chapter 7

# Collecting and paying child support

**This chapter covers:**
1. Introduction (below)
2. Payment of child support (p136)
3. Collection of other payments (p145)

## 1. Introduction

Once a decision on liability for, and the amount of, child support have been made, payment can be made in different ways. The non-resident parent can pay directly to the person with care without the payment going through the Child Maintenance Service (CMS). Alternatively, the CMS can collect and enforce child support,[1] and certain other maintenance payments (see p145).[2] **Note:** the CMS usually refers to the non-resident parent as the 'paying parent' and the person with care as the 'receiving parent'.

Fees are charged for using the CMS's collection service (see p138) and when some types of enforcement action are taken (see p187).[3]

If the collection service is used, a payment schedule is set up. If this breaks down and arrears accrue, debt management procedures may be put in place and the CMS may decide to take enforcement action. If child support is being paid directly and payments are missed, the person with care can inform the CMS, and debt management and enforcement action can also be taken. If the non-resident parent has arrears, see Chapter 8.

The CMS does not have discretion about the amount of child support due.[4] The amount of child support cannot be altered, except by a revision, supersession, appeal or variation. The CMS does not suspend the current collection just because the non-resident parent states that s/he cannot afford to pay. However, it may agree to lower payments if a decision on a revision, supersession, appeal or variation is pending (see p153).

Decisions on how payment is enforced *are* discretionary and should take into account all the circumstances of the individual case and the welfare of any child(ren) likely to be affected (see p126). This should allow scope for negotiation between the CMS and the individuals involved. Ask the CMS to investigate the circumstances fully in order to allow it to use its discretion appropriately.

## 2. **Payment of child support**

The Child Maintenance Service (CMS) can require the non-resident parent to pay child support:[5]
- directly to the person with care (see below); *or*
- directly to a child applicant in Scotland; *or*
- to, or via, the CMS, provided the person with care, non-resident parent or child applicant in Scotland has requested this (see below); *or*
- to, or via, another person.

The CMS has broad discretion to decide how payment is to be arranged. This includes the payment of any collection or enforcement fees.[6] Before making these decisions, the CMS must, as far as possible, give the non-resident parent and the person with care an opportunity to make representations and must take these into account.[7]

### Direct payment

The CMS prefers the parties to agree that child support should be paid by the non-resident parent directly to the person with care. If direct payments are agreed, once the CMS has calculated the amount owed, the parties make their own arrangement about when and how payments will be made. This is known as '**direct pay**'.

The CMS informs each parent about the amount of any initial arrears and the date regular payments should start. It recommends payment by standing order or a money transfer service (such as PayPal or MoneyGram) if the person with care does not want to disclose financial details to the non-resident parent. The CMS can also advise the person with care about setting up a 'non-geographic' bank account (an account with a central or national sort code rather than one linked to a local branch) and can then pass the account details securely to the non-resident parent. This type of sort code does not give any information about the area in which the person with care lives.[8]

Direct payments are not monitored by the CMS. Both parties should therefore keep careful records of the payments made. If the payment arrangement breaks down, the person with care can ask to use the collection service (see below).

**Note:** if the non-resident parent in a closed '1993 rules' or '2003 rules' case who has transferred to the '2012 rules' was subject to enforced methods of payment (such as a deduction from earnings order) for the old case, the CMS offers her/him a '**compliance opportunity**'. This is an opportunity to comply voluntarily (eg, by paying by direct debit or one of the other voluntary methods of payment (see p140) over the first six months of the '2012 rules' case. During this period, in most cases, half of the child support due is paid by voluntary methods, and half by a deduction from earnings order (see p162) or by deduction from a bank account (see p170) in order to safeguard some payment. The non-resident parent is only then offered the option of 'direct pay' if s/he pays on time and in full throughout the six-month period. If s/he refuses or fails to comply, enforced methods of payment continue.[9]

If the non-resident parent is on benefit at the start of this compliance opportunity, or moves onto benefit during the period, the above does not apply. The case is administered by the CMS's collection service and child support payments are made by deductions from benefit in the usual way (see p141). A decision on whether the non-resident parent is likely to pay, and should be allowed to make direct payments, is made on the information already available. If s/he is considered likely to pay, the case is administered under 'direct pay'. If not, it continues under the collection service, with the collection fees due (see p138).[10]

## The collection service

The person with care (or child applicant in Scotland) can request that payment of child support be made via the CMS.[11] The CMS calls this collection service '**collect and pay**'. The non-resident parent pays child support to the CMS, which then passes it on to the person with care. The CMS can only provide the collection service if the person with care (or child applicant in Scotland) requests the service.[12] It can only do so if the non-resident parent agrees, or if the CMS thinks that s/he is unlikely to pay otherwise.[13] The non-resident parent can apply to switch to 'direct pay' without the agreement of the person with care at any time, but the CMS will only agree to that if it considers it to be in the best interest of the qualifying child(ren). The CMS will always agree if a person with care asks to switch to direct pay.[14]

If the non-resident parent is on benefit, the person with care may want to use the collection service to obtain direct deductions from the benefit. This is particularly useful if a voluntary arrangement cannot be reached. However, there is a collection fee for direct deductions from benefit through the collection service (see p141).

The collection service can be requested at a later date – eg, if payments become irregular. The request can be made verbally or in writing.

If the collection service is being used, the CMS has discretion to decide:

- the method by which the non-resident parent pays;[15]
- the person to whom child support is paid;[16]
- the method by which payment is made to the person with care;[17]

- the timing of payments;[18] *and*
- the amount of payments towards any arrears.[19]

The CMS must notify the non-resident parent in writing of the amounts and timing of payments due, to whom and how s/he must make payment, and details of any amount that is overdue and remains outstanding. If a previous '1993 rules' or '2003 rules' case has been closed and outstanding arrears were transferred to the new computer system when the parties applied under the '2012 rules', this notice must also include those outstanding arrears.[20] The notice is sent as soon as possible after the child support calculation is made and again after any change in the details in the notice.[21] A copy is sent to the person with care.

Only payments actually received by the CMS can be passed on. The CMS aims to make the first payment to the person with care within six weeks of making the initial payment arrangements with the non-resident parent. It also aims to transfer payments as soon as it receives them and no later than one week after receiving them from the non-resident parent.[22]

Using the collection service removes the need for direct contact between the non-resident parent and person with care (although using a non-geographic bank account and having the CMS pass the details to the non-resident parent can also remove the need for direct contact – see p136). It should also help ensure regular payments by starting enforcement action (see p161) as soon as payments are missed, although this does not always happen.

Even if the collection service is used, you should always keep your own records and evidence of payments in case you need to query the accuracy of arrears or the standard of service in handling payments. A payment statement is only issued periodically or on request (see p142).

## Fees

Both the non-resident parent and the person with care must pay regular fees if the 'collect and pay' service is used.[23] These are intended to encourage people to make direct payments instead.[24]

The following fees apply.[25]

- The **non-resident parent** must pay an additional fee of 20 per cent of her/his child support liability for each day for which 'collect and pay' arrangements are in place. If s/he is paying child support to more than one person with care and not all are paid by 'collect and pay', the fee is only charged on those payments for which 'collect and pay' has been arranged.[26]

Four per cent of the amount of child support due is deducted before paying the **person with care**.[27]

If the amount actually paid by the non-resident parent is lower than the amount due, the CMS still deducts a fee of 4 per cent of the amount paid before making the payment of child support to the person with care.[28]

*Example*

Joe is the non-resident parent of four children who live with his former partner, Susan. Joe has been assessed as liable to pay £35 a week in child support to Susan. If the collection service is used, Joe must, in fact, pay £42 a week (£35 + (20% x £35)) to the CMS. The CMS also deducts £1.40 (4% x £35) from the child support due to Susan, so she receives £33.60 a week. The balance of £8.40 a week is retained by the CMS.

If the calculation of fees results in a fraction of a penny, this is disregarded if it is less than a half. If a half or over, it is rounded up to the next penny.[29]

In certain circumstances, the CMS can waive the fees for cases which are related to previous '2003 rules' or '1993 rules' cases that were subject to enforced methods of payment (such as a deduction from earnings order) and which have now been closed (see p1). The CMS intends to waive the fees for a limited period to allow the non-resident parent a 'compliance opportunity' (see p136) to determine whether it is appropriate to allow her/him to pay directly. In order to manage the 'compliance opportunity', payments must be administered by 'collect and pay'. Fees can be waived if:[30]

- the person with care, non-resident parent and qualifying child in a '2012 rules' application are the same as in a previous '2003 rules' or '1993 rules' case; *and*
- a notice of liability ending was issued on or after 23 May 2016 in relation to the previous case; *and*
- the previous case was one in which payment was being enforced on the date the notice of liability ending was issued; *and*
- the new application under the '2012 rules' was made before liability in the previous case ended; *and*
- the CMS has specified that child support due under the new '2012 rules' calculation is to be paid by certain methods (eg, standing order, direct debit, automated credit transfer, credit card, debit card, cheque, postal order, banker's draft or cash), or by a combination of one of those methods and a deduction from earnings order (see p162), in order to allow the non-resident parent to demonstrate that s/he is still likely to pay without an enforced method of payment; *and*
- the first payment made in accordance with these payment arrangements is the first payment of child support due under the '2012 rules' calculation.

In such cases, collection fees can only be waived from the effective date of the '2012 rules' calculation to the date the CMS decides that the payment arrangements are to end – ie, the end of the 'compliance opportunity', usually expected to be the first six months of the '2012 rules' calculation. The power for the CMS to waive fees in these cases will end on 22 May 2021.[31]

### If someone is both a person with care and a non-resident parent

In some child support calculations, someone might be both a person with care and a non-resident parent at the same time – eg, if the qualifying children from a relationship live with different parents after the relationship has ended. In this situation, both parents may be liable to pay child support to each other and a separate calculation is made for each. The CMS can offset their liabilities so that only the person liable to pay the higher amount pays, but only if the collection service is being used.[32] (Where direct pay is used, parties could arrange between themselves to offset liabilities so that only one party pays the net amount due.)

*Example*
Ali and Nazia have two children, Mohammed and Faisal. When they separate, Mohammed lives with Ali and Faisal lives with Nazia. Both parents apply to use the collection service. Ali works full time and is liable to pay child support of £60 a week. Nazia works part time and is liable to pay child support of £20 a week.
Instead of the CMS collecting and distributing two sets of payments, it deducts Nazia's liability from Ali's:
£60 – £20 = £40
Ali pays Nazia £40 per week. Nazia does not pay anything.

If someone's liability is offset in this way, collection fees are only calculated on the net amount paid, rather than on the actual liabilities – ie, in the above example, Ali pays £48 a week (£40 plus 20 per cent) and Nazia receives £38.40 a week (£40 minus 4 per cent).

If both parties to a child support calculation are non-resident parents and persons with care and both fall into arrears, these can also be offset so that the CMS only has to pursue the party with the largest debt (see p154).[33]

### Method of payment

The CMS can specify that the non-resident parent make payments by whichever of the following methods it considers appropriate:[34]

- standing order;
- direct debit;
- automated credit transfer;
- credit card;
- debit card;
- cheque;
- postal order;
- banker's draft;
- voluntary deductions from earnings (a deductions from earnings order can also be used as a method of enforcing payment if the non-resident parent has arrears or fails to agree a payment method – see p162);
- cash.

If the collection service is being used, the CMS asks for payment to be made by direct debit or by deductions from earnings.[35] The CMS can direct a non-resident parent to take all reasonable steps to open a bank or building society account for the purposes of paying child support and any collection fees.[36] However, there is no penalty for failing to do so.

When deciding the method of payment, the CMS should give the parties the opportunity to make representations and must take these into account.[37]

If the non-resident parent is receiving certain benefits, the CMS normally deducts the amount for child support directly from the benefit before s/he receives it (see below).[38]

If payment is made via the CMS, the person with care is usually paid by automated credit transfer, unless the CMS considers that it is necessary to use another method.[39] The person with care is asked to provide details of a bank, building society or post office account. If you do not have an account, or experience difficulty opening one, contact the CMS.

## Deductions from benefit

If a non-resident parent on benefit is required to pay child support at the flat rate (see p60), s/he may pay this directly to the person with care. Direct pay is available to non-resident parents on benefit, in the same way as for other non-resident parents. However, the CMS prefers that non-resident parents on benefit use collect and pay.

If the collection service is being used, the CMS asks Jobcentre Plus to make a deduction from the non-resident parent's benefit for child support.[40] Although child support is calculated weekly, the frequency of the deductions aligns with the frequency of her/his benefit payments.

Deductions can be made from the benefits that qualify a non-resident parent for the flat rate (see p60).[41] From July 2019, deductions can also be made from universal credit (UC) if the non-resident parent has earned income.[42]

If someone should pay at the flat rate but a variation has been made which results in the reduced or basic rate being payable instead, deductions can be made towards the new amount of child support calculated.

If a non-resident parent and her/his partner are on one of the means-tested benefits that qualify for the flat rate (see p60) and each is a non-resident parent, the flat-rate deduction of £7 is split between them so that each contributes half the amount to their respective persons with care.[43]

The CMS requests the deduction and Jobcentre Plus must make it in full wherever possible. The parent must be left with at least 10 pence a week (one penny for UC).[44] Partial deductions are not made. The deduction for child support is always made, whatever other deductions are due.

**Note:** deductions from benefit also cover any fee due, making the total deduction £8.40 a week (and the amount received by the person with care is then £6.72 – ie, £7 minus four per cent). If the non-resident parent was offered a 'compliance opportunity' at the start of the '2012 rules' case (see p136) and has been accepted as likely to pay voluntarily, deductions from benefit do not include an element for collection fees.[45]

Both the person with care and the non-resident parent are notified that deductions are to be made.

If there are arrears of child support, see p154.

## Timing of payments

Whether direct pay or collect and pay is used, the CMS calculates the total amount of child support (and any collection fees) due to be paid over a 'reference period' of 52 weeks, beginning on the effective date (see p131) or on the annual review date (see p75).[46] This total amount due is based on the assumption that the amount of child support will remain unchanged for the 52-week period. The non-resident parent is then required to pay child support in equal instalments. The frequency of payments (usually weekly or monthly) is agreed with the non-resident parent, and is usually at the same frequency as her/his wages are paid if s/he is employed. The non-resident parent is sent a 'payment plan', showing how much is due to be paid, the start and end dates of the reference period and the frequency of payments.[47] The person with care is sent an 'expected payment plan' showing the same information.[48] New payment plans are issued if the amount due changes.

Unless undue hardship would be caused to any of the parties, the frequency of payments to the person with care is the same as the frequency set for the non-resident parent's payments (but see p165 for deduction from earnings orders).[49]

Unless payments are to be by direct debit or standing order, the non-resident parent is advised to make each payment three to four days before the due date in order to ensure that payments are received on time and to avoid arrears. Clearance times are allowed for each method of payment, but the CMS aims to make payments to the person with care within a week of receiving them from the non-resident parent.[50] If a delay in payments is caused by maladministration on the part of the CMS, the person with care may wish to complain and claim compensation (see Chapter 11).

## Records and evidence of payments

It is important to keep records of both the payments made and received, in case mistakes are made. Records can be in the form of bank statements or receipts if payments are made in cash. If either party disputes the amount that the CMS says is owed, the CMS can be asked to provide a statement of transactions and a breakdown of its calculations.

## Overpayments

An overpayment can arise because:
* a calculation has been changed and the amount of child support due for a past period has been reduced; *or*
* the non-resident parent has paid more than the regular payment due for some other reason (including making voluntary payments in the initial payment period); *or*
* there has been a CMS error.

If the CMS receives an unexpected payment from the non-resident parent, it should check to determine the reason for this – eg, it could be for an overdue collection to offset arrears or an amount towards a future collection.

If there is an overpayment, the CMS has discretion about how it deals with it.[51] The amount may be allocated to reduce arrears due under a previous calculation or, if there are no arrears, it can be used to reduce the amount payable under the current calculation.[52] Adjustments may also be made if there are overpayments of voluntary payments in the initial payment period (see p150).[53] If this is the case, the CMS first makes adjustments to balance out the overpayment.

An adjustment of the amount due under the current child support calculation may reduce the amount to nil.[54] If it does, the parent with care will not receive any more child support until the overpayment has been recovered.

If all, or some, of an overpayment made by the non-resident parent remains after offsetting it against regular child support, arrears and other liability, the CMS can make a refund to the non-resident parent.[55] Refunds are only usually made if there are no overdue collections or arrears on the case. The CMS should refund overpayments made because of CMS error – eg, if a person was told to pay more than the calculation required. If you are in this situation, you may also wish to complain and request compensation (see Chapter 11).

### Recovery of overpayments from the person with care

Allocating overpayments against arrears or regular child support payments is a discretionary decision, and so the person with care may wish to negotiate with the CMS about the rate at which the amount is to be recovered, or for repayment to be made in a different way.

If it is not possible to reduce previous arrears or regular child support payments (perhaps because there is no current calculation and no arrears owed), or if the CMS decides that recovering arrears in this way is not appropriate, it can decide to reimburse all or part of an overpayment directly to a non-resident parent.[56] If the CMS reimburses the non-resident parent, it can recover all, or part, of it from the person with care if s/he has benefited from being overpaid.[57] This also applies to reimbursing overpayments caused by the non-resident parent making voluntary payments.[58]

The CMS aims to recover all overpayments, and contacts the person with care to ask for repayment and to discuss options for how repayment will be made. However, CMS guidance states that recovery of an overpayment from the person with care is not enforceable if there is no current child support calculation in force.[59] If the person with care does not agree to make the repayment, recovery is suspended. An overpayment cannot be recovered from the person with care if s/he was on income support (IS), income-based jobseeker's allowance (JSA), income-related employment and support allowance or pension credit at any time during the period in which the overpayment occurred or on the date the non-resident parent was reimbursed.[60] CMS guidance also states that recovery of an overpayment becomes temporarily unenforceable when a person with care starts to receive benefits, such as IS or income-based JSA, and it should be suspended. It may be reconsidered for recovery at a future date. In addition, the guidance states that the CMS cannot enforce the recovery of overpayments caused by its own administrative error, but the person with care will be asked whether s/he is prepared to repay them.

All decisions relating to recovery of overpayments are discretionary. When making them, the CMS must consider the welfare of any child(ren) likely to be affected by the decision (see p126). Before allocating overpayments against arrears or regular child support payments, the CMS must also consider, in particular:[61]

- the circumstances of the non-resident parent and person with care; *and*
- the amount of the overpayment and the period over which it would be reasonable to adjust the child support payable in order to rectify the overpayment.

If you dispute whether an overpayment should be recovered from you, or if it appears to have been caused by an administrative error by the CMS, you should obtain advice. You may wish to complain (see Chapter 11) about any maladministration, taking into account all the loss and inconvenience caused. You should argue that a past overpayment caused by an error by the CMS should not have an impact on you and your child(ren) now.

## Payments made to a third party

The CMS can treat certain payments made to a third party (eg, a mortgage lender) as payments of child support. This can include voluntary payments made between the effective date and the date of the calculation (used to offset any initial arrears – see p149) and payments made after the effective date.[62]

If the person with care agrees to receive payments from the non-resident parent outside the usual child support collection service (eg, if a non-resident parent agrees to pay an urgent utility bill on behalf of the person with care), these may be offset against the amount of child support owed by the non-resident parent.[63] Payments can only be offset if child support is collected by the CMS's collection service.[64] The amount can be offset against any arrears owed, or from her/his ongoing liability if there are no arrears.

For a payment to be offset, it must have been agreed by the person with care and must be for one of the following, in relation to the home in which the qualifying child lives:[65]

- a mortgage or loan either to purchase the property or to pay for essential repairs to it;
- rent on the property;
- mains-supplied gas, water or electricity charges;
- council tax payable by the person with care;
- essential repairs to the heating system;
- essential repairs to 'maintain the fabric' of the home.

Non-resident parents who pay child support directly can reach their own offsetting agreement, but the CMS does not monitor it.[66]

If the CMS intends to reduce ongoing payments of child support to the person with care, it should take into account the circumstances of both parties and the period over which it would be reasonable to adjust the payments.[67] If the current calculation is adjusted, the amount payable may be reduced to nil.[68]

The decision to offset payments made to third parties is discretionary and there is no right of appeal against it. If you are unhappy, you could complain about how the CMS has used its discretion (see Chapter 11).

# 3. **Collection of other payments**

The Child Maintenance Service (CMS) can collect and enforce other forms of maintenance if child support is being collected.[69] Some parents may have, for example, 'top-up' maintenance under a court order in addition to child support (see p19).

The CMS's power to collect other maintenance is discretionary. The CMS can only collect other maintenance that falls due after it gives the non-resident parent written notice that it will do so.[70]

The following payments under a court order can be collected by the CMS:[71]

- additional child maintenance in excess of the CMS maximum;
- maintenance for a child's education or training;
- maintenance paid to meet the additional expenses of a child with a disability;
- maintenance paid for a stepchild – ie, a child living with the person with care who is not a qualifying child, but who was accepted by the non-resident parent as a member of her/his family when the child used to live with her/him;
- spousal or civil partner maintenance for a person with care of a child for whom child support is being collected.

The methods used by the CMS for collecting and enforcing other types of maintenance are the same as for child support.[72] If a non-resident parent is paying more than one type of maintenance and pays less than the total amount required, s/he should stipulate how the amounts are to be allocated. The CMS allocates as requested, except that if arrears of child support are specified, current child support is paid before arrears. If the non-resident parent does not stipulate, the CMS has discretion on how to apportion the payments.[73]

## Collection of court costs

If the CMS applies to a court to decide whether a person is a parent, the court can order her/him to pay the CMS's costs in bringing the case to court, including the cost of any DNA tests (see p47).

The CMS negotiates with the liable person about how these costs should be paid. It initially requests the full amount due, but payment by instalments may be agreed.

Payment of these costs can only be enforced through further court action – the rules for enforcement of child support (see p161) do not apply. The relevant court is the county court in England and Wales or the sheriff court in Scotland. If the case is contested, a hearing is arranged in the court with jurisdiction for the area in which the parent lives. The usual debt enforcement procedures can be applied by the court.

# Notes

**1. Introduction**
1 s29(1) CSA 1991
2 s30(1) CSA 1991
3 DWP, *Supporting Separated Families: securing children's futures*, Cm 8399, July 2012; CSF Regs
4 R(CS) 9/98

**2. Payment of child support**
5 s29 CSA 1991; reg 2 CS(C&E) Regs
6 Reg 1(2A) CS(C&E) Regs
7 Reg 6 CS(C&E) Regs
8 CMS factsheet CMSB029GB, *Managing Your Payments With Direct Pay*, October 2013, available at gov.uk

9 Written ministerial statement by the Minister for State, DWP, House of Commons, *Hansard*, 20 May 2013, col 58WS; CS(DOF) Regs, Explanatory Memorandum
10 CS(DOF) Regs, Explanatory Memorandum
11 s29(1)(b) CSA 1991
12 s29(1)(b) CSA 1991
13 ss4(2) and (2A) and 7(3) and (3A) CSA 1991
14 DWP, *Supporting Separated Families: securing children's futures*, Cm 8399, July 2012; CMS leaflet CMSB001GB, *About the Child Maintenance Service: a guide for paying parents and receiving parents*, April 2019

15 Reg 3 CS(C&E) Regs
16 Reg 2 CS(C&E) Regs
17 Reg 5 CS(C&E) Regs
18 Reg 4 CS(C&E) Regs
19 Reg 4 CS(MPA) Regs
20 Reg 7(1) CS(C&E) Regs
21 Reg 7(2) CS(C&E) Regs
22 CMS leaflet CMSB013GB, *Receiving Child Maintenance: information for receiving parents with a Collect and Pay arrangement*, October 2013
23 s6 CMOPA 2008; CSF Regs 2014
24 DWP, *Supporting Separated Families: securing children's futures*, Cm 8399, July 2012
25 DWP, *Supporting Separated Families: securing children's futures*, Cm 8399, July 2012
26 Reg 7(2) CSF Regs 2014
27 Reg 7(3) CSF Regs 2014
28 DWP, *Government Response to the Consultation Supporting Separated Families: securing children's futures*, Cm 8742, November 2013; reg 7(3) CSF Regs 2014
29 Reg 7(5) CSF Regs 2014
30 Reg 12A CSF Regs 2014; CS(DOF) Regs, Explanatory Memorandum
31 Reg 1(2) CS(DOF) Regs
32 s41C(3) CSA 1991; reg 5 CS(MPA) Regs
33 Reg 7 CS(MPA) Regs
34 Reg 3(1) CS(C&E) Regs
35 CMS leaflet CMSB009GB, *Paying Child Maintenance: information for receiving parents with Collect and Pay arrangement*, October 2013
36 Reg 3(2) CS(C&E) Regs
37 Reg 6 CS(C&E) Regs
38 CMS leaflet CMSB009GB, *Paying Child Maintenance: information for receiving parents with Collect and Pay arrangement*, October 2013
39 Reg 5(1) CS(C&E) Regs
40 This system tag automaticly created in DB.
41 s43 CSA 1991; Sch 9B SS(C&P) Regs
42 Reg 8(2) CS(MA) Regs 2019 and Explanatory Memorandum
43 Sch 1 para 4(2) CSA 1991; reg 44(2) and (3) CSMC Regs
44 Reg 35(l) and Sch 9B SS(C&P) Regs; Sch 7 para 2(4) UC,PIP,JSA&ESA(C&P) Regs
45 CS(DOF) Regs, Explanatory Memorandum
46 s29(3)(ca) and (3A) CSA 1991; reg 4 CS(C&E) Regs, as substituted by reg 4(1) CS(MOC&NCR) Regs
47 CMS leaflet CMSB009GB, *Paying Child Maintenance: information for receiving parents with a Collect and Pay arrangement*, October 2013
48 CMS leaflet CMSB013GB, *Receiving Child Maintenance: information for receiving parents with Collect and Pay arrangement*, October 2013
49 Reg 5(3) CS(C&E) Regs
50 CMS leaflet CMSB009GB, *Paying Child Maintenance: information for receiving parents with a Collect and Pay arrangement*, October 2013
51 Regs 8 and 9 CS(MPA) Regs
52 Reg 8 CS(MPA) Regs
53 Reg 9 CS(MPA) Regs
54 Regs 8(3) and 9(3) CS(MPA) Regs
55 s41B(2) CSA 1991
56 s41B(2) CSA 1991
57 s41B(3) and (4) CSA 1991
58 s41B(7) CSA 1991
59 CSA online procedures, release No.153, December 2012
60 Regs 10A and 10B CS(AIAMA) Regs
61 Regs 8(2) and 9(2) CS(MPA) Regs
62 Regs 6 and 7 CS(MPA) Regs
63 Reg 6(1) CS(MPA) Regs
64 s41C(3) CSA 1991
65 Reg 6(3)(a)-(f) CS(MPA) Regs
66 CS(MPA) Regs, Explanatory Memorandum
67 Reg 7(2) CS(MPA) Regs
68 Reg 7(3) CS(MPA) Regs

### 3. Collection of other payments
69 s30 CSA 1991; CS(CEOFM) Regs
70 Reg 5 CS(CEOFM) Regs
71 Reg 2 CS(CEOFM) Regs
72 Regs 3 and 4 CS(CEOFM) Regs
73 s30(3) CSA 1991

# 8

# Chapter 8

# Arrears

**This chapter covers:**
1. Arrears (below)
2. Enforcement action (p161)
3. Fees for enforcement action (p187)
4. Delays in collection and enforcement (p189)

## 1. Arrears

The Child Maintenance Service (CMS) can only act on arrears if child support is being collected and paid through its collection service (see p137).[1] If the collection service is being used, the CMS can take enforcement action as soon as payments are missed.

If a non-resident parent pays child support directly to the person with care, the person with care must notify the CMS that payments have stopped. The CMS is otherwise not aware of this. The CMS may then decide to take enforcement action. If it does, it also starts managing ongoing future payments through the collection service. It does not pursue arrears if payments are being made directly, even if they arose from a past period when the collection service was being used. However, it can add the arrears to the payment schedule.

If direct payment arrangements break down and the case is moved onto the collection service (see p137), the CMS will ask for payment records for the time direct payment was in place, pursue arrears due for this time and charge fees (see p138) on these arrears.

Alternatively, if a private family-based arrangement for child maintenance is made instead, the CMS closes the case, then treats it as an 'arrears-only' case and pursues the arrears.

The CMS cannot take enforcement action on non-payment of maintenance in a private agreement. If a private agreement breaks down, the person with care can apply to the CMS for child support instead. The CMS can pursue all arrears of child support from the date the child support calculation is requested, but not any missed payments under the private agreement before that date.[2]

The CMS's priority is to collect arrears in cases where child support is still in payment, so that children for whom child support is being paid can benefit from the arrears recovered. Historic arrears in cases where child support is no longer being paid are a lower priority, and may be written off (see p157).

If the non-resident parent now resides in another European Union country, the CMS can enquire about assets and enforce certain arrears that accrued while both parents were resident in the UK (see p161).

When '1993 rules' and '2003 rules' cases closed as part of the case closure process (see p1) and a new application for child support was made, any outstanding arrears from the closed cases were verified at that point and further action considered (see p159 for further details).[3]

## Initial arrears

As the first child support calculation is usually made after its effective date (see p131), there are almost always initial arrears.

The CMS draws up a 'payment plan', which shows payments for the following 12 months, including initial arrears. The proposed schedule is discussed and agreed with the non-resident parent. Written confirmation of the collection schedule is issued once the non-resident parent has agreed to it.[4]

The written notification states:[5]

• the amount due and to whom it is to be paid;
• how it is to be paid – ie, method, day and interval between payments;
• any amounts that are overdue and outstanding.

The CMS may request payment of the initial arrears as a lump sum. If a non-resident parent cannot pay this all at once, s/he may negotiate an agreement to pay in instalments or a collection schedule to cover both the initial payment and ongoing liability (see p151).

A parent who fails to pay the outstanding arrears within seven days of the written notification of the amount due may face further enforcement action.

If you think the calculation is wrong, you may be able to challenge the decision (see Chapters 9 and 10). If you object to the way the CMS is dealing with collecting the amount you owe, you can make a complaint (see Chapter 11).

**Note:** if a court order made on or after 3 March 2003 has been in force for more than a year and there is an application to the CMS, any payments due under that order which the non-resident parent has made after the effective date are treated as payments of child support.[6] This helps to avoid additional liability for child support accumulating if there is a gap between the effective date (at which point the court order ceases to have effect) and the date the calculation is actually made. If the payments made under the court order are at a higher rate than those due under the calculation, this is treated as an overpayment of child support and the calculation can be adjusted accordingly.

## Voluntary payments made in the initial period

If the non-resident parent makes voluntary payments through the CMS (or, if the CMS agrees, directly to the person with care or a third party) after the effective date, but before the calculation is made and notified, these may be offset against arrears of child support.[7] The CMS may seek the views of the parties when considering whether a payment should be classed as a voluntary payment.[8] By accepting a payment as a voluntary payment, the CMS can be deemed to have agreed to its being made directly to the person with care or a third party.[9] As these are discretionary decisions, the CMS must consider the welfare of any child likely to be affected (see p126). There is no right of appeal against these decisions.

Only the following types of payment can be offset:[10]

- in lieu of child support;
- in respect of a mortgage or loan on the child's home, or for repairs or improvements to the property;
- rent on the child's home;
- mains gas, water or electricity at the child's home;
- council tax payable at the child's home;
- repairs to the heating system at the child's home;
- repairs to the child's home.

Payments can be made by cash, standing order, cheque, postal order, debit card or other method or arrangement from an account of the non-resident parent or on her/his behalf – eg, credit card.[11]

If the payments are made to the CMS, it passes them on to the person with care. Once the CMS has made the calculation, the voluntary payments are offset against the initial arrears.

If the payments are made directly to the person with care or a third party, the CMS checks with the person with care whether payments have been made.[12] This is normally done by phone. If the person with care confirms the payments, this is usually accepted without any further need for proof. If there is a dispute about whether a payment has been made, the CMS asks the non-resident parent to verify the payments by providing bank statements, duplicates of cashed cheques, receipts, paid bills or invoices, or a written or verbal statement from the person with care.[13] It is in the interests of both parties to ensure payments are recorded, and the CMS should explain to the non-resident parent the importance of keeping a record and provide a form on which to do so.

If either party disagrees with a decision about offsetting, s/he can make a complaint (see Chapter 11).

If offsetting means that the non-resident parent has overpaid child support, the calculation may be adjusted to compensate her/him, or a refund may be made.[14]

If the non-resident parent makes payments outside the usual collection service after the calculation is made (eg, if s/he pays an urgent bill on behalf of the parent with care), see p144.

## Arrears notice

The CMS may begin to consider action to recover arrears when:

- a payment from the non-resident parent to the CMS is not received; *or*
- child support is being paid directly to the person with care and s/he notifies the CMS that a payment due has not been received.

The CMS aims to begin action within three days of a payment being missed.[15] The CMS contacts the non-resident parent to discuss the issue, normally by telephone at first and followed up in writing if no response is received. The non-resident parent may request an appointment at a local office to discuss payment face to face with CMS staff.

If the non-resident parent has missed one or more child support payments, the CMS must send her/him an arrears notice stating the amount of all the outstanding arrears owed. The notice also explains the rules about arrears and requests payment of the outstanding amount.[16]

The arrears notice only shows the total amount of outstanding arrears, but the non-resident parent can ask the CMS at any time to provide an itemised list of payments due but not received.[17]

If you have received an arrears notice, you should check that the amount owed is correct and tell the CMS of any mistakes. If you think that the balance is incorrect, ask for a payment statement (see p142) and compare this with your own records. It is important to keep the CMS informed so that it does not start enforcement action in the meantime.

The non-resident parent can contact the CMS to negotiate payment by instalments (see below). Once an arrears notice has been issued, another does not have to be sent if arrears remain uncleared, unless the non-resident parent has paid all the arranged payments for a 12-week period.[18]

The CMS does not send an arrears notice if direct pay arrangements are in place, or the collection service is being used but no enforcement action is being taken, and the CMS has notified the non-resident parent during the previous 12 months that it will consider taking collection and enforcement action if payments are missed. In this case, the CMS can take enforcement action and start managing ongoing payments if the non-resident parent has missed one or more payments.[19]

## Negotiating repayments

If you have received an arrears notice, you should contact the CMS to negotiate an agreement to pay the arrears.

You can contact the CMS before this point – eg, when you receive the collection schedule or if you have difficulty making ongoing payments. The CMS does not normally agree to defer payment of current liability, although it may do so if a revision, supersession or appeal is pending (see p153).

If you intend to pay the arrears, the CMS may:
- accept a delayed payment, setting a time limit by when payment must be received; *or*
- reschedule the amount to include it within the arrears.

If you indicate that a change of circumstances is causing you difficulty in making payments, the CMS may investigate whether there should be a supersession (see p204). In all cases, if you want to co-operate, try to renegotiate an agreement in good time before any anticipated change in circumstances – eg, redundancy. If you have paid regularly and the change would reduce the amount due, the CMS may accept a lower amount. You could also try to negotiate a suspension in payments if your personal circumstances make it difficult or insensitive to enforce recovery – eg, if you are unemployed, sick or in prison.

**Note:** if your income changes significantly due to coronavirus (COVID-19) – eg, due to the need to self-isolate or 'shield', or if you have lost your job or had to claim statutory sick pay – you should report this to the CMS as soon as possible.

The CMS has the discretion to make an agreement with a non-resident parent about how arrears will be recovered, so to avoid other methods of recovery, you should come to an agreement (see p151) as soon as possible and comply with it.

There are no set rules on the level of payments or how quickly the arrears must be cleared. Although CMS staff always begin by requesting full payment of the outstanding arrears, it may be possible to reach an agreement to pay the amount in instalments. The CMS aims to agree repayment plans that are affordable and that will be kept to.

In making these discretionary decisions, the CMS must take into account the welfare of any child likely to be affected (see p126) and should consider:
- the needs of the non-resident parent or any new family;
- any representations from the non-resident parent about hardship;
- the needs of the person with care and the qualifying child.

If you have other financial priorities (eg, fuel) or other large debts, you should get independent money advice: preparing a financial statement and sending it to the CMS may assist in reaching an agreement. However, existing arrangements with other creditors may have to be renegotiated to take into account the child support calculation. As the CMS has several methods of recovery, it is unlikely to agree to a non-resident parent making low payments over a very long period. It is in your interests to come to an agreement in order to avoid further enforcement action, and to keep the CMS informed so that it does not assume that you are refusing to co-operate. For more information on preparing a financial statement and negotiating with creditors, see CPAG's *Debt Advice Handbook*.

The CMS aims to collect arrears within two years, at a rate of up to 40 per cent of a non-resident parent's net income.[20]

It may accept a plan to pay arrears by instalments over more than two years, but it is likely to obtain a liability order (see p180) if there will be more than £1,000 outstanding at the end of two years. A liability order gives the CMS the power to use a wide range of methods to enforce payment, should the plan not be completed. The CMS may also consider other methods of recovery.

Repayments spread over several years may help non-resident parents who are in financial hardship, but this means that the person with care will receive payments very late and may want to make representations to the CMS. No interest is paid to the person with care in respect of arrears. If arrears have accrued because of CMS delay or error, you may wish to make a complaint and request compensation (see Chapter 11).

The person with care and qualifying children are not consulted about the level at which arrears are collected, but are informed when the decision has been made. This practice may be contrary to the European Convention on Human Rights' protection of private property,[21] but there has been no reported caselaw on this point (see also p190 on the fact that a person with care cannot directly enforce the payment of child support).

### If the non-resident parent does not reach an agreement or defaults

The CMS aims to take prompt action on arrears. If a repayment agreement is not reached, legal enforcement should begin. There is no set timescale for how quickly action should begin if no arrangement has been agreed, but it should begin as quickly as possible.[22]

If the non-resident parent fails to reach or keep a repayment agreement:

- a penalty payment may be imposed,[23] although in practice, this power is not currently used; *and*
- a deduction from earnings order or other method of enforcement may be considered (see p161).

The CMS informs her/him of its powers to collect and enforce child support.

### If there is a revision, supersession, variation or appeal pending

The CMS can suspend the collection of arrears if a decision on a revision, supersession, variation or appeal is pending. If the calculation is likely to be reduced, the CMS may agree to suspend collection of some of the ongoing payments. However, this does not happen often; the CMS prefers to speed up considering the case and aims to supersede calculations to reflect changes quickly in order to minimise arrears.[24]

If you are a non-resident parent and have requested a revision, supersession or appeal and you are having problems paying current child support or any arrears, ask the CMS for lower regular payments.

## Payment of arrears

Arrears do not have to be paid by the same method as ongoing child support payments – eg, they could be collected via the CMS, with ongoing payments made directly to the person with care. However, in practice, the CMS prefers to use the same method of payment for both.

Arrears of child support may be retained by the CMS and not passed to the person with care if they are in respect of a period before 12 April 2010 during which time the person with care (or her/his partner) was in receipt of income support (IS), income-based jobseeker's allowance (JSA), income-related employment and support allowance (ESA) or pension credit (PC). (Before this date, child support payments were treated as income for means-tested benefits.)

The CMS can keep any arrears payments that would not have been passed to the person with care had the child support been paid when due[25] – ie, the CMS can retain an amount equal to the difference between the amount of benefit that was paid to the person with care and the amount that would have been paid had the non-resident parent not been in arrears.[26] Payments of arrears are allocated between the CMS and the person with care in the same way as overpayments (see p143).

### If the non-resident parent is on benefit

If the non-resident parent is in receipt of one of the benefits that would qualify her/him for the flat rate (see p60), a deduction of £8.40 a week may be made from the benefit towards any child support arrears. That will also apply if the non-resident parent or her/his partner gets universal credit (UC) and s/he has earnings, provided her/his income level would otherwise qualify to pay the flat rate.[27] This deduction is a £7 payment towards arrears, plus a 20 per cent collection fee. The amount of the deduction that is for fees is retained by the CMS.[28] Deductions for arrears are separate to other deductions made from benefit and are not affected by the priority rules to decide which deductions should be made first. For more information on the priority rules on deductions from benefit, see CPAG's *Welfare Benefits and Tax Credits Handbook*.

The CMS cannot deduct an amount for both arrears and ongoing child support at the same time, so the maximum that can be deducted from a parent's benefit is £8.40 a week.

If you are a person with care and you believe that arrears owed by a non-resident parent who is on benefit and is paying ongoing child support should be pursued in some other way, contact the CMS to explain your reasons. If the CMS is unwilling to take action, a complaint may be made (see Chapter 11).

## Offsetting arrears

'Offsetting' is a way of balancing payments or arrears that are owed by a person with care and a non-resident parent to each other, so that the CMS only has to pursue arrears from one of them. Similarly, the amount of child support a non-resident parent is required to pay can be reduced to take account of arrears owed to her/him by the other person for a period when s/he was a person with care. Offsetting therefore reduces any arrears due under any current or previous child support calculation made in respect of the same relevant people – ie, a person with care and non-resident parent (and child applicant in Scotland).[29]

Arrears may be offset if:

- a non-resident parent becomes a parent with care; *or*
- arrears are owed by both parties to a calculation.

*Example*

Stephen and Zoe divorced five years ago. They have one child, Luke, who has lived with Zoe since the divorce. Zoe applied for child support and used the collection service. However, Stephen has not paid child support regularly for the past few years. Luke decides that he wants to live with Stephen, who becomes the parent with care. Zoe is now the non-resident parent. If Stephen applies for child support, the amount that Zoe must pay to Stephen each week can be reduced as a way of recovering the arrears still owed to her.

Luke has lived with his father, Stephen, for two years. His mother, Zoe, made regular child support payments for the first year, but when Stephen moves in with his new partner, she starts to miss payments. Luke then returns to live with Zoe, who becomes the parent with care again. At this time, Zoe owes Stephen £1,000 in arrears. However, there are still £500 arrears that are yet to be recovered from when Stephen was the non-resident parent and did not make regular payments. Rather than both sets of arrears being pursued, Stephen's arrears are deducted from Zoe's. Zoe has to pay Stephen £500 in arrears. Only Zoe is pursued for arrears. Stephen's liability under the new calculation could be reduced to recover these.

Arrears can only be offset in this way if the collection service is being used. Those with an arrangement to pay child support directly can reach their own offsetting agreements, but the CMS does not monitor them.[30] Offsetting is a discretionary power. The decision to offset arrears does not require the agreement of either parent, but the CMS should notify all relevant parties to the calculation when it is considering offsetting and ask for their views. You are given 14 days in which to respond. The CMS should take into account parents' wishes and should also have regard to the welfare of any child likely to be affected by the decision (see p126).[31]

If there are no arrears of child support due, or an amount remains to be offset after any arrears have been taken into account, the CMS can reduce the amount payable under the current calculation. When reducing ongoing payments to the person with care, the CMS should take into account the circumstances of all the parties and the period over which it would be reasonable to adjust payments. Payments can be reduced to nil.[32]

If the current child support calculation is reduced, either the person with care or the non-resident parent can contact the CMS at any time to ask that it be reviewed. The CMS should then discuss with both parties alternative ways of collecting any outstanding arrears.[33]

## Accepting part payment in full and final settlement

In certain circumstances, the CMS can treat a part payment of arrears of child support owed by a non-resident parent as 'full and final settlement' of all the arrears owed.[34] This flexibility is intended to act as an incentive for the non-resident parent to pay at least something, where s/he may not otherwise have done so.

Before accepting a part-payment offer from the non-resident parent, the CMS must obtain the written consent of the person with care (or child applicant in Scotland, and person with care of that child).[35]

The decision to accept an offer of part payment is discretionary. The CMS only uses this power if an offer is made by the non-resident parent or suggested by the person with care. It then investigates the circumstances of the non-resident parent, and also considers the likely success of continued enforcement action in recovering the full arrears.[36] The CMS must also consider the welfare of any child likely to be affected (see p126). See also p157 for when arrears may be written off.

If the CMS intends to accept the offer, it prepares a written agreement setting out:[37]

- the name of the non-resident parent;
- the name of the person with care (or child applicant in Scotland) if her/his consent is required (but see below);
- the amount of arrears and the period to which they relate;
- the amount that the CMS proposes to accept as settlement of those arrears;
- who the amount will be paid to and by what method; *and*
- the date by which the payment must be made.

A copy is sent to the non-resident parent and to each person with care (or child applicant in Scotland) affected for their agreement.[38]

If the CMS considers the offer to be unreasonable, it may decide not to contact the person with care. In some circumstances, it may insist on the full amount of the arrears being paid – eg, if it thinks that the non-resident parent has the ability to pay and there is a reasonable prospect of recovering the arrears.[39]

If there are arrears due both to a person with care and to the Department for Work and Pensions (DWP) (ie, because, for a period prior to 12 April 2010, the person with care would have received less benefit if the child support due had been paid), any part payment agreed is allocated to pay the person with care first. **Note:** if it is only the DWP that will not be paid in full if the offer is accepted, the CMS does not need the consent of the person with care (or child applicant in

Scotland) before accepting the offer.[40] In such a case, the CMS has discretion to decide whether the amount offered is reasonable in the non-resident parent's current financial circumstances.

If the non-resident parent has arrears that are due to more than one person with care, these are treated as separate amounts.[41] The CMS does not ask the non-resident parent to identify which person with care should receive the part payment.[42] If the non-resident parent does not state a preference, the CMS apportions the payment between them. Each person with care is notified of how much of the part payment s/he will receive if s/he agrees to accept this as a full and final payment. If one or more person(s) with care rejects the offer, the CMS may apportion the amount between those who have accepted it. Arrears due to those who have rejected the offer remain outstanding and are pursued by the CMS.

If the offer is accepted and the agreed payment made, the person with care cannot change her/his mind and ask the CMS to reinstate and pursue the arrears. So a person with care may wish to accept an offer where, for example, s/he would rather receive some arrears than wait for the enforcement process to run its course. If the non-resident parent pays all the agreed amount, her/his liability on any outstanding arrears ends and the CMS cannot take further action on them.[43] If the non-resident parent fails to make all of the agreed part payment, s/he remains liable for the full amount of the outstanding arrears and the CMS pursues recovery.[44] The CMS can make a further proposed agreement for part payment in the future, even if the non-resident parent has failed to keep to the terms of a previous agreement. The new agreement replaces any previous one.[45]

The part payment offered must be paid in one lump sum. At some point in the future, part payments may be able to be made by instalments.[46] However, there are no plans to introduce this at present.

## Writing off arrears

The CMS has the power to write off certain arrears.[47] Before 10 December 2012, a decision not to pursue recovery resulted in the arrears being suspended, but the liability still remained. Suspended arrears can be revived by the CMS in certain circumstances, but many arrears have remained on record, even though there is no prospect of their ever being collected.

The power to write off arrears is limited. The CMS can only write off arrears if it considers that it would be unfair or inappropriate for it to enforce the liability and:[48]

- the person with care (or child applicant in Scotland) has requested that the CMS stop taking action on the arrears; *or*
- the person with care (or child applicant in Scotland) has died; *or*
- the non-resident parent died before 25 January 2010 and it is not possible to recover the arrears from her/his estate; *or*

- the arrears have accrued from an interim maintenance assessment (see previous editions of this *Handbook* for details of these) in force between 5 April 1993 and 18 April 1995. These arrears are not legally recoverable;[49] *or*
- the CMS has advised the non-resident parent that the arrears have been permanently suspended and that no further action would ever be taken to recover them. This may happen if, for example, the arrears resulted from a delay (which was not the non-resident parent's fault) in establishing child support liability; *or*
- in Scotland, the arrears relate to debt that is subject to sequestration (Scottish bankruptcy) once the period of sequestration has ended. Debt in these circumstances is not legally recoverable;[50] *or*
- in Scotland, the non-resident parent has been subject to a protected trust deed (a formal agreement between a debtor and her/his creditors) that has expired.[51] Arrears in these circumstances are also not legally recoverable; *or*
- the arrears relate to liability for child support in a closed '1993 rules' or '2003 rules' case in certain circumstances (see p159).

The CMS has discretion whether to use this power to write off arrears. Before doing so, it must consider all the circumstances of an individual case, the principles of child support law and the welfare of any child affected by the decision.

If the non-resident parent has arrears that are due to more than one person with care, these are treated as separate amounts and separate decisions are made.[52]

If it is considering writing off arrears, the CMS must give written notice to the person with care and non-resident parent (and a child applicant in Scotland).[53] The notice must set out:[54]

- the person with care (or child applicant in Scotland) who is owed the arrears;
- the amount of arrears and the period to which they relate;
- the reasons why the CMS believes that it would be unfair or inappropriate to enforce the arrears;
- the effect of writing off the arrears; *and*
- an explanation of the right to make representations to the CMS about the proposal to write off the arrears within 30 days of receiving the notice.

The notice is treated as being received two days after it was sent by the CMS to the person's last known or notified address.[55]

The requirement for the CMS to give written notice does not apply if:[56]

- the person in question has died or cannot be traced; *or*
- the arrears relate to debt that is subject to sequestration; *or*
- in certain circumstances, the arrears arise from liability for child support in closed '1993 rules' or '2003 rules' cases (see below).

When making its decision, the CMS must consider any written representations made by any relevant party.[57] If no written representations are made within 30 days, the CMS can decide to write off the arrears.[58] It must give written notice of its decision to the person with care (and a child applicant in Scotland) and non-resident parent (unless the person in question has died or cannot be traced or, in certain circumstances, the arrears arise from liability for child support in closed '1993 rules' or '2003 rules' cases – see below).

If the CMS does not write off the arrears, it may continue to pursue recovery. There is no right of appeal against its decision.

## Arrears in closed cases

The DWP has said that it will use the closure of existing '1993 rules' and '2003 rules' cases (see p1) to validate arrears and prioritise recovery action.[59]

Arrears in historic cases are only transferred to the CMS computer system if there is an ongoing liability for child support under a '2012 rules' application. Before being transferred, the arrears are checked for accuracy. Only arrears that have been validated in this way are transferred. This process could take up to six months. Existing enforcement action on the historic case is expected to continue while this is going on. The parties are informed of any balance of arrears that is transferred to the new case.

Once arrears have been validated and transferred, no new enforcement action is started by the CMS unless the non-resident parent has failed to pay her/his ongoing liability in the '2012 rules' case. This means that, once enforcement action in the historic case has ended, no further enforcement action will be started until the CMS accepts that a direct payment arrangement (see p136) is not suitable in the '2012 rules' case.[60]

If a historic case has been closed and there are arrears, but no ongoing liability for child support in a new '2012 rules' case, action to recover the outstanding arrears is expected to be treated as a low priority.[61]

The CMS can consider writing off arrears that arise from liability for child support in closed '1993 rules' or '2003 rules' cases.[62] It intends to do this proactively to address historic arrears as it considers it too costly to maintain records of these arrears on its computer systems.[63]

The CMS can consider writing off these arrears if they are:[64]

- over £1,000 and the effective date in the case was on or before 1 November 2008; *or*
- over £500 and the effective date was after 1 November 2008; *or*
- over £500 and arose in a closed '1993 rules' or '2003 rules' case which has been transferred to the CMS computer system.

If the non-resident parent has not made any payments within the previous three months, the CMS can send written notice to the person with care (or child applicant in Scotland), inviting her/him to make representations on whether the arrears should be written off. Representations must be made by post within 60 days of receiving the notice. The CMS describes this as an opportunity for the person with care to ask for a last attempt to be made to collect the arrears. Representations could include information (eg, about a non-resident parent's current whereabouts, employment or assets) that could help with successful collection of the arrears. The CMS only takes action to attempt collection if it is cost-effective to do so and it is reasonably certain that action may be successful.[65] If no representations are made within 60 days, the CMS can decide to write off the arrears. In such a case, it does not need to notify the parties of its decision.[66]

If the CMS receives written representations within 60 days saying that the person with care (or child applicant in Scotland) wants the arrears to be collected, it then considers whether it can successfully collect the arrears and gives written notice to the non-resident parent. S/he can make written representations within 21 days of receiving the notice.[67]

In these cases, the notice to each party must include the usual information about the arrears (see p158), except that it does not have to set out the period to which the arrears relate (or, if the arrears are over £1,000 and the effective date was on or before 1 November 2008, the amount of the arrears).[68]

The CMS can then decide whether to write off the arrears. When making its decision, the CMS must consider any written representations made by any relevant party.[69] It must give written notice of its decision to the person with care (and a child applicant in Scotland) and non-resident parent (unless the person in question has died or cannot be traced).[70]

The CMS can also consider writing off smaller arrears amounts. That can be done if the non-resident parent has not made any payments within the previous three months and the arrears are:[71]

- £1,000 or less and the effective date in the case was on or before 1 November 2008; *or*
- £500 or less and the effective date was after 1 November 2008; *or*
- £500 or less and arose in a closed '1993 rules' or '2003 rules' case which has been transferred to the CMS computer system.

The CMS is not required to invite representations from the parties before making its decision. It must, however, give written notice of its decision to the person with care (and a child applicant in Scotland) and non-resident parent (unless the person in question has died or cannot be traced).[72]

If the arrears are under £65 and no payment has been received in the last three months, the CMS can write off the arrears without giving notice of its decision to the parties.[73] There is no right of appeal against a CMS decision on writing off arrears.

## 2. **Enforcement action**

The Child Maintenance Service (CMS) should usually consider enforcement action as soon as it is clear that the non-resident parent has failed to keep to the agreed payment arrangements for child support and any fees due and has not responded to warnings.[74]

In many cases, in order to enforce payment, the CMS must first obtain a **liability order** from the county court or, in Scotland, sheriff court (see p180). However, for an increasing number of enforcement options, the CMS does not need a liability order and no court action is required.

A liability order is *not* required for:
- a deduction from earnings order. This is usually appropriate when the non-resident parent is employed (see p162);
- making deductions from bank or building society accounts. This is likely to be used if the non-resident parent is not an employee (see p170);
- collecting arrears from a deceased person's estate (see p179).

However, the CMS must first obtain a liability order (see p180) if it wants to:
- take control of and sell goods (see p182);
- disqualify the non-resident parent from driving or from holding or obtaining a passport or other travel authorisation (see p184);
- imprison the non-resident parent (see p184).

**Note:** the rules on collecting and enforcing payments of child support also apply to payment of any fees for enforcement action due, except that the CMS cannot seek to disqualify the non-resident parent from driving or from holding or obtaining a passport or other travel authorisation, or to imprison her/him, when enforcement action is being taken solely to recover fees.[75]

A decision concerning collection and enforcement cannot be challenged by seeking a revision and then appealing to the First-tier Tribunal.[76] However, certain enforcement decisions can be appealed in the courts. A deduction from earnings order can be appealed to a magistrates' court (England or Wales) or the sheriff court (Scotland). Orders to deduct amounts from bank accounts can be appealed in the family court (England and Wales) or the sheriff court (Scotland). Decisions of the courts on disqualification from driving or from holding or obtaining a passport can also be appealed. It may be possible to challenge other decisions by judicial review (see p198). A complaint can also be made about the way the CMS has used its discretion (see Chapter 11).

The CMS can enforce certain arrears that accrued while both parents were resident in the UK if the non-resident parent now resides in another European Union (EU) country. The CMS may also make enquiries about assets a non-resident parent may own in another EU state.[77] Enforcement of arrangements made or decisions recognised before the end of the transition period following the UK leaving the EU will be under the EU law that is in force in the UK on that date (currently 31 December 2020). After that date, rules on recognition and enforcement of maintenance arrangements contained in the various Hague Conventions are likely to apply unless other reciprocal provision is made between the UK and EU member states.[78]

The CMS can also assist parents with care to obtain a court order for ongoing maintenance, which can then be enforced by applying (in England and Wales) to the Reciprocal Enforcement of Maintenance Orders (REMO) Unit at the office of the Official Solicitor and Public Trustee or HM Courts and Tribunals Service Maintenance Enforcement Business Centres, or (in Scotland) the Scottish government's Central Authority and International Law Team.[79] These arrangements relate to a range of countries with which the UK has reciprocal agreements.[80]

## Deduction from earnings orders

### When a deduction from earnings order is made

The CMS may make a deduction from earnings order, instructing the non-resident parent's employer to make deductions from her/his wages or salary and pay them to the CMS.[81] The CMS does not need a court order to do this and it is the first enforcement option that is likely to be used against an employed non-resident parent who cannot provide a good reason for the arrears, or who has failed to agree a method of payment with the CMS.[82]

A non-resident parent can also choose a voluntary deduction from earnings order as the method of making regular child support payments, even if s/he is not in arrears (see p140).

*Earnings*

'Earnings' include wages, salary, fees, bonuses, commission, overtime pay, occupational pension or statutory sick pay, any other payment made under an employment contract and a regular payment made to compensate for loss of wages.[83] Earnings do not include working tax credit, any social security benefit or disablement benefit, a payment by a foreign government or the government of Northern Ireland, or a payment to a special member of a British reserved armed force.[84] 'Net earnings' is the amount remaining after income tax, national insurance (NI) and contributions towards a pension scheme have been deducted.[85]

A deduction from earnings order cannot be made if there is a good reason not to use one.[86] For what is considered 'good reason', see p169.

The best way for a non-resident parent to avoid a deduction from earnings order being made is to negotiate an arrears agreement (see p151) and keep to it wherever possible. However, making ongoing payments in full may be enough to prevent an order from being made. If a non-resident parent objects to an order, this is likely to be rejected if s/he is unlikely to make regular payments using a different method.

The decision to make a deduction from earnings order is discretionary and the welfare of any child(ren) must be considered (see p126).[87] If the non-resident parent is advised that the CMS intends to make an order, s/he should tell the CMS, preferably in writing, how any children would be affected.

A deduction from earnings order can be made while the non-resident parent is waiting for a decision on a revision, supersession or appeal, but the CMS should consider the grounds of the revision, supersession or appeal before making one. A non-resident parent can also make representations about the amount and method of payments (see p140 and p148). The CMS may accept lower payments, but may still impose an order.

A deduction from earnings order cannot be made if the employer is based outside the UK and has no place of business in the UK, but can be made in Great Britain against an employer in Northern Ireland and vice versa.[88]

A deduction from earnings order cannot be made if the non-resident parent is in the armed forces. Instead, the CMS can request the armed forces to make deductions for child support under armed forces law, known as a deduction from earnings request, which sets limits on the amounts that can be deducted.[89]

If the full amount requested by the CMS cannot be deducted from earnings, the CMS uses other methods to collect and enforce the remainder.

**Note:** a deduction from earnings order may also have been made as part of 'compliance opportunity' arrangements (see p136) offered to a non-resident parent when a previous '2003 rules' or '1993 rules' case closed. If a child support application was made under the '2012 rules' before the date the existing case closed, the CMS may have allowed the non-resident parent to pay a portion of the '2012 rules' child support liability by a voluntary method of payment for a period of time and make a deduction from earnings order for the remainder. In this situation, the CMS does not have to consider whether there is a good reason not to make an order, and there is therefore no right of appeal on this ground against the order being made.[90]

If a deduction from earnings order is made, the non-resident parent can appeal against it to the magistrates' court in England and Wales, or sheriff court in Scotland (see p169).

## Information the non-resident parent must provide

The non-resident parent must provide the name and address of her/his employer, the amount of her/his earnings and anticipated earnings, place of work and the nature of her/his work within seven days of being asked to do so in writing by the CMS.[91] Once a deduction from earnings order is in force, s/he must inform the CMS within seven days of leaving employment or becoming employed or re-employed.[92] Failure to take all reasonable steps to comply with any of these requirements is an offence, punishable by a fine of up to £500.[93]

For these purposes, information sent to the CMS is treated as having been given or sent on the day that it is received.[94] Any notice sent from the CMS is treated as though it was given or sent on the day that it was posted.[95]

## What the employer must do

A copy of the deduction from earnings order must be 'served' on the employer and the non-resident parent.[96] The employer must comply with it within seven days of receiving it,[97] and can be fined up to £1,000 for providing false or misleading information, or deliberately withholding information from the CMS.[98]

The order must state:[99]

- the name and address of the non-resident parent;
- the name of the employer;
- the non-resident parent's place of work, employee number and NI number (if known by the CMS), and the nature of her/his work;
- the normal deduction rate(s) (see p165) and the date on which each takes effect;
- the 'protected earnings proportion' (see p165);
- the address to which the deductions must be sent.

An employer must inform the CMS in writing within 10 days of being served with an order if it does not, in fact, employ the non-resident parent.[100]

If a parent who is subject to a deduction from earnings order leaves her/his job, the employer must notify the CMS within 10 days.[101] If an employer finds out that an order is in force against an employee, it must notify the CMS within seven days of becoming aware of this.[102] Failure to take all reasonable steps to comply with any of these requirements is an offence, punishable by a fine of up to £500.[103]

The employer must inform the non-resident parent in writing of the amount of each deduction no later than the date of the deduction or, if not practicable, by the following payday.[104] If the deduction will always be the same amount, this can be done by a statement given at least annually.[105] If the employer does not give you notice, you can complain to an employment tribunal, which can order the employer to pay you a fine up to the total amount of the unnotified deductions, even if paid to the CMS.[106] This fine does not affect any deductions already paid to the CMS.

For other duties about providing information, see p36. The CMS and the child maintenance section of the gov.uk website provide further information for employers.

Employers can manage deduction from earnings orders through a self-service website.[107]

If an employer implements a deduction from earnings order incorrectly and you dispute this, you should ask the CMS to intervene.

For these purposes, information sent to the CMS is treated as having been given or sent on the day that it is received.[108] Any notice sent from the CMS is treated as though it was given or sent on the day that it was posted.[109]

## How much is deducted

The deduction from earnings order states a 'normal deduction rate' and a 'protected earnings proportion'.[110]

The **'normal deduction rate'** is the amount that will be deducted each payday, provided it does not bring the parent's net earnings below a certain amount (the protected earnings proportion). The normal deduction rate can include the current child support liability and an amount for any arrears, penalty payments (see p153) and any fees due. There are no special rules on how quickly the CMS should aim to clear the liability, although often the maximum deduction rate of 40 per cent of net earnings is applied (see p151). You may wish to discuss with the CMS how it has chosen to apply its discretion.

**Note:** more than one normal deduction rate can be set, each applying to a different period.[111]

The **'protected earnings proportion'** is 60 per cent of net earnings.[112] Deductions must not reduce earnings below this level.

The CMS does not know the non-resident parent's net earnings or pay frequency, as it receives only gross income information from HM Revenue and Customs. The employer is therefore responsible for calculating the protected earnings proportion. The CMS provides employers with pay frequency options for weekly, fortnightly, four-weekly and monthly pay, from which the employer selects the normal deduction rate corresponding to the parent's pay frequency.[113] If the parent is paid at a different frequency, the CMS must cancel the order (see p168).[114]

These amounts also apply to deduction from earnings orders made after 10 December 2012 in 'arrears only' cases under the '1993 rules' and '2003 rules' (ie, cases where there are arrears outstanding but no regular ongoing child support liability), provided the CMS gives written notice to the non-resident parent. Any deduction from earnings order made before this date continues under the previous rules until it is cancelled or lapses.[115]

**Note:** if an order is made as part of a 'compliance opportunity' (see p163), payments under the order do not need to be made in equal instalments.

## Payment

The employer must pay the CMS monthly by the 19th of the month following the month in which the deduction is made.[116] This means that there is always a delay before the person with care receives the first payment from the CMS. The person with care receives monthly payments, even if the non-resident parent is having weekly deductions made. These monthly payments may not always be for the same amount (see p167).

The payment by the employer may be made by credit transfer, cheque or any other method to which the CMS agrees.[117] The deduction from earnings order reference number must be given so that the CMS can identify the person with care.

It is an offence, punishable by a fine of up to £500, for an employer to fail to take all reasonable steps to pay the CMS on time.[118]

### Administration of the deductions

An employer can deduct a charge for administrative costs each time a deduction is made under a deduction from earnings order. This means that employees paid weekly can be charged more for administrative costs. The charge must not exceed £1 per deduction and can be made even if this would bring someone's earnings below the protected earnings proportion.

Each payday, the employer should make a deduction from net earnings at the normal deduction rate plus any administration charge. If deducting the normal deduction rate would reduce net earnings below the protected earnings proportion, the amount of the deduction is the excess of net earnings over the protected earnings proportion.[119]

If the employer fails to make a deduction, or it is less than the normal deduction rate, arrears build up and are deducted at the next payday in addition to the normal deduction, applying the same rules for protected earnings.[120]

If, on a payday, the non-resident parent is paid for a longer period than that for which the normal deduction rate is set, the deduction is increased in proportion to the length of the pay period.[121]

Such fluctuations in deductions may mean that the person with care receives irregular payments.

*Example*

Ed is due to pay child support of £48 a week and has net earnings of £240 a week. When a deduction from earnings order is considered, there are arrears of £432. The order shows a normal deduction rate of £60 (child support due plus £12 towards arrears) and a protected earnings proportion of £144. The employer can deduct £1 administrative costs for weeks in which a deduction is made.

| Payday | Net pay | Child support due | Deduction | Pay | Unpaid |
|--------|---------|-------------------|-----------|------|--------|
| 5/7    | £240    | £60               | £61       | £179 |        |
| 12/7   | £250    | £60               | £61       | £189 |        |
| 19/7   | £160    | £60               | £17       | £143 | £44    |
| 26/7   | £160    | £104              | £17       | £143 | £88    |
| 2/8    | £240    | £148              | £97       | £143 | £52    |
| 9/8    | £250    | £112              | £107      | £143 | £6     |
| 16/8   | £250    | £66               | £67       | £183 |        |

| Payday | Net pay | Child support due | Deduction | Pay | Unpaid |
|--------|---------|-------------------|-----------|-----|--------|
| 23/8 | £240 | £60 | £61 | £179 | |
| 30/8 | £120 | £60 | Nil | £120 | £60 |
| 6/9 | £240 | £120 | £97 | £143 | £24 |
| 13/9 | £240 | £84 | £85 | £155 | |
| 20/9 | £250 | £60 | £61 | £189 | |
| 27/9 | £240 | £60 | £61 | £179 | |

In the week of 19/7, the full deduction cannot be made, as this would take income below the protected earnings proportion. A deduction is made of £16 plus a £1 administration fee. The amount of the deduction from earnings order outstanding is added to the next amount due on 26/7. As earnings are again low, the full deduction cannot be taken and is carried forward. In the week of 30/8, earnings are too low for a deduction to be made and, therefore, there is no deduction and no administrative charge.

## Payment to the person with care

When payments under the order have reached the CMS, they should be passed on to the person with care within approximately 10 days. If s/he was on income support, income-based jobseeker's allowance, income-related employment and support allowance or pension credit in the period to which the arrears relate, some of the payments may be retained in lieu of benefit paid.[122] This only applies to arrears of child support payments that were due to be made before 12 April 2010 (when child support was taken into account as income for means-tested benefits).

### Example

Following on from the previous example, Ed's ex-wife Claire will receive the following payments.

| Month | Payment by the 19th of the month | Current liability paid (£48 a week due) | Arrears paid (assigned to oldest debt) |
|-------|----------------------------------|------------------------------------------|-----------------------------------------|
| July | | Nil | Nil |
| August | £156 | £156 | Nil |
| September | £328 | £192 | £136 |
| October | £300 | £192 | £108 |

By the time Claire gets the first payment from the deduction from earnings order in August, s/he is owed £624 (£432 + £192 (July)), but because of Ed's fluctuating earnings, s/he receives less than the amount due. It is only in September that s/he begins to obtain arrears of child support, even though the order was put in place in July.

## Priority of orders

A deduction from earnings order takes priority over an attachment of earnings order made by a county court and any arrestment of earnings under Scottish law.[123] In England and Wales, if a deduction from earnings order is served on an employee who is already subject to an attachment of earnings order made by a magistrates' court to recover a fine, council tax or maintenance, the earliest order has priority.[124]

Any deductions under a lower priority order are taken from the net earnings left after deductions under the first order have been made.

### Reviews, cancellations and lapsed orders

The CMS must **review** a deduction from earnings order if there is a change in the amount of the calculation, or if any arrears, penalty payments and any collection or enforcement fees included have been paid off.[125] This does not apply if a normal deduction rate that takes into account the change has already been specified (see p165). An order can be changed on this review.[126] An employer must comply with the change within seven days of the new order being served on it.[127]

If the non-resident parent is paid at a frequency other than weekly, fortnightly, four-weekly or monthly, the CMS *must* **cancel** the order.[128]

The CMS *can* cancel the order if:[129]

- no further payments are due under it; *or*
- liability in an existing case has ended under the case closure process (see p1); *or*
- it is ineffective or there appears to be a more effective way of collecting the payments;
- it is defective (see p169) or does not comply with a procedural requirement; *or*
- the CMS did not have, or has ceased to have, jurisdiction to make it; *or*
- using it to enforce a default maintenance decision or interim maintenance decision is no longer appropriate, given the compliance or attempted compliance of the non-resident parent; *or*
- it has agreed with the non-resident parent an alternative method for payment of the child support and any fees due, and it considers that it is reasonable.[130]

If the order was made as part of a 'compliance opportunity' (see p163), the CMS can also cancel it if:[131]

- the non-resident parent receives a benefit that means the flat rate applies (see p60); *or*
- the non-resident parent has made payments by the agreed voluntary method for the agreed period and the CMS considers that it is reasonable in the circumstances to cancel the order.

If an order was in force for a '1993 rules' or '2003 rules' case and there were outstanding arrears when that case closed and an application was made under the '2012 rules', the order is treated as cancelled when the arrears are transferred to the '2012 rules' computer system. The order therefore continues until the arrears are validated. If there are no outstanding arrears, the order is treated as cancelled on the date the first deduction is made under an order under the '2012 rules'.[132]

The CMS must send written notice of cancellation to the non-resident parent and employer.[133]

A deduction from earnings order **lapses** when a non-resident parent leaves the employment.[134] The CMS can **revive** it if s/he finds a new job with the same or a different employer.[135] If it is revived, copies of the notice must be served on the parent and new employer.[136] Any shortfall under the order before the revival cannot be carried over to the revived order.[137]

## Appeals

A non-resident parent can appeal against a deduction from earnings order to the magistrates' court in England and Wales or sheriff court in Scotland.[138] The appeal must be made within 28 days of the order being made (56 days if the parent is not resident in the UK).[139] An appeal can only be made on the grounds that:

- the order is 'defective' (see below); *or*
- the payments made to the parent are not earnings (see p162);[140] *or*
- unless the order is made as part of a 'compliance opportunity' (see p163), there is 'good reason' not to use an order (see below).[141]

A deduction from earnings order is **defective** if it is impracticable for an employer to comply with it because it does not include the correct information required.[142] Many orders may include incorrect information (such as errors in names, addresses and dates), but an appeal will not succeed on this basis if the employer can still comply with it. Although some early appeals were upheld because the order was unsigned, a signature is not legally required.

When determining whether there is a **good reason** not to use an order, the CMS must consider whether making the order is likely to result in the disclosure of the parentage of a child and the likely impact of this on the non-resident parent's employment or on any relationship between the non-resident parent and a third party.[143] The impact of a third party becoming aware of the non-resident parent's deduction from earnings order is not considered to be a good reason in any other circumstances.[144]

A good reason for not imposing an order may also exist if a relative of the non-resident parent or parent with care is employed by the same employer as the non-resident parent and s/he is likely to find out about the order. If her/his employment or family relationships may be adversely affected as a result, this should be a good reason not to impose an order.[145]

The fact that a non-resident parent may prefer a different method of payment or would prefer the employer not to be informed about her/his child support liability are not considered good reasons to refrain from using a deduction from earnings order.[146]

In England and Wales, there is no specific application form for the appeal. In Scotland, the form of the application for an appeal is laid out in the sheriff court child support rules.[147]

Once the application is made, the court notifies the CMS. The CMS checks the deduction from earnings order and contacts the employer to check the earnings. If the order is based on incorrect amounts, the CMS varies and reissues it. If the case gets as far as a court hearing, the magistrates/sheriff may quash the order or specify which payments, if any, constitute earnings.[148] The court cannot question the child support calculation itself.[149]

Even if the court quashes the order, it cannot order the CMS to repay deductions to the non-resident parent.[150] For this reason, if deductions are being made from payments that are not earnings, or on the basis of an incorrect normal deduction rate or protected earnings proportion, it may be better to challenge the order by judicial review.

Either party can be represented by a lawyer. The CMS appoints its own staff to conduct deduction from earnings order appeals and appear at related court hearings.[151] The non-resident parent can also be represented by a lay person, if the magistrate or sheriff accepts that s/he is suitable. An authorised lay representative does not have the full rights of a legal representative, but may be entitled to expenses.

**Note:** if you think the CMS has not properly used its discretion in making a deduction from earnings order, you can make a complaint (see Chapter 11) and/or consider a judicial review (see p198).

## Deductions from bank accounts

If a non-resident parent has failed to pay child support, the CMS can make an order requiring a bank or building society to make deductions from her/his account and pay the CMS. The CMS can make an order without the non-resident parent's consent, and without applying to court or obtaining a liability order.[152] The deductions can be either regular (see p171) or made as a lump-sum payment (see p174).[153] As soon as a non-resident parent is in arrears, a deduction order becomes possible as a method of enforcement.

An order is most commonly made if a non-resident parent is self-employed and a deduction from earnings order is therefore not possible.

The CMS has discretion to choose the most suitable account from which to make deductions. Generally, regular deduction orders are directed at current accounts and lump-sum deduction orders at savings accounts. The use of deduction orders on more complex accounts, such as notice accounts or stocks and shares accounts, may also be considered.[154]

Since 14 December 2018, deduction orders can also be made in respect of a joint account.[155] This may be a personal joint account or an account used by a partnership in England and Wales in which the non-resident parent is a partner.[156] This does not apply to partnerships in Scotland.

A regular deduction order and, since 14 December 2018, a lump-sum deduction order can also be made in respect of an account which is used by a non-resident parent as a sole trader. Deduction orders cannot be made in respect of any other accounts (ie, apart from partnership accounts in England and Wales and sole trader accounts) which are used wholly or partly for business purposes.[157]

The CMS always attempts to make deductions from a non-resident parent's individual accounts first. If there are insufficient funds, it then considers deductions from any joint accounts. Joint personal accounts are considered before any partnership accounts. In order to protect the interests of other partners, deductions are not made from a partnership account if the account balance is less than £2,000.[158]

Before making a deduction order on a joint account, the CMS can require the bank or building society to provide information on:[159]

- the name and home address (or correspondence address) of each account holder;
- the type of account, account number and sort code;
- the balance in the account; *and*
- details of any transactions on the account in the previous six months.

The bank or building society must provide this information within 14 days of the request. If the information does not allow the CMS to establish how much of the funds in the account belongs to the non-resident parent, the CMS assumes that each account holder owns an equal share.[160]

When a bank or building society is sent a deduction order, it must notify the CMS of certain matters within seven days – eg, if the account does not exist, has been closed or is in a different name from that specified in the order. It must also notify the CMS within seven days if the name of a joint account holder is changed, provided the order remains in force at any time during that seven-day period.[161]

It is an offence, punishable by a fine of up to £500, for a bank or building society not to comply with the requirements of a regular deduction order or to fail to provide information when required to do so, unless it can show that all reasonable steps were taken to comply.[162]

The bank or building society can take an amount from the account to cover its administrative costs. The maximum amounts that can be charged are:[163]

- £10 for each deduction made under a regular deduction order;
- £55 for each deduction made under a lump-sum deduction order.

## Regular deduction orders

A regular deduction order can be used to collect both arrears and ongoing child support payments.[164]

Before a regular deduction order is made on a joint account, notice must be given to each account holder, giving her/him an opportunity to make representations on the proposed order and the amounts to be deducted.[165]

Each account holder must be told:

- the name of the non-resident parent and that the order is in respect of her/his child support liability;
- the number and sort code of the account;
- the proposed dates on which deductions will be made;
- that they can make representations about the proposed order, the amounts to be deducted and the dates on which deductions will be made. Representations must be made within 14 days of receiving the notice, although the CMS may allow longer if it is reasonable in the circumstances. An order cannot be made until this period has expired; *and*
- that the order is likely to be made in the terms set out in the notice unless representations are received.

The CMS can also provide any further information about the non-resident parent that it considers essential to allow joint account holders to make representations.[166]

When a regular deduction order is made, a copy is sent to the bank or building society, the non-resident parent and, if it is on a joint account, each of the other account holders. The order must specify the amount of the regular deduction and the dates on which deductions are due to be made.[167]

The maximum that can be deducted is 40 per cent of the non-resident parent's gross weekly income (net weekly income in '1993 rules' and '2003 rules' cases). The weekly income is to be calculated as the date of the current child support calculation or, if arrears are being collected for a calculation no longer in force, at the date of the most recent previous calculation. If a default maintenance decision has been made, the maximum that can be deducted is £80 a week.[168]

### Priority of payments

If the non-resident parent's account is subject to other deduction orders, such as a third-party debt order, these are generally paid first before a regular deduction order is dealt with. The exception to this is if a third-party debt order is served on the bank or building society after the regular deduction order, but on or before the date a payment is due to be made under the deduction order. In this case, the deduction order is paid first on that occasion, unless the bank or building society has already taken steps to process the other orders. For future payments, it is assumed that the other orders take priority.[169]

### Minimum amounts

A deduction cannot be made if the amount of credit in the relevant account is below a certain level on the date a deduction is due to be made. The minimum amounts are:

- £40, if deductions are made monthly;
- £10, if deductions are made weekly;
- if deductions are made for any other period, £10 for each whole week in that period, plus £1 for each additional day in that period.

In addition to these amounts, there must be sufficient funds in the account to pay the administrative costs.[170] Deductions are not made from a partnership account if the account balance is less than £2,000.

### Reviews and variations

A non-resident parent, a bank or building society or, if the order is on a joint account, any other account holder can apply to the CMS for a **review** of a regular deduction order if:[171]

- the parent does not have a beneficial interest in some, or all, of the money in the account; *or*
- there has been a change in the amount of the child support calculation; *or*
- any amount payable under the order has been paid; *or*
- there has been a change in the non-resident parent's current income (net weekly income in '1993 rules' and '2003 rules' cases);[172] *or*
- because of an official error, an incorrect amount has been specified in the order; *or*
- the order does not contain the correct information or exceeds the maximum deduction rate; *or*
- in the case of an order on a joint account:
  - another account holder satisfies the CMS that the amount contributed by the non-resident parent to the account has decreased, or will decrease within three months of the date of the application for review; *or*
  - another account holder who did not make representations within the 14-day period before the order was made (see p172) satisfies the CMS that s/he had a reasonable excuse for not doing so and applies for a review within three months of the expiry of that period.

A regular deduction order can be **varied** to change the amount that is deducted if:[173]

- the CMS accepts that the non-resident parent has made a payment of child support arrears, or a payment towards an enforcement fee, and no alternative method of payment is in place; *or*
- there has been a successful appeal against a child support calculation; *or*
- the order has been changed following a successful review or appeal to the family court (sheriff court in Scotland); *or*
- there are arrears that are not included in the order; *or*
- in the case of an order on a joint account, the CMS believes that the amount contributed by the non-resident parent to the account has changed, or will change within three months of the date of the order being made or varied.

The CMS has discretion to vary the deduction period or the deduction dates at any time.[174]

Before varying a regular deduction order on a joint account to increase the amount deducted or change the deduction dates, the CMS must serve a notice on each account holder.[175] This notice must contain the same types of information about the account as before an order is first made (see p172). It must also explain:

- why the CMS proposes to vary the order;
- that each account holder can make representations about the proposal to vary the order, the amounts to be deducted and the dates on which deductions will be made. Representations must be made within 14 days of receiving the notice, although the CMS may allow longer if it is reasonable in the circumstances. The order cannot be varied until this period has expired; *and*
- that the order is likely to be varied in the terms set out in the notice unless representations are received.

## Lump-sum deduction orders

If it is established that the non-resident parent owes arrears of child support, the CMS considers whether a lump-sum deduction order is the most appropriate method of recovering them.

Once the CMS has decided to make a lump-sum deduction order, it serves an interim order to the non-resident parent's bank or building society. This acts as an instruction to secure funds up to the amount of the order in a specified account until further notice. The bank or building society is expected to prevent these from being moved or reduced below the amount that is ordered or, if funds are already below this amount, not to allow them to decrease further (unless the CMS permits it to do so – eg, because of hardship).[176]

Once funds have been secured, a copy of the interim order is served on the non-resident parent. The bank or building society and the parent each have 14 days (unless it is a joint account – see below) in which to make representations to the CMS.[177] In the case of a joint account, the notice must tell each account holder:[178]

- the name of the non-resident parent and that the order is in respect of her/his child support liability;
- that the interim order is an instruction to the bank or building society to secure the funds and that the CMS proposes to make a final order;
- the earliest proposed date on which a deduction under the final order will be made;
- that each account holder can make representations about the proposal, the proposed amount to be deducted and the earliest date proposed for deducting the amount. Representations must be made within 28 days of receiving the notice, although the CMS may allow longer if it is reasonable in the circumstances; *and*
- that the order is likely to be made in the terms set out in the notice unless representations are received.

The CMS can also provide any further information about the non-resident parent that it considers essential to allow joint account holders to make representations.[179]

Once an interim order has been made, the CMS can issue a final lump-sum deduction order. It must not do this until the period for making representations (14 days or, for an order on a joint account, 28 days) has expired and it has considered any representations made. The order is served on the bank or building society, and a copy on the non-resident parent and, in the case of an order on a joint account, each of the other account holders.[180]

A final order instructs the bank or building society to pay to the CMS either the amount due or, if less, the amount in the account. The bank or building society must pay the amount to the CMS once the period for appealing has expired (see p179) or, if an appeal has been made, once the appeal has been concluded and any period for appealing further has expired.[181]

The amount sought by the CMS in the final order must not be more than the amount specified in the interim order.[182] The CMS must ensure that the amount deducted from a joint account does not exceed an amount that is fair, given all the circumstances. In considering what amount to deduct, the CMS must pay particular attention to the amounts contributed to the account by each of the account holders.[183]

An order is treated as having been 'served' on a person at the end of the day on which the copy is posted to her/his last known address.[184]

The non-resident parent, a bank or building society or, in the case of an order on a joint account, another account holder can ask the CMS not to instruct the bank or building society to secure funds – ie, to allow money in the account to be moved or reduced. The CMS can agree to this if:[185]

- the non-resident parent, her/his partner or any relevant other child is experiencing hardship in meeting her/his ordinary living expenses; *or*
- in the case of an order on a joint account, another account holder, her/his partner or any child for whom s/he is a person with care is experiencing hardship; *or*
- the non-resident parent (or a joint account holder) has any written, contractual obligations regarding the money that were made before the order was made; *or*
- the non-resident parent (or a joint account holder) has made an agreement with the bank or building society and the availability of an amount in the account is required as security for that agreement; *or*
- there are any other circumstances that the CMS considers appropriate in the particular case.

In deciding whether to allow funds to be moved or reduced, the CMS must take into account:[186]

- any adverse impact the decision may have on the non-resident parent or anyone else; *and*
- any alternative arrangements which may be made by the parent, any other account holder and the bank or building society.

If it agrees, the CMS serves a notice on the bank or building society instructing it to move or remove the funds.

### Priority of payments

In **England and Wales**, if there is a final lump-sum deduction order and another interim third-party debt order, a bank or building society must comply with them in the order in which they were served on it. If an interim lump-sum deduction order is served after an interim third-party debt order, the final versions of these other orders take priority.[187]

In **Scotland**, a bank or building society must give priority to the lump-sum deduction order and any other orders, according to the order in which they were served on it.[188]

### Minimum amounts

A deduction should not be made if the amount of credit in the relevant bank account is below a minimum level. The current minimum level is £55 plus the amount of administrative costs charged by the bank or building society.[189] The administrative costs must not be more than £55.[190] Deductions are not made from a partnership account if the account balance is less than £2,000.

### Variations

In certain circumstances, a non-resident parent, her/his bank or building society or a joint account holder can ask the CMS to use its discretion to vary the order. A variation reduces the amount specified in the order.[191] The circumstances include if:[192]

- the CMS accepts the parent's agreement to make a payment;
- there has been a revision or supersession of, or a successful appeal against, the child support calculation;
- there has been an appeal to the family court (sheriff court in Scotland) against making an order, or against a refusal by the CMS to consent to funds being moved or reduced;
- the CMS allows money in the account to be moved or reduced because it agrees that otherwise hardship may be caused (see p175);
- the parent is under a written contractual obligation made before the lump-sum deduction order was made.

## Lapsed, discharged and revived orders

A **regular deduction order** lapses if the CMS considers it reasonable and:[193]

- an alternative method of payment of the child support due, including any fees, has been agreed between the CMS and the non-resident parent; *or*
- on two consecutive deduction dates (or more if the CMS decides this is appropriate), there have been insufficient funds in the account to make the deduction; *or*

- in the case of an order on a joint account, the CMS is satisfied that the non-resident parent has stopped making contributions to the account or will stop making contributions to the account in the next deduction period.

If the order lapses, this takes effect on the day the bank or building society receives notification of this from the CMS.

A lapsed regular deduction order is treated as remaining in force for certain purposes. It can be **revived** if:[194]
- the non-resident parent fails to comply with an agreement about an alternative method of payment; *or*
- the CMS has reason to believe that there are now sufficient funds in the account to make a deduction; *or*
- in the case of an order on a joint account, the non-resident parent has started to make contributions to the account again.

Before reviving a lapsed regular deduction order on a joint account, the CMS must serve a notice on each account holder and consider any representations received. The CMS must provide the same information as for varying a regular deduction order, and the process and timescale for representations are the same (see p174).[195]

A regular deduction order *may* be **discharged** by the CMS if it considers it appropriate and *must* be discharged if:[196]
- the account specified in the order has been closed; *or*
- the child support calculation is no longer in force and the amount due, including any fees, has been paid in full; *or*
- the non-resident parent has complied with any alternative methods of payment agreed with the CMS for a period it considers appropriate; *or*
- the CMS has reviewed the order and the amount to be deducted has been reduced to nil or a court has set aside the order on appeal; *or*
- six months have passed since the order lapsed (and, in the case of an order on a joint account, the account holders have not been informed that the CMS is considering reviving the order), unless an appeal has been made (see the bullet point below); *or*
- an appeal has been made against a lapsed order and one month has passed since either the appeal was concluded or the time limit for a further appeal expired, whichever is the later; *or*
- the non-resident parent has died; *or*
- in the case of a joint account, the non-resident parent is no longer an account holder.

**A lump-sum deduction order lapses** if the CMS considers it reasonable and:[197]
- there is no money in the account (including if the amount has reduced to nil because the CMS has given permission for money to be used, for instance, in cases of hardship – see p175); *or*

- an alternative method of payment of the child support due, including any fees, has been agreed between the CMS and the non-resident parent.

If the order lapses, this takes effect on the day the bank or building society receives notification of this from the CMS.

A lapsed lump-sum deduction order is treated as remaining in force for certain purposes. It can be **revived** if:[198]

- there was no money in the account specified in the order, but the bank or building society has informed the CMS that there is now money in the account (even if it is not sufficient to pay the whole amount specified in the order); *or*
- the order lapsed because there was no money in the account because the CMS had given permission for money to be used (eg, in cases of hardship) and the bank or building society has informed the CMS that there is now money in the account (even if it is not sufficient to pay the whole amount specified in the order); *or*
- money is still due under the order and the non-resident parent has failed to comply with an agreed alternative method of payment of the child support due.

**A lump-sum deduction order may be discharged** by the CMS if it considers it appropriate in all the circumstances, and *must* be discharged if:[199]

- the account specified in the order has been closed; *or*
- in the case of an order on a joint account, the non-resident parent is no longer an account holder in relation to that account; *or*
- the amount of arrears specified in the order, including any fees, has been paid in full; *or*
- the non-resident parent has paid the total amount of arrears due, including any fees, by an alternative method of payment agreed with the CMS; *or*
- after considering representations about making an interim order, the CMS has decided not to make a final order; *or*
- six months have passed since the order lapsed, or since a deduction was made if the amount of the deduction was for all the funds in the account but less than the amount due under the order (unless an appeal has been made – see the bullet point below); *or*
- an appeal has been made against a lapsed order and one month has passed since the appeal was concluded or the time limit for a further appeal expired, whichever is the later; *or*
- the non-resident parent has died.

If the order is discharged, this takes effect on the day the bank or building society receives notification of this from the CMS.

## Appeals

A non-resident parent and, in the case of an order on joint account, another account holder have the right to appeal against a regular deduction order or a lump-sum deduction order and related decisions made by the CMS. The appeal is made to the family court in England and Wales or the sheriff court in Scotland.

You can appeal against:[200]

- the making of a regular deduction order;
- any decision by the CMS on a request to review a regular deduction order;
- a refusal to allow funds which are the subject of an interim lump-sum deduction order to be moved or used – eg, in the case of hardship (see p175). In this case, the non-resident parent, her/his partner and any relevant other child (and, in the case of an order on a joint account, another account holder, her/his partner and any child for whom the other account holder is a person with care) all have the right of appeal;
- the making of a final lump-sum deduction order.

An appeal must be made within 21 days of the date you receive notice of the order or decision. In England and Wales, this time limit cannot be extended by the court. In Scotland, an appeal may be accepted late if the court accepts that there are special reasons.[201] A non-resident parent or another account holder is considered to have received the notice of the order or decision at the end of the day on which it was posted to her/his last known address.[202]

## Recovery of arrears from an estate

If a non-resident parent dies on or after 25 January 2010, any arrears for which s/he was liable immediately before her/his death become a debt, payable to the CMS from her/his estate.[203] The CMS can request the payment of arrears of child support (and any collection fees) from an estate without having to apply to court or obtain a liability order. The decision to recover arrears is a discretionary one. The CMS can contact the administrator or executor of the estate to request payment.

The CMS aims to avoid legal action where possible when using this power and to avoid delaying or obstructing the administration of an estate.[204]

The CMS is notified electronically when other government departments are informed of the death of a non-resident parent. However, the person with care may also wish to inform the CMS that the non-resident parent has died.

The administrator or executor has the same rights of appeal, following the same procedures and time limits, as the non-resident parent had before s/he died.[205]

The CMS must disclose relevant information to enable the administrator or executor to make a decision about whether to pay or appeal the arrears. The CMS has discretion to decide whether the information requested is essential and, therefore, whether it should be disclosed.[206] The CMS should not disclose the address of any person involved in the case unless s/he has given written consent, and should also prevent the disclosure of any information that could lead to the person with care, or any other relevant person, being located.[207]

It is intended that child support arrears will be treated in the same way as other debts – eg, unpaid utility or council tax bills. It does not appear that they take priority over other payments.

Before making a claim on an estate, the CMS should thoroughly check the amount of outstanding debt, including completing any outstanding reassessments relating to periods before the death.[208] Administrators of the estate should check that the CMS has carried out this process and that the amount of debt to be recovered is accurate.

### When arrears should not be recovered

The CMS should not pursue arrears from an estate without the consent of the person with care. If s/he does not wish to pursue the arrears, the CMS should not take any further action.[209] For further details on when arrears may be written off, see p157. The CMS also has a duty to take into account the welfare of any child likely to be affected (see p126). This includes a child(ren) of the non-resident parent who may not have been the subject of the child support calculation, or other dependent children who would otherwise benefit from the estate. When the CMS registers its claim against the estate, it may not be aware of other children or the potential implications for them. If the CMS later becomes aware of any potentially adverse impact on other children, it should reconsider whether to pursue the arrears.[210] The CMS also takes into account the administrative cost of recovering arrears in this way.[211]

If the arrears recovered from an estate would be retained by the CMS in lieu of any benefit paid, they should not be pursued if this would have a detrimental effect on a person with care or a qualifying child. This only applies to arrears relating to a period before 12 April 2010, when child support was counted as income for means-tested benefits. The CMS should contact the person with care to establish what impact the recovery would have before approaching the administrators of the estate.[212]

### Obtaining a liability order

If enforcement methods, such as a deduction from earnings order, are inappropriate (eg, because the non-resident parent is not employed) or have been tried but proved ineffective, the CMS may apply to the magistrates' court in England and Wales, or sheriff court in Scotland, for a liability order.[213]

A liability order provides legal recognition of the debt, and allows the CMS to take further enforcement measures. A liability order is required before the CMS can take action to:

- take control of and sell goods (see p182);
- disqualify the non-resident parent from driving or from holding or obtaining a passport or other travel authorisation (see p184);
- imprison the non-resident parent (see p184).

The CMS must give the non-resident parent seven days' notice of its intention to seek a liability order (28 days if s/he is not resident in the UK).[214] The notice must state the amount of child support outstanding, including any collection or enforcement fees.

If the court decides that the payments are due but have not been made, it must make the order.[215] The court cannot question the child support calculation itself.[216] When making a liability order, the court can take into account payments made by the non-resident person by a method other than that specified by the CMS.[217]

An order (including one made in Northern Ireland) can be enforced anywhere in the UK.[218]

If the court makes the liability order, it usually orders the non-resident parent to pay the CMS's legal expenses.

### Time limits

Since 12 July 2006, there has been no time limit for applying for a liability order. Debts that were older than six years on 12 July 2006 (ie, that became due on or before 12 July 2000) and were not subject to a liability order cannot be enforced through a liability order and will be recovered by other methods.[219] The six years do not begin to run until the non-resident parent is notified of the calculation. Although a calculation can be backdated, liability does not exist until it is made.[220]

The CMS does not need to act on a liability order immediately after it is granted. If an order is made, there may be a long delay before the CMS takes any further action. Action that directly aims to recover money (eg, taking control of goods) must be taken within six years from the date of the order.[221] The six-year time limit does not apply to action that does not, in itself, recover money, such as imprisonment or disqualification from driving.[222]

### England and Wales

The non-resident parent is sent a summons, giving 14 days' notice of the hearing. The magistrates' court decides whether or not to issue the liability order, but cannot consider whether the parent is liable or the calculation has been properly made.[223] If an appeal against a decision of the CMS on those issues is pending, however, the court may decide to adjourn.

The court may decide not to issue an order if the non-resident parent appears to be co-operating. However, the CMS may still ask for the order to be granted on the understanding that it will not be enforced if the parent continues to co-operate. If the parent does not attend the court, the CMS may still obtain the order, unless the application has not been properly made. It is unusual for a non-resident parent to attend a liability order hearing. If s/he does attend, the court may adjourn and arrange another hearing to ensure that there is sufficient time for her/him to speak. She can be represented by a lawyer or another person.

The liability order must specify the outstanding amounts of child support, fees and other forms of maintenance.[224]

### Scotland

The non-resident parent is sent a notice of the application for a liability order and has 21 days to object to its being made. This should be done in writing by returning the notice stating the grounds of the objection and enclosing evidence. If objections are received, a court hearing is held. Even if the parent does not attend, the sheriff must still consider her/his objections.[225] The court cannot question the non-resident parent's liability for child support, or the calculation itself. An extract of the liability order may be issued 14 days after the order is actually made.

## Taking control of goods and other enforcement action

If a liability order has been made, in England and Wales, the CMS can instruct enforcement agents to take control of the non-resident parent's goods or take court action (see below). In Scotland, a liability order can be enforced by 'diligence' (the term for various processes of debt enforcement in Scottish law – see p183).[226] The law on taking control of goods and diligence can be complex. The following is not a full statement of the law, but a summary of the processes that can be used by the CMS.[227] If you are subject to enforcement action by the CMS, get help from a money adviser.

The CMS aims to use the full range of sanctions available, including taking control of goods, removing a driving licence, disqualifying the non-resident parent from holding or obtaining a passport, and imprisonment, where appropriate.[228]

### England and Wales

If a liability order has been made, the amount on the order can be enforced in England and Wales by **taking control of and selling the non-resident parent's goods**.[229] The enforcement agent (a private bailiff) carrying this out must give the person written notice at least seven clear days before taking action. The notice must include details of the liability order and the debt.[230] It must also explain how payment of the debt in full can be made to avoid the taking and subsequent sale of goods.[231]

Certain items cannot be taken. These include:[232]

- tools, books, vehicles and other items necessary for work, up to a total value of £1,350; *and*

- clothing, bedding, furniture, household equipment and provisions reasonably required to meet the basic domestic needs of the non-resident parent and every member of her/his household.

Fees can be charged at each of the stages involved in the process.[233]

For more information about bailiffs, including how to complain about them, see CPAG's *Debt Advice Handbook*.

Once a liability order has been made, the CMS can **register the order as if it were a judgment debt**.[234] This record is publicly available and damages the non-resident parent's credit rating (see also p55 for when the CMS can disclose information directly to credit reference agencies). The CMS can also use the county court to recover any amount that remains unpaid.[235]

A **charging order** allows a debt to be registered against the non-resident parent's property (and certain other assets, such as land, stocks, shares and any interest s/he may have in a trust). When the property is sold, the debt due under the liability order can be recovered from the proceeds of the sale. In some cases, it may not be possible to register a charge, in which case a caution against dealings may be obtained to prevent the property from being sold without the CMS's knowledge. Once a charge or caution has been registered, the CMS can consider applying to the court for an order of sale, forcing the non-resident parent to sell the property and pay the debt.

A **third-party debt order** can be obtained by the CMS if it is aware that the non-resident parent has a bank account or is owed money by a third party. The order freezes funds in the account and requires that person to release funds to the CMS up to the amount of the liability order.

## Scotland

In Scotland, the CMS can ask sheriff officers to issue a 'charge for payment', a formal request in writing demanding that the non-resident parent pay the debt within a specific period, usually 14 days. If s/he does not, various enforcement processes (known as 'diligence') can be used.

The CMS can ask the sheriff court to freeze money or goods through an **arrestment**. This prevents money in an account being used, and prevents any money owed to the non-resident parent being paid into the account. A company holding any goods owed to the parent can be required to cancel the transaction and transfer the money used to pay for the goods to the CMS instead.

The sheriff court can also make an **attachment order**, preventing the non-resident parent from selling or transferring belongings. If the parent still does not pay the arrears, the goods can be seized and sold at public auction and the proceeds paid to the CMS.

The CMS can instruct sheriff officers to register the debt against any heritable property (eg, a house, garage, land or business premises). This is known as

**inhibition**, and prevents the non-resident parent selling or transferring the property until s/he has paid the debt.

## Orders preventing the disposal of assets

In England, Wales and Scotland, the CMS can take action in the High Court or family court (England and Wales) or the Court of Session or sheriff court (Scotland) to prevent a non-resident parent disposing of assets or transferring them out of the UK in order to avoid paying child support arrears.[236]

If the asset has already been disposed of, the court can make an order to 'set the transaction aside' or, in Scotland, to 'reduce the disposition' – ie, to reverse the disposal.[237] If the parent is about to dispose of an asset, the court can make an order to prevent this.[238]

The court can review any disposal of assets by the non-resident parent, except if the asset was given as part of a contract with an innocent party who acted in good faith.[239] For example, if the parent disposes of a sum of money to purchase goods from an individual who had no knowledge of her/his intention to avoid paying child support, the transaction cannot be reversed. An asset transferred to another as part of a marriage agreement or the formation of a civil partnership can, however, be reviewed by the court.[240] Assets transferred under a will are not treated as having been disposed of.

If the court is satisfied that the CMS would be able to take action to recover arrears from the asset in question, the burden of proof is on the non-resident parent to show that s/he did not dispose of, or was not about to dispose of, the asset with the intention of avoiding paying child support.[241] If an order is made in Scotland, the parent can apply to the court to have it reviewed, varied or recalled at any time.[242]

## Disqualification from driving or holding a passport, and imprisonment

If other methods of recovery have failed, the CMS may take action to disqualify the non-resident parent from driving for up to two years or to imprison her/him for up to six weeks (but not both).[243] From 14 December 2018, the CMS can also take action to disqualify the non-resident parent from holding or obtaining a passport or other UK travel authorisation for up to two years.[244] The CMS cannot seek both disqualification from holding a passport and imprisonment. **Note:** the CMS can only take action if the other enforcement proceedings have been tried unsuccessfully. It is not enough that they have been considered, but not pursued.[245]

Before taking action, the CMS must attempt to contact the parent. If no phone contact has been successful during the enforcement action, a face-to-face visit may be appropriate. These powers are only used as a last resort where all other methods of recovery have failed. The CMS has said that disqualification from holding or obtaining a passport will be used only in exceptional circumstances and where arrears of over £1,000 remain outstanding.[246] Suspended prison sentences and suspended disqualifications from driving are more common than actual committals and disqualifications.[247] Disqualification from holding or obtaining a passport can also be suspended.[248]

These powers are discretionary, and when deciding whether to take these types of action, the CMS must consider the welfare of any child likely to be affected (see p126).

The CMS must apply to the magistrates' court (or, in Scotland, sheriff court) for an order disqualifying the non-resident parent from driving or a warrant committing her/him to prison.[249] The CMS makes one application to the court, and the court decides whether either disqualification from driving or committal to prison is appropriate. The CMS can make representations to the court on which it thinks is more appropriate, and the parent can respond to any such representations.[250]

From 14 December 2018, the CMS can also apply to the court for an order disqualifying the parent from holding or obtaining a passport or other UK travel authorisation. The court cannot disqualify the parent from holding or obtaining a passport *and* commit her/him to prison.[251] **Note:** the power to disqualify a parent from holding or obtaining a passport does not apply in Northern Ireland.

The non-resident parent must attend the hearing.[252] The court can summon her/him to appear in court and produce her/his driving licence or passport (if s/he has one).[253] If s/he does not appear, the court may issue a warrant for her/his arrest.[254]

The court must enquire into the parent's means, whether s/he needs a driving licence or passport to earn a living and whether there has been 'wilful refusal or culpable neglect' on her/his part to pay the child support due.[255] It cannot question the child support calculation or the liability order. The court can only disqualify the non-resident parent from driving or holding or obtaining a passport, or commit her/him to prison, if there has been 'wilful refusal or culpable neglect'.[256] The decision whether to make the order is at the court's discretion. The CMS must prove beyond reasonable doubt that the non-resident parent has the ability to pay and has wilfully refused.[257]

A written statement from an employer is accepted as proof of earnings.[258]

### Disqualification from driving or holding a passport

If the court decides that there has been wilful refusal or culpable neglect and it is appropriate to disqualify the non-resident parent from driving or holding a passport, it issues an order.[259] If the CMS applied for an order but the court did not make one, the CMS can apply again if the parent's circumstances have changed.[260]

The order states the amount outstanding, including child support, collection and enforcement fees and the expenses incurred by the CMS in making the application.[261] If an order is made, the non-resident parent must give up her/his driving licence and counterpart or any passport or travel authorisation to the court.

The implementation of the order may be suspended for a particular period or on particular conditions – eg, that the parent makes regular payments (or, in the case of an order on holding a passport, if the court is satisfied that exceptional circumstances justify the order being suspended).[262]

The maximum period of disqualification from driving or holding a passport is two years.[263] If, after the order has been issued, part payment is made, either the non-resident parent or the CMS can apply to the court to have the order revoked or the period of disqualification reduced.[264] The CMS can make representations to the court about how much of the outstanding arrears should be paid before it would be appropriate for the court to revoke the order. When the court makes an order on holding a passport, it can order that the non-resident person be searched and any money found can be paid towards the arrears due. If part payment is made this way, the court then has discretion to decide whether to reduce the period of disqualification or revoke the order.[265]

If the amount is paid in full, the order must be revoked.[266] If the arrears have not been paid in full at the end of the period of disqualification, the CMS may apply again for disqualification or imprisonment.[267]

You can appeal against the court's decision. An an appeal should be made within 21 days of the court's decision (28 days in Scotland – in Scotland, the court can accept a late appeal if it considers there are good reasons).[268]

### Imprisonment

If the court decides that there has been 'wilful refusal or culpable neglect' and it is appropriate, a warrant for imprisonment is issued.[269] If the CMS has applied for the court to consider disqualification from driving or committal to prison, the court should explain the reasons why this is preferred.

A warrant for imprisonment cannot be issued against a non-resident parent who is under 18.[270]

Instead of immediate committal to prison, the court usually fixes a term of imprisonment and postpones it on conditions, usually of regular payments.[271] A warrant of commitment is issued, stating the total amount outstanding, including child support, collection and enforcement fees and the expenses incurred by the CMS in making the application.[272] If the amount is paid in full, the non-resident parent will not be imprisoned.

The maximum period of imprisonment is six weeks.[273] If, after the warrant has been issued, part payment is made, the period of imprisonment is reduced by the same proportion as that by which the debt has been reduced.[274]

If the parent is imprisoned, s/he can be released immediately if the liability order debt is paid in full. If part of the debt is paid, the prison sentence can be reduced.[275] Advisers should check whether the payment needs to be made to the prison or to the CMS.

The court cannot write off the arrears, so if full payment is not made, arrears still exist following the period of imprisonment. If a warrant is not issued or the court does not fix a term of imprisonment, the CMS can renew the application at a later date on the grounds that the non-resident parent's circumstances have changed.[276]

If the non-resident parent builds up a new debt (eg, by not keeping up with current child support payments), the CMS can go back to court to request a warrant in respect of each new debt.[277]

## Bankruptcy

A non-resident parent may have child support arrears when s/he is made bankrupt. The CMS is not a creditor that can be bound by an individual voluntary arrangement (in England and Wales, this is a binding compromise agreement with creditors to avoid the consequences of bankruptcy) made by a non-resident parent and so any liability for arrears of child support cannot be reduced by means of an individual voluntary arrangement.[278]

The CMS cannot take enforcement action while a non-resident parent is being made bankrupt. Therefore, if the CMS is notified of bankruptcy, any ongoing enforcement action must cease until the bankruptcy order has been made.

In this case, the CMS may decide not to enforce the liability order because it may not be practical – eg, a charging order/inhibition of sale may not be effective, as any property may already have been sold to pay creditors.

As part of bankruptcy proceedings, the non-resident parent can inform the court of her/his child support liabilities. The administrator of the bankruptcy should take this into account when deciding how much money the parent needs to meet her/his basic living expenses. This decision is made before any available funds are distributed among creditors.

The CMS may still consider further enforcement measures, such as disqualification from driving or imprisonment, against a non-resident parent who is bankrupt, particularly if s/he has a steady income. In these circumstances, you must show that you cannot afford to meet your child support liability. This may be more difficult if the administrator of the bankruptcy has already made provision for the current child support payments when deciding how much money you need to meet basic living expenses. In the vast majority of cases, the CMS still pursues child support.[279]

If a non-resident parent is sequestrated in Scotland, any child support debt is no longer legally recoverable and may be written off (see p157).

---

## 3. **Fees for enforcement action**

If the Child Maintenance Service (CMS) takes certain enforcement action, fees are imposed on the non-resident parent as follows:[280]

- £50 for making a deduction from earnings order (see p162);
- £50 for making a regular deduction order (see p171);
- £200 for making a lump-sum deduction order (see p174);
- £300 for applying for a liability order (see p180).

Enforcement fees may be waived by the CMS if:[281]
- an additional fee would otherwise be due because:
  - more than one deduction from earnings order is sought by the CMS because the non-resident parent has more than one employer or has recently changed jobs; *or*
  - more than one regular deduction order or lump-sum order is sought because the non-resident parent has more than one bank or building society account, or has recently changed accounts; *or*
  - the amount being collected under a deduction from earnings order or regular deduction order has changed; *or*
- the CMS has sought a liability order, but it was not granted; *or*
- the CMS's action to impose a deduction from earnings order, regular deduction order or lump-sum deduction order has been successfully challenged by the non-resident parent by appeal or judicial review; *or*
- due to error or maladministration by the CMS, the deduction from earnings order, regular deduction order or lump-sum deduction order has lapsed or been discharged; *or*
- a deduction from earnings order is made because the non-resident parent has chosen to use this as the method of paying her/his child support liability; *or*
- a deduction from earnings request (see p163) is made for a non-resident parent in the armed forces when that parent is deployed on operational duty.

**Note:** there are no fees for enforcement action on remaining cases under the '2003 rules' and '1993 rules' until these are closed (see p1).

From 23 May 2016, enforcement fees can also be waived in certain circumstances (see p139) while the non-resident parent is being offered a 'compliance opportunity' (see p136) to prove that s/he will pay voluntarily in order to be allowed to use 'direct pay' in a '2012 rules' case. In such cases, if a deduction from earnings order is imposed during the compliance period to cover a portion of the payments due, the fee for the order can be waived.[282] At the end of the compliance opportunity, if the order is varied (ie, because the non-resident parent has not complied and it has to be varied to cover the full amount of child support due), an enforcement fee of £50 is due. This fee is only due the first time the deduction from earnings order is varied, and can be waived by the CMS for one of the usual reasons listed above.[283] The power to impose and waive these fees in these circumstances ends on 22 May 2021.[284]

An enforcement fee is payable to the CMS, not the person with care. It is recovered by the CMS from any arrears owed by the non-resident parent before the balance is paid to the person with care.[285] If an enforcement fee is charged, the CMS must send the non-resident parent a notice as soon as possible stating the amount of the fee and the enforcement action in respect of which it has been imposed.[286]

**Note:** the rules on collecting and enforcing payments of child support also apply to payment of fees, except that the CMS cannot seek to disqualify a non-resident parent from driving or from holding or obtaining a passport or other travel authorisation, or imprison her/him, where enforcement action is being taken against her/him solely to recover fees.[287]

# 4. **Delays in collection and enforcement**

Many cases may accumulate arrears. In recent years, the Child Maintenance Service (CMS) has said that it has been pursuing a more vigorous approach to enforcement and taking enforcement action more quickly in response to a non-resident parent's failure to pay.

If you are a person with care and concerned about the speed of pursuit, contact the CMS and explain the effects of this on the welfare of the child(ren). In particular, you may want to request that a deduction from earnings order be issued. If a deduction from earnings order or another form of enforcement is refused, the reasons for this should be explained.

**Note:** enforcing the obligation to pay child support is at the discretion of the CMS.[288] This means that a person with care cannot decide which method of enforcement is used. If you believe that there has been undue delay by the CMS, or that it has not used its discretion reasonably or rationally, you can make a complaint (see Chapter 11). Judicial review (see p198) could also be considered. Get specialist advice before considering an application for judicial review.

If arrears of over £100 have built up because of CMS maladministration, you may be eligible for an advance payment (see below). This may be in addition to any payment of compensation (see p243).

## Advance payments

An advance payment of child support is not compensation. The payment is to ensure that a person with care is not worse off as a result of maladministration by the CMS. Essentially, it is advance payment of arrears that the CMS is collecting from the non-resident parent. The decision on whether or not to make an advance payment is discretionary and there are no guidelines in the legislation. Some details of when the CMS considers making an advance payment are available on the child maintenance section of the gov.uk website.

For an advance payment to be considered, there must be clear evidence of maladministration by the CMS. 'Maladministration' may include:

- rudeness;
- delay;
- refusing to answer reasonable questions;
- knowingly giving advice which is misleading or inadequate;
- incompetence;
- bias – eg, because of gender or ethnicity; *or*
- disregarding guidance that should be followed.

A request for an advance payment could also be considered even if the CMS is not able to recover arrears from the non-resident parent. This could apply if arrears of child support have become unenforceable – eg, because enforcement action was not taken within the time limits, or the non-resident parent has subsequently moved abroad and is outside the CMS's jurisdiction. If the arrears could have been collected had the CMS taken timely action, a request for an advance payment can be made. Although the power is discretionary, the Independent Case Examiner (ICE – see p247) has recommended payment in such cases.[289]

The CMS may consider an advance payment on its own initiative or at the request of the person with care. If an advance payment is to be made, the amount is the arrears that would have been due but for the maladministration. Allowances are made for normal processing time, so only delay over and above this is considered.

If a decision is made not to make a payment, there is no right of appeal. You can provide further information to support the case, complain (see Chapter 11), contact your MP or possibly seek a judicial review (see p198). If a complaint is made, the CMS may still refuse to make an advance payment. However, ICE and the Ombudsman have the power to recommend advance payments, so it may be worthwhile moving to the next stage of the complaints procedure if you have reasonable grounds.

Where maladministration has occurred, there is also provision for the CMS to pay compensation or a consolatory special payment (see p243).

## Enforcement by the person with care

Although there is no provision in child support legislation for the person with care to bring her/his own court action against the non-resident parent for the child support due, it may be possible to do so. In practice, however, such action may be difficult. The European Court of Human Rights has confirmed that only the CMS has the legal standing to enforce child support, and that a lack of direct access to the courts by a person with care to enforce child support payments from a non-resident parent does not breach the right to a fair hearing under the European Convention on Human Rights.[290]

In certain circumstances, legal action against the CMS may be possible if there has been a serious breach of statutory duties (such as discrimination). If you are considering legal action, get legal advice. However, it is not possible to sue the CMS for negligence in the way it deals with your case.

Using the complaints procedure is more likely to be an effective means of obtaining redress within a reasonable timescale (see Chapter 11).

# Notes

**1. Arrears**
1 ss4(2)(b) and 7(3)(b) CSA 1991
2 CMS leaflet CMSB006GB, *What Happens if a Paying Parent Doesn't Pay Child Maintenance?* November 2013
3 DWP, *Supporting Separated Families: securing children's futures,* Cm 8399, July 2012; DWP, *Preparing for the Future, Tackling the Past: child maintenance – arrears and compliance strategy 2012-2017,* January 2013
4 CMS leaflet CMSB009GB, *Paying Child Maintenance: information for receiving parents with a Collect and Pay arrangement,* October 2013
5 Reg 7 CS(C&E) Regs
6 Reg 8A CS(MAJ) Regs
7 s28J CSA 1991
8 Reg 2(2) CS(VP) Regs
9 *DP v CMEC (CSM)* [2012] UKUT 63 (AAC)
10 Reg 3(b) CS(VP) Regs
11 Reg 3(a) CS(VP) Regs
12 Regs 2(2) and 4(b) CS(VP) Regs
13 Reg 4(a) CS(VP) Regs
14 s41B(1A) and (2) CSA 1991; reg 9 CS(MPA) Regs
15 DWP, *Preparing for the Future, Tackling the Past: child maintenance – arrears and compliance strategy 2012-2017,* January 2013
16 Reg 3(3) CS(MPA) Regs
17 Reg 3(3)(a) CS(MPA) Regs; DWP, *Child Support (Miscellaneous Amendments) Regulations 2012: government response to consultation,* March 2012
18 Reg 3(4) CS(MPA) Regs
19 Reg 3A CS(MPA) Regs

20 DWP, *Child Maintenance Frequently Asked Questions,* August 2012
21 First Protocol, Art 1 European Convention on Human Rights
22 DWP, *Preparing for the Future, Tackling the Past: child maintenance – arrears and compliance strategy 2012-2017,* January 2013
23 s41A CSA 1991 and reg 7A CS(C&E) Regs; Sch 7, para 3(1) UC,PIP,JSA&ESA(C&P) Regs
24 DWP, *Preparing for the Future, Tackling the Past: child maintenance – arrears and compliance strategy 2012-2017,* January 2013
25 s41(2) and (2A) CSA 1991; reg 8 CS(AIAMA) Regs
26 Reg 8 CS(AIAMA) Regs
27 Regs 3-8 CS(MA) Regs 2019 and Explanatory Memorandum
28 Sch 9B para 3(1) SS(C&P) Regs
29 Reg 7(1) CS(MPA) Regs
30 Child Maintenance and Enforcement Commission, *Child Maintenance and Other Payments Act Summary of Responses to the Consultation on Draft Regulations,* November 2009, para 3
31 Child Maintenance and Enforcement Commission, *Child Maintenance and Other Payments Act Summary of Responses to the Consultation on Draft Regulations,* November 2009, para 3
32 Reg 7(3) CS(MPA) Regs
33 Child Maintenance and Enforcement Commission, *Child Maintenance and Other Payments Act Summary of Responses to the Consultation on Draft Regulations,* November 2009, para 3.5

34  s41D CSA 1991
35  s41D(3) and (5)-(7) CSA 1991
36  DWP, *The Draft Child Support
    Management of Payments and Arrears
    (Amendment) Regulations 2012:
    government response to consultation on
    draft regulations*, October 2012
37  Reg 13D(1) and (2) CS(MPA) Regs
38  Reg 13D(3) CS(MPA) Regs
39  DWP, *The Draft Child Support
    Management of Payments and Arrears
    (Amendment) Regulations 2012:
    government response to consultation on
    draft regulations*, October 2012
40  Reg 13C(1) CS(MPA) Regs
41  Reg 13B CS(MPA) Regs
42  DWP, *The Draft Child Support
    Management of Payments and Arrears
    (Amendment) Regulations 2012:
    government response to consultation on
    draft regulations*, October 2012
43  Reg 13E(1) and (2) CS(MPA) Regs
44  Reg 13E(3) CS(MPA) Regs
45  Reg 13E(4) and (5) CS(MPA) Regs
46  DWP, *The Draft Child Support
    Management of Payments and Arrears
    (Amendment) Regulations 2012:
    government response to consultation on
    draft regulations*, October 2012
47  s41E CSA 1991
48  s41E(1) CSA 1991 and reg 13G
    CS(MPA) Regs
49  DWP, *Preparing for the Future, Tackling
    the Past: child maintenance – arrears and
    compliance strategy 2012-2017*, January
    2013
50  CS(MA) Regs 2018, Explanatory
    Memorandum, para 7.30
51  Reg 9 CS(MA) Regs 2019 and
    Explanatory Memorandum CS(MA)
    Regs 2019
52  Reg 13F CS(MPA) Regs
53  The duties on the CMS to give written
    notice do not apply to someone who
    cannot be traced or who has died: regs
    13(2) and 13H(2) CS(MPA) Regs.
54  Reg 13H CS(MPA) Regs
55  Reg 13H(5) CS(MPA) Regs
56  Reg 13H(2) CS(MPA) Regs
57  Reg 13I CS(MPA) Regs
58  Reg 13H(4) CS(MPA) Regs
59  DWP, *Supporting Separated Families:
    securing children's futures*, Cm 8399, July
    2012; DWP, *Preparing for the Future,
    Tackling the Past: child maintenance –
    arrears and compliance strategy 2012-
    2017*, January 2013

60  DWP, *Supporting Separated Families:
    securing children's futures*, Cm 8399, July
    2012
61  DWP, *Preparing for the Future, Tackling
    the Past: child maintenance – arrears and
    compliance strategy 2012-2017*, January
    2013
62  Regs 13G(g) and (h) and 13K CS(MPA)
    Regs
63  CS(MA) Regs 2018, Explanatory
    Memorandum, paras 7.21-7.23
64  Regs 13G(g) and (h) and 13K(1)(c) and
    (e) and (2)(c) CS(MPA) Regs
65  Reg 13H(3)(da)(i) CS(MPA) Regs;
    CS(MA) Regs 2018, Explanatory
    Memorandum, para 7.23
66  Reg 13J(2) CS(MPA) Regs
67  Reg 13H(1A) and (3)(da)(ii) CS(MPA)
    Regs
68  Reg 13H(3)(b) CS(MPA) Regs
69  Reg 13I CS(MPA) Regs
70  Reg 13J CS(MPA) Regs
71  Regs 13G(g) and (h) and 13K(1)(b) and
    (d) and (2)(b) CS(MPA) Regs
72  Regs 13H(2) and 13J CS(MPA) Regs
73  Regs 13G(g) and (h), 13K(1)(a) and
    (2)(a) and 13J(2) CS(MPA) Regs

## 2. Enforcement action

74  CMS leaflet CMSB006GB, *What
    Happens if a Paying Parent Doesn't Pay
    Child Maintenance?*, November 2013
75  Reg 13 CSF Regs
76  *KA v CMEC* [2009] UKUT 99 (AAC)
77  House of Commons, *Hansard*, Written
    Answers, 20 July 2011, col 1063W
78  Jurisdiction and Judgments (Family)
    (Amendment etc.) (EU Exit) Regulations
    2019, No. 519
79  *Child Maintenance: cases where someone
    lives overseas (England and Wales)*, House
    of Commons Library, January 2018
80  Details available at: gov.uk/child-
    maintenance-if-one-parent-lives-abroad
81  s31 CSA 1991
82  CMS leaflet CMSB006GB, *What
    Happens if a Paying Parent Doesn't Pay
    Child Maintenance?*, November 2013
83  Reg 8(3) and (4) CS(C&E) Regs
84  Reg 8(4) CS(C&E) Regs
85  Reg 8(5) CS(C&E) Regs
86  s29(4)(a) CSA 1991
87  *R v Secretary of State for Social Security ex
    parte Biggin* [1995] 2 FCR 595, [1995] 1
    FLR 851
88  Sch 1 para 10 CS(NIRA) Regs

89 CSA(CA)O; s342(1)(e)(ii) Armed Forces Act 2006; reg 10 Armed Forces (Forfeitures and Deductions) Regulations 2009 SI No.1109
90 Regs 3(3) and 6 CS(DEOAMMA) Regs
91 Reg 15 CS(C&E) Regs
92 Reg 15(1) CS(C&E) Regs
93 s32(8) and (11) CSA 1991; reg 25(ab) and (b) CS(C&E) Regs
94 Reg 1(3)(a) CS(C&E) Regs
95 Reg 1(3)(b) CS(C&E) Regs
96 s31(6) CSA 1991
97 s31(7) CSA 1991
98 s14A CSA 1991; reg 4(2)(b) CSI Regs; CMS, *Make Child Maintenance Deductions From an Employee's Pay*, gov.uk/child-maintenance-for-employers
99 Reg 9 CS(C&E) Regs
100 Reg 16(1) CS(C&E) Regs
101 Reg 16(2) CS(C&E) Regs
102 Reg 16(3) CS(C&E) Regs
103 s32(8) and (11) CSA 1991; reg 25(aa), (b) and (c) CS(C&E) Regs
104 Reg 13 CS(C&E) Regs; s8(2)(b) ERA 1996
105 s9 ERA 1996
106 s12(3)-(5) ERA 1996
107 childmaintenanceservice.direct.gov.uk
108 Reg 1(3)(a) CS(C&E) Regs
109 Reg 1(3)(b) CS(C&E) Regs
110 Reg 9 CS(C&E) Regs
111 Reg 9(d) CS(C&E) Regs
112 Reg 11(2) CS(C&E) Regs
113 Regs 10(1) and (2) and 11 CS(C&E) Regs, as substituted for '2012 rules' cases and other 'arrears only' cases by reg 4(4) CS(MOC&NCR) Regs
114 Reg 10(3) CS(C&E) Regs, as substituted for '2012 rules' cases by reg 4(4) CS(MOC&NCR) Regs
115 Regs 1(4), 11 and 12 CS(MOC&NCR) Regs
116 Reg 14(1) CS(C&E) Regs
117 Reg 14(2) CS(C&E) Regs
118 s32(8) and (11) CSA 1991; reg 25(aa) CS(C&E) Regs
119 Reg 12(2) CS(C&E) Regs
120 Reg 12(4) CS(C&E) Regs
121 Reg 12(3A) CS(C&E) Regs
122 Reg 8 CS(AIAMA) Regs
123 Reg 24(2)(a) and (4) CS(C&E) Regs
124 Reg 24(2)(b) CS(C&E) Regs
125 Reg 17 CS(C&E) Regs
126 Reg 18 CS(C&E) Regs
127 Reg 19 CS(C&E) Regs

128 Regs 10(3) and 20(1)(g) CS(C&E) Regs, as substituted for '2012 rules' cases and other 'arrears only' cases by regs 4(4) and (6) and 11 CS(MOC&NCR) Regs
129 Reg 20(1) CS(C&E) Regs
130 Reg 20(1A) CS(C&E) Regs
131 Reg 36 CS(C&E) Regs, as inserted by reg 3(3) CS(DEOAMMA) Regs, modifying reg 20 by inserting paras (1)(i) and (1B) until 21 May 2021
132 Reg 4 CS(DEOAMMA) Regs, amending reg 12 CS(MOC&NCR) Regs until 21 May 2021
133 Reg 20(2) CS(C&E) Regs
134 Reg 21(1) CS(C&E) Regs
135 Reg 21(4) CS(C&E) Regs
136 Reg 21(5) CS(C&E) Regs
137 Reg 21(6) CS(C&E) Regs
138 Reg 22(1) CS(C&E) Regs
139 Reg 22(2) CS(C&E) Regs
140 Reg 22(3) CS(C&E) Regs
141 Reg 22(3A) CS(C&E) Regs
142 Reg 8(1) CS(C&E) Regs
143 Reg 3(4) CS(C&E) Regs
144 Reg 3(6)(c) CS(C&E) Regs
145 Reg 3(5) CS(C&E) Regs
146 Reg 3(6) CS(C&E) Regs
147 r5 and Form 6 AS(CSR)
148 Reg 22(4) CS(C&E) Regs
149 s32(6) CSA 1991
150 *Secretary of State for Social Security v Shotton* [1996] 2 FLR 241
151 ss48 and 49 CSA 1991; r6 AS(CSR)
152 ss32A and 32F CSA 1991
153 Reg 25A CS(C&E) Regs
154 Child Maintenance and Enforcement Commission, *Deduction Order Review*, Research Report No.2, March 2011, p16

155 Reg 25XA CS(C&E) Regs
156 Reg 25A(1), definition of 'joint account', CS(C&E) Regs
157 Reg 25X CS(C&E) Regs
158 DWP, *Child Maintenance: changes to compliance measures*, December 2018
159 Reg 25XC CS(C&E) Regs
160 CS(MA) Regs 2018, Explanatory Memorandum, para 7.11
161 Regs 25E(5A) and 25O(5A) CS(C&E) Regs
162 ss32D and 32K CSA 1991; regs 25E, 25O and 25AC CS(C&E) Regs
163 Reg 25Z CS(C&E) Regs
164 s32A CSA 1991
165 s32B(1) CSA 1991; reg 25A1 CS(C&E) Regs
166 Reg 25XB CS(C&E) Regs
167 s32A(5) and (7) CSA 1991; reg 25B(1) CS(C&E) Regs

168 Reg 25C CS(C&E) Regs, as amended by reg 4(7) CS(MOC&NCR) Regs for '2012 rules' cases
169 Reg 25H CS(C&E) Regs
170 Reg 25D CS(C&E) Regs
171 Reg 25G CS(C&E) Regs
172 Reg 25G(2)(d) CS(C&E) Regs
173 Reg 25I CS(C&E) Regs
174 Reg 25I(3) CS(C&E) Regs
175 Reg 25IA CS(C&E) Regs
176 ss32E and 32G CSA 1991; reg 25N CS(C&E) Regs
177 s32E(6) CSA 1991; reg 25M CS(C&E) Regs
178 Reg 25MA CS(C&E) Regs
179 Reg 25XB CS(C&E) Regs
180 s32F CSA 1991; reg 25MA(4) CS(C&E) Regs
181 ss32G(5) and (6) and 32H(1) CSA 1991
182 s32F(3)(a) CSA 1991
183 s32F(3)(b) and (4) CSA 1991
184 Reg 25A(3)(b) CS(C&E) Regs
185 s32I CSA 1991; reg 25N(1) and (2) CS(C&E) Regs
186 Reg 25N(3) and (4) CS(C&E) Regs
187 Reg 25P(1) and (2) CS(C&E) Regs
188 Reg 25P(6) CS(C&E) Regs
189 Reg 25Q CS(C&E) Regs
190 Reg 25Z(b) CS(C&E) Regs
191 s32J(3) CSA 1991; reg 25R CS(C&E) Regs
192 Regs 25R and 25N CS(C&E) Regs
194 Reg 25K CS(C&E) Regs
195 Reg 25KA CS(C&E) Regs
197 Reg 25S CS(C&E) Regs
198 Reg 25T CS(C&E) Regs
199 Reg 25U CS(C&E) Regs
200 Reg 25AB CS(C&E) Regs
201 **EW** paras 9.17 and 9.19 *Practice Direction 30A: appeals*, Family Procedure Rules 2010; *AH v SSWP (CSA)* [2017] EWFC 9
**S** rr5AB and 5AC AS(CSR); r2.6 Act of Sederunt (Summary Applications, Statutory Applications, Appeals etc. Rules) 1999, No.929
202 Reg 25A(3)(b) and (4) CS(C&E) Regs
203 s43A CSA 1991; reg 11 CS(MPA) Regs
204 Child Maintenance and Enforcement Commission, *Child Maintenance and Other Payments Act Summary of Responses to the Consultation on Draft Regulations*, November 2009, para 4.9
205 Reg 12 CS(MPA) Regs
206 Reg 13 CS(MPA) Regs
207 Reg 13(3) CS(MPA) Regs

208 Child Maintenance and Enforcement Commission, *Child Maintenance and Other Payments Act Summary of Responses to the Consultation on Draft Regulations*, November 2009, para 4.11
209 Child Maintenance and Enforcement Commission, *Child Maintenance and Other Payments Act Summary of Responses to the Consultation on Draft Regulations*, November 2009, para 4.6
210 Child Maintenance and Enforcement Commission, *Child Maintenance and Other Payments Act Summary of Responses to the Consultation on Draft Regulations*, November 2009, para 4.8
211 DWP, *Preparing for the Future, Tackling the Past: child maintenance – arrears and compliance strategy 2012–2017*, January 2013
212 Child Maintenance and Enforcement Commission, *Child Maintenance and Other Payments Act Summary of Responses to the Consultation on Draft Regulations*, November 2009, para 4.7
213 s33 CSA 1991
214 Reg 27 CS(C&E) Regs
215 s33(3) CSA 1991
216 s33(4) CSA 1991
217 *Bird v SSWP* [2008] EWHC 3159 (Admin)
218 Reg 29 CS(C&E) Regs; r3 AS(CSR)
219 Reg 28(2) and (2A) CS(C&E) Regs; DWP, *Preparing for the Future, Tackling the Past: child maintenance – arrears and compliance strategy 2012-2017*, January 2013
220 *R (Sutherland) v SSWP* [2004] EWHC 800 (Admin)
221 s9 Limitation Act 1980
222 *CMEC v Mitchell* [2010] EWCA Civ 333
223 *Farley v CSA and another* [2006] UKHL 31
224 Reg 29(1) and Sch 1 CS(C&E) Regs
225 *Secretary of State for Social Security v Nicol* [1996] SLT 34
226 ss35(1) and 38(1) CSA 1991
227 s38 CSA 1991
228 DWP, *Preparing for the Future, Tackling the Past: child maintenance – arrears and compliance strategy 2012-2017*, January 2013
229 s35 CSA 1991; Part 3 TCEA 2007
230 Regs 6-8 Taking Control of Goods Regulations 2013, No.1894
231 Sch 12 para 58 TCEA 2007
232 Reg 4 Taking Control of Goods Regulations 2013, No.1894
233 Taking Control of Goods (Fees) Regulations 2014, No.1
234 s33(5) CSA 1991
235 s36 CSA 1991

236 s32L CSA 1991
237 s32L(2) CSA 1991
238 s32L(1) CSA 1991
239 s32L(5) CSA 1991
240 s32L(5) CSA 1991
241 s32L(7) CSA 1991
242 s32L(11)(b) CSA 1991
243 ss39A, 40, 40A and 40B CSA 1991
244 ss39B-39G CSA 1991
245 ss39A(1) and 39B(1)(a) and (b) CSA
1991; *Karoonian v CMEC and Gibbons v
CMEC* [2012] EWCA Civ 1379
246 DWP, *Preparing for the Future, Tackling
the Past: child maintenance – arrears and
compliance strategy 2012-2017,* January
2013; DWP, *Child Maintenance: changes
to compliance measures,* December 2018
247 DWP/National Statistics, *CSA Quarterly
Summary Statistics for Great Britain,*
December 2015
248 s39C(2)-(4) CSA 1991
249 ss39A(2), 39B, 40 and 40A CSA 1991
250 s39A(4) CSA 1991
251 s39B(1) and (6) CSA 1991
252 ss39A(3) and 39B(4) CSA 1991
253 **EW** Regs 35(1) and 35A(1) CS(C&E)
Regs
**S** rr5A and 5AZA and Forms 5A and
5AZA AS(CSR)
254 **EW** Reg 35(1) CS(C&E) Regs
**S** r5B(1) AS(CSR)
255 ss39A(3) and 39B(4) CSA 1991
256 ss39B(5), 40(3), 40A(1) and 40B(1) CSA
1991
257 *Karoonian v CMEC and Gibbons v CMEC*
[2012] EWCA Civ 1379
258 **EW** Regs 35(2) and 35A(2) CS(C&E)
Regs
**S** r5C AS(CSR)
259 ss39B and 40B CSA 1991
260 **EW** Regs 35(3) and 35A(3) CS(C&E)
Regs
**S** r5F AS(CSR)
261 **EW** Regs 35(4)-(5) and 35A(4) and (5)
and Schs 4 and 5 CS(C&E) Regs
**S** Regs 35(5) and 35A(5) CS(C&E) Regs;
rr5E and 5EA and Forms 5E and 5EA
AS(CSR)
**All** ss39B(8) and 40B(3) CSA 1991
262 ss39C(2)-(4) and 40B(1)(b) CSA 1991
263 ss39C(1) and 40B(1) CSA 1991
264 ss39E(1) and (3) and 40B(5)(a) CSA
1991
265 ss39D and 39E(4) CSA 1991
266 ss39E(2) and 40B(5)(b) CSA 1991
267 ss39C(5) and 40B(7) CSA 1991

268 **EW** s111A Magistrates Court Act 1980
**S** r6.3 Act of Sederunt (Sheriff Appeal
Court Rules) 2015, No.356
**All** ss39B(11)(b) and 40B(8)(c) CSA
1991
269 ss40 and 40A CSA 1991
270 ss40(5) and 40A(3) CSA 1991
271 ss40(3)(b) and 40A(1)(b) CSA 1991
272 **EW** Sch 3 CS(C&E) Regs
**S** Reg 2 Child Support (Civil
Imprisonment) (Scotland) Regulations
2001, No.1236; r5D and Form 5D
AS(CSR)
273 ss40(7) and 40A(5) CSA 1991
274 **EW** Reg 34(5) and (6) CS(C&E) Regs
**S** Reg 3 Child Support (Civil
Imprisonment) (Scotland) Regulations
2001, No.1236
275 CMS leaflet CMB006GB, *What Happens
if a Paying Parent Doesn't Pay Child
Maintenance?,* November 2013
276 **EW** Reg 33(3) CS(C&E) Regs
**S** r5F AS(CSR)
277 CMS leaflet CMB006GB, *What Happens
if a Paying Parent Doesn't Pay Child
Maintenance?,* November 2013
278 *CMEC v Beesley* [2010] EWCA Civ 1344;
s382(5) Insolvency Act 1986, as
amended by s142 WRA 2012
279 DWP, *Preparing for the Future, Tackling
the Past: child maintenance – arrears and
compliance strategy 2012-2017,* January
2013

## 3. Fees for enforcement action
280 Reg 10 CSF Regs 2014
281 Reg 12 CSF Regs 2014
282 Reg 12A CSF Regs 2014; CS(DOF) Regs,
Explanatory Memorandum
283 Regs 10(2) and 12(1A) CSF Regs 2014
284 Reg 1(2) CS(DOF) Regs
285 Reg 11 CSF Regs 2014
286 Reg 7(1B) and (4) CS(C&E) Regs
287 Reg 13 CSF Regs 2014

## 4. Delays in collection and enforcement
288 *Kehoe v UK* [2009] 48 EHRR, [2008] 2
FLR 1014
289 Independent Case Examiner for the
DWP, *Annual Report 1 April 2011 – 31
March 2012,* July 2012
290 *Kehoe v UK* [2009] 48 EHRR, [2008] 2
FLR 1014

# Chapter 9

**Challenging a decision: revisions and supersessions**

**This chapter covers:**
1. Changing a decision (below)
2. Revisions (p199)
3. Supersessions (p204)

## 1. Changing a decision

Most decisions can be changed or challenged by a revision or supersession. However, there are some decisions that cannot (see p198).

The Child Maintenance Service (CMS) can also correct an accidental error in a decision or in the record of a decision at any time. The correction is then treated as part of the record of the decision.[1]

A revision or supersession is a decision that changes an earlier decision.

- **A revision** means that the decision which is wrong is itself changed. The revised decision usually takes effect from the date the original decision had effect.
- **A supersession** means that the original decision is replaced by a new decision, which takes effect from a later date.

As with all decisions, revisions and supersessions are made by officials who work for the CMS and who make decisions on behalf of the Secretary of State for Work and Pensions. A revision or supersession usually happens because the CMS is told that something is wrong or has changed since the initial decision was made. The CMS may also initiate a revision or supersession itself.

If a decision is challenged within 30 days, it may be revised. Outside this time period, a decision can only be revised if the CMS accepts a late application (see p200), or in special circumstances where the original decision was wrong in such a way that it can be revised at any time – eg, if there has been an official error (see p202). If these special circumstances are not met, the decision may be superseded instead. A decision can also be superseded if circumstances have changed since it was made.

The table below shows when decisions are revised and superseded.

If the original decision is not incorrect, but the CMS has not dealt with the case properly in some way (eg, you have experienced intimidating or unnecessary intrusive questioning, or unwarranted demands for evidence and documentation), a complaint can be made at any time (see Chapter 11).

In some cases where the original decision is wrong (eg, where maladministration has led to an official error), it may be appropriate to make a complaint as well as applying for the decision to be revised.

### Revisions and supersessions

| Why is the decision being challenged? | When? | What can be done? |
| --- | --- | --- |
| The decision is wrong for any reason. | Within 30 days of being told the decision. | The decision can be revised. |
| The CMS made a mistake (an 'official error'), or it was misled or did not know about something that would have affected its decision, or someone is not a parent of a child to whom a calculation relates. | At any time. | The decision can be revised. If the CMS did not know something or was misled, the decision can only be revised in certain circumstances (see p199). If these do not apply, the decision can be superseded. |
| The decision is wrong for any reason (other than one of the above reasons). | More than than 30 days after being told the decision. | The decision may be superseded. A late application for a revision to be considered can also be made (see p200). |
| Something that affects the decision has changed. | At any time. | The decision can be superseded. |

A variation is an element of the child support calculation. This means that if an application for a variation is made after a calculation is in force and the CMS accepts it, it then revises or supersedes the original calculation to include the variation. See Chapter 5 for details.

For how to change a decision on deductions of child support from benefits, see CPAG's *Welfare Benefits and Tax Credits Handbook*.

If you believe that the other parent is fraudulently claiming a benefit, you cannot directly challenge this decision, but can raise the issue with the CMS, which contacts the other part of the Department for Work and Pensions, which then investigates.

Decisions of the First-tier Tribunal and the Upper Tribunal (see Chapter 10) can also be superseded or revised, but only in certain circumstances (see p200 and p204).

## Challenging a decision that cannot be revised or superseded

Some decisions cannot be revised or superseded. These are mainly about information gathering, collection and enforcement (including decisions about fees), and refusals to make an interim or default maintenance decision.

If you want to challenge a decision that cannot be revised or superseded, provide the CMS with further information and ask it to reconsider. If the decision involved the CMS exercising its discretion, there may be further information that could be put to the CMS about the welfare of any child(ren) affected (see p126). If the CMS refuses to change the decision, you could make a complaint. An accidental error in a decision or in the record of a decision can also be corrected at any time.[2]

Some decisions on the enforcement of arrears cannot be revised or superseded, but can be appealed to a court (see p162).

### Judicial review

Judicial review is the legal procedure that allows a court to examine the way in which a public body has exercised its decision-making power to ensure that it has done so lawfully.[3] A person affected by a decision or action of a public body or one of its officers can ask the High Court (or Court of Session in Scotland) to carry out a judicial review of the decision or action. Unlike tribunals, these courts have the power to order you to pay the other side's costs as well as your own.

A judicial review looks at the validity of the process by which a decision was made, rather than the actual result of the decision.

The court can 'set aside' the decision and can also order the public body which made the decision to consider it again in a lawful way. Judicial review is a 'last resort' process and is not usually possible if there is a right to raise the issue in an appeal to the First-tier Tribunal, Upper Tribunal or court. If you are considering a judicial review of a CMS decision, you should seek legal advice as soon as possible after the decision is made.

In England and Wales, before you can apply for a judicial review in the High Court you must follow a 'pre-action protocol'. This is designed to avoid expensive litigation, and the majority of straightforward cases are resolved at this stage. It is, therefore, a valuable way of getting a decision changed when you cannot appeal against it. This protocol does not apply in Scotland, but it is good practice to avoid litigation and sending a 'letter before claim' can provide a way of doing so.

Judicial review can be used to challenge a decision of the Upper Tribunal to refuse permission to appeal against a First-tier Tribunal decision, and occasionally to challenge First-tier Tribunal decisions in the Upper Tribunal.

In England and Wales, an application must be made to the High Court promptly and, in any event, within three months of the decision being challenged.[4] In Scotland, an application must be made within three months (or a longer time if the Court of Session considers it equitable in the circumstances).[5] The court's permission must be obtained before making an application.[6]

Judicial review of a child support decision may succeed if:[7]

- the CMS makes an error in law – eg, it does something it has no power to do; *or*
- the CMS fails to take into account a relevant matter or takes an irrelevant matter into account, or where a decision is 'so outrageous in its defiance of logic or of accepted moral standards that no sensible person who had considered the question could have arrived at it'; *or*
- there has been procedural unfairness.

## 2. **Revisions**

The Child Maintenance Service (CMS) can revise a decision:[8]

- on its own initiative; *or*
- if requested by a person with care, non-resident parent or child applicant in Scotland; *or*
- if a person applies for a variation.

### Decisions that can be revised

Most child support decisions can be revised, including:[9]

- a decision to make a calculation (including a variation on a calculation), an interim maintenance decision or a default maintenance decision;
- a decision not to make a calculation, unless the CMS has made an interim or default maintenance decision instead (in which case, this decision can be revised). A refusal to make an interim or default maintenance decision cannot be revised;
- a decision of the First-tier Tribunal to make, or refuse to agree to, a variation to a calculation following a referral by the CMS;
- any supersession decision made by the CMS (see p204);
- a decision which has previously been revised.

A decision can only be revised on the basis of the circumstances at the time the decision took effect. It cannot be revised because of a change in circumstances after the date the decision was made, or because of an expected change.[10] Instead, the decision may be superseded (see p204) or a new child support application could be made.

For revisions of default maintenance decisions, see p130.

**Note:** under the test case rules (see p236), the CMS may postpone revising a decision until the outcome of an appeal in the 'test' case is known.

## When a decision can be revised

A decision can be revised:
- on any grounds, provided an application for a revision is within the time limit or a late application is accepted (see below); *or*
- at any time if there are specific grounds (see p201).

## Time limits for a revision on any grounds

The CMS can revise a decision on any grounds if:
- a person applies within 30 days of the decision (or of the date an accidental error in the decision, or in the record of the decision, was corrected); *or*
- a person applies for a variation within 30 days, provided the grounds for a variation existed from the date of the decision being revised; *or*
- the CMS initiates the revision within 30 days of the original decision.

To apply for a revision on any grounds, you do not have to provide a reason for challenging the decision. It is enough that you think the decision is wrong.

If you apply within the 30-day time limit, but the CMS refuses to carry out a revision because there is insufficient information or evidence, it may allow you more time to provide this. (The CMS generally allows 14 days to provide information and extends this to 16 days to allow for the time taken to reach the CMS by post.) If the CMS does not allow this extra time to provide information and evidence, it could still revise the decision at a later date if it accepts a late application for a revision (see below).

If you miss the time limit, it may be possible to make a late application (see below).[11] In addition, check whether there are specific grounds to apply for a revision at any time (see below).

### Late applications

The CMS can extend the 30-day period for applying for a revision on any grounds if it considers that:[12]
- the application has merit; *and*
- there are 'special circumstances' (see below) which mean that it was not practicable to apply within the time limit; *and*
- it is reasonable to allow the application.

'**Special circumstances**' are not defined. Any special circumstances can count. Include as much detail as possible to explain why an application is late. The application for an extension must identify the decision you want revised and explain why an extension should be granted.[13] There is no absolute time limit for seeking a revision on any grounds. However, the longer the delay in applying for a revision, the more compelling the special circumstances must be.[14]

**Note:** if you have difficulty meeting a time limit for any reason related to coronavirus (COVID-19), explain that to the CMS as soon as possible.

When the CMS is considering whether to accept a late application, any days before an accidental error in a decision or in the record of a decision is corrected are not counted towards the time limit.[15]

An application that is refused may not be renewed,[16] although the CMS may have power to reconsider a refusal to extend.[17] If a late application for a revision is refused, the CMS should go on to consider whether the decision can be revised on one of the specific grounds on which a decision can be revised at any time (see below) or whether it can be superseded.[18]

If the CMS refuses to accept a late application for an 'any grounds' revision, this means it has considered whether to revise the original decision. There is no right of appeal against the decision not to extend the time limit, but you can appeal to the First-tier Tribunal against the original decision.[19]

Judicial review of a refusal to extend the time limit for making a revision may also be possible (see p198).

**Note:** because a supersession (see p204) cannot usually lead to a decision being backdated to the original effective date, if possible you should make a late application for a revision. However, in case this is not accepted, an application for a supersession can be made at the same time, if appropriate. For example, a decision may be based on the wrong information about a child's education. If you have missed the deadline for applying for a revision, you can make a late application (giving special reasons) and also apply for a supersession on the grounds that there has been a mistake about a fact (see p204).

## Revisions on specific grounds

The CMS can revise a decision at any time if:

- an appeal has been made in time (or within the time allowed for late appeals) and it has not yet been determined.[20] If an appeal is lodged, the CMS checks whether the decision should be revised. This allows the CMS to take into account any new information that has come to light in the appeal process. If a decision is revised in these circumstances, the appeal may lapse (see p203); *or*
- there has been an 'official error' (see p202);[21] *or*
- the decision is wrong because of a misrepresentation or failure to disclose a material fact (see p202) and, because of this, the decision is more advantageous to the person who misrepresented or failed to disclose than it would otherwise have been;[22] *or*
- it is an interim maintenance decision or default maintenance decision;[23] *or*

- the information on historic income (or unearned income for a variation) given to it by HM Revenue and Customs (HMRC) has since been amended;[24] *or*
- the decision is wrong because a child support calculation has been made for someone who was not, at the time it was made, a parent of the qualifying child.[25]

If the CMS makes a decision which is then appealed and, while that appeal is pending, the CMS makes a second decision on the same case, when the First-tier Tribunal decides the appeal on the first decision, the CMS can revise its second decision at any time if it would have been made differently had the CMS known about the tribunal's decision.[26]

### Official error

'Official error' is a mistake made by an officer of the CMS, another part of the Department for Work and Pensions or HMRC, which was not caused, or contributed to, by anyone outside these bodies.[27] This includes mistakes of law (see p205), except those only shown to be an error by a decision of the Upper Tribunal or court. It also includes mistakes of fact, such as:

- a mistake of arithmetic;
- a wrong assumption about a person's circumstances where there was no evidence for it;
- a mistake made because CMS staff failed to ask something that was relevant, failed to take specific evidence into account, or did not pass information or evidence to the officer who made the decision, when they should have done.

**Note:** if the official error appears to be accidental (eg, a mistake of arithmetic), you can ask the CMS to correct this. The CMS can correct an accidental error in a decision, or in the record of a decision, at any time. If the CMS does this, the time limit for requesting a revision of the decision begins from the date of the correction.[28]

### Misrepresentation and failure to disclose

A '**misrepresentation**' is a written or spoken statement of fact which is untrue.[29] This applies to an untrue statement, even if the person making it believes it to be true.[30]

There is only a '**failure to disclose**' a fact if there is a legal duty to report that fact to the CMS.[31] Therefore, a person who is asked to give information, but does not, has failed to disclose that information. However, if a person is not asked for the information, there can be no failure to disclose unless it is one of the facts that a parent with care or non-resident parent must always report. There is no general duty to report all changes of circumstances to the CMS, but there are some changes which must be reported (see p53).

The CMS can only consider a revision if the original decision was more advantageous to the person who misrepresented or failed to disclose.[32]

## How to apply for a revision

The notification of a decision also explains how to ask for a revision of that decision.[33] The request for a revision may be made by telephone. However, unless the issue is straightforward, it is best to follow up any telephone call with a letter to the CMS, confirming the reason for the request.

The CMS is not required to notify the parties that it is considering a revision or to inform one party that the other has applied for a revision. However, if there is an application for a variation that has had a preliminary consideration[34] or a request for a revision of a calculation with a previously agreed variation,[35] the other parties are usually contacted and asked for their representations.

There are rules about what information the CMS should disclose (see p53).

If you request a revision, you must show that there are grounds for doing so,[36] unless you are applying within the time limit or a late application is accepted (see p200) (in which case, it is enough that you simply think that the decision is wrong).

Provide a full explanation of your reasons for seeking the revision, and any supporting information or evidence.

If you do not provide sufficient information or evidence for the CMS to make a decision, the CMS may allow more time in which to do so (see p200).

The CMS may decide to:
- revise the decision; *or*
- make a default maintenance decision (see p129); *or*
- refuse to revise the decision.

If someone has lodged an appeal (see Chapter 10), the CMS can still consider whether the decision should be revised. If it is revised and the revised decision is more advantageous for the person who appealed, the appeal lapses.[37] S/he can then decide to lodge a fresh appeal against the revised decision within the usual time limits. The CMS should try to inform all the relevant people that the appeal has lapsed. If the revised decision does not benefit the person appealing, the appeal goes ahead against the decision as revised. The person who appealed is given one month to make any further representations on the appeal.[38]

## The revised decision

All the parties must be notified of the decision and given the usual details (see p130).[39] If there is more than one person with care in relation to a non-resident parent, all must be notified. The normal rules on disclosure of information apply (see p53).[40]

If the decision is revised, this normally has the same effective date as the decision it replaces,[41] unless the effective date was wrong, in which case the revised decision has the effective date it should have had.[42]

If a revision is refused, the notification of the decision must include the reasons for the refusal and details of how to appeal.

The time limit for appealing against a decision that has been revised runs from the date of the notice of the revised decision.[43]

## 3. **Supersessions**

The Child Maintenance Service (CMS) can supersede a decision at any time, with or without an application, if certain rules are met. Usually a decision is superseded because of a change in circumstances since the decision was made. There is no general duty to tell the CMS of all changes of circumstances. See p53 for the changes that must be notified. A decision can also be superseded if it was wrong in law (see p205).

The main difference between a revision and a supersession is that a superseded decision generally takes effect from the date on which it is made (see p208), whereas a revision generally takes effect from the effective date of the decision that is being revised. However, there are exceptions to this general rule.

A child support calculation is likely to be subject to regular supersessions. See p75 for the rules about annual reviews and p77 for the rules about periodic current income checks.

### Decisions that can be superseded

Most child support decisions (whether made by the CMS, the First-tier Tribunal or the Upper Tribunal) can be superseded.[44] Decisions that can be superseded include:

- a decision to make a child support calculation (including a variation of a calculation), an interim maintenance decision or a default maintenance decision (see p130);
- a decision of a First-tier Tribunal on a CMS referral of a variation application;
- a revised decision (see p199).

### When a decision can be superseded

The CMS can normally supersede a decision if:[45]

- there has been a relevant change of circumstances since the decision had effect, or it is expected that there will be such a change. In some circumstances, there must be a significant change in the amount of the calculation as a result (see p206);

- it was made in ignorance of, or was based on a mistake about, a material fact; *or*
- there is an application for a variation of the calculation.

A decision made by the CMS can also be superseded if it is wrong in law (see below).

If the CMS is notified of a change of circumstances, it does not have to consider anything apart from that change when it is considering whether to supersede the decision. If the CMS is acting on its own initiative to supersede the decision, it does not have to consider anything other than the change that caused it to act.[46] It does not have to investigate whether all the other circumstances are still correct. However, the CMS might decide to incorporate the supersession process into a 'case check', which could result in other changes or errors being identified, and subsequent revisions or supersessions being carried out.

Under the 'test case rules', the CMS may delay superseding a decision until the outcome of an appeal in another 'test' case is known (see p236 for details).

## Wrong in law

If a decision is wrong in law, it can be superseded. However, this could also constitute an official error and also be grounds for a revision at any time (see p202). This may be more advantageous than a supersession, as a revised decision normally takes effect from the date the original decision took effect.

A decision is wrong in law if:[47]

- when making it, the CMS misinterpreted or overlooked part or all of an Act of Parliament, a regulation or relevant caselaw; *or*
- there is no evidence to support it; *or*
- the facts are such that no reasonable person applying the law could have come to such a conclusion; *or*
- there is a breach of 'natural justice' – ie, the procedure used has led to unfairness, or the officer who took the decision appeared to be biased;[48] *or*
- the CMS has not given sufficient reasons for the decision; *or*
- when exercising its discretion, the CMS took something irrelevant into account or ignored something relevant – eg, the welfare of a child (see p126).[49]

A decision is also wrong in law if the regulation under which it is made was not made lawfully.

A decision is also wrong in law if it is contrary to European law – ie, European Union (EU) law and the European Convention on Human Rights. EU law will rarely be relevant to child support issues (and, depending on changes to UK law after the UK leaves the EU, may no longer apply). Caselaw has established that European law on the equal treatment of men and women in social security matters does not apply to child support.[50]

## When a decision cannot be superseded

The CMS cannot supersede a decision:

- which can be revised instead (see p199);[51]
- refusing to make or cancelling a child support calculation.[52] A further application for a calculation should be made instead.

In a case in which gross income is determined on the basis of current income (see p72), a decision cannot be superseded on the basis that there has been, or it is anticipated that there will be, a change in the non-resident parent's current income, unless the new income level is at least 25 per cent different from the previous income.[53] This 'tolerance level' does not apply if the superseding decision:[54]

- is made by the CMS as part of an annual review of gross income or a periodic check of current income; *or*
- is made because of an error of law; *or*
- supersedes a calculation decision that was based on an estimate of current income.

The CMS intends calculations to remain in place for a reasonable period. In many cases, the calculation is likely to remain in place for the year ahead.

## Deciding whether to request a supersession

Before requesting a supersession because of a change of circumstances, you may wish to establish whether a fresh calculation would be to your advantage. Unless it is a change that must be reported to the CMS (see p53), you need only tell the CMS about the changes in your favour. If the change only relates to one party, the CMS may not tell the other person. However, if it does, s/he might tell the CMS about other changes. These may cancel out the effect of the changes which led you to ask for a supersession.

If you believe that the other parent's circumstances have changed (eg, a non-resident parent no longer has relevant other children living with her/him), you can ask for a supersession and for the CMS to investigate (see Chapter 3). The CMS does not have to, but any changes it is aware of must be taken into account when it decides whether or not to supersede.

## How to apply for a supersession

A party to the calculation can apply for a supersession at any time. There are no time limits. If an application is made, the CMS must consider it and supersede if the conditions on p204 are met.

The CMS can also initiate a supersession. It must take into account the welfare of any child(ren) affected (see p126) when considering whether or not to do so.

The CMS learns of some changes automatically from Jobcentre Plus or may do so from a third party.

If the supersession is in relation to an application for a variation that has had a preliminary consideration (see p111),[55] or a supersession of a previously agreed variation,[56] the other relevant parties are contacted and notified of the grounds of the application and any relevant information or evidence the applicant has given. They are not told details of any long-term illness or disability of a relevant other child (if the application for variation was made on that basis), harmful medical evidence or the address of a relevant person or qualifying child if that would cause a risk of harm or undue distress.[57]

Otherwise, the other parties are not notified of the application for a supersession. The normal rules about disclosure apply to the information given in any notification (see p53).[58]

The CMS does not have to check all the facts again. It can just consider the issues raised in the application.[59] You should therefore include all available information and evidence that supports your case for the decision to be changed in the application. Information provided may need to be verified in the normal way (see Chapter 3).

## The superseding decision

The CMS may decide that:

- there are no grounds for a supersession to be made; *or*
- there are grounds for a supersession, but the calculation remains unchanged; *or*
- there are grounds for a supersession and the calculation should be changed; *or*
- the calculation should be cancelled.

If the decision results in a supersession, whether or not a new calculation is made (including an interim maintenance decision (see p113) or default maintenance decision – see p129), the parties must be notified of the decision and given the usual details (see p130).[60] The notice must also state how to apply for a revision or supersession, and how to appeal.[61]

If a supersession is refused, notification is also given, including the reasons for the refusal and the right to challenge the decision.[62]

You can ask for a supersession decision to be revised and can then, if the decision is one against which there is a right of appeal, appeal to the First-tier Tribunal (see Chapter 10).

If the CMS intends to cancel the case, it must notify each party. If the reason for cancellation is a child applicant in Scotland's ceasing to be a qualifying child, the CMS must inform any other potential child applicants in the case.[63]

## Effective date of the superseding decision

The general rule is that a supersession takes effect from the day on which the decision is made or the application for the supersession/variation was made.[64] However, the effective date may be different in certain circumstances (see the table below, but note that this does not cover all the circumstances in which a calculation is cancelled – see p131).

| Circumstances | Effective date |
|---|---|
| Gross income is based on current income and the non-resident parent is required to report a change because her/his current income has changed by at least 25 per cent. | The day on which the change occurred.[65] |
| There is a new qualifying child in relation to the non-resident parent. | The day that would be the initial effective date (ie, two days after the day on which written notification would be sent to the non-resident parent) if a new application were made for that child, if there were no calculation already in force.[66] |
| The application is made by one of the parties. | The day the application is received by the CMS.[67] |
| The CMS has acted on its own initiative. | If the CMS acts on the basis of information provided by a third party, the day that information is provided.[68] In any other case, the day on which the decision is made.[69] |
| There is an anticipated change in circumstances. | The day on which the change is expected to occur.[70] |
| There is an expected change in circumstances which is a ground for a variation. | The day on which the change is expected to occur.[71] |
| A qualifying child dies or ceases to be a qualifying child. | The day on which the change occurred.[72] |
| A relevant other child (or a child supported under other maintenance arrangements) dies or ceases to be a qualifying child for child support purposes. | The day on which the change occurred.[73] |

| | |
|---|---|
| A person with care ceases to be a person with care in relation to a qualifying child. | The day on which the change occurred.[74] |
| A person with care, non-resident parent or a qualifying child ceases to be habitually resident in the UK. | The day on which the change occurred.[75] |
| A non-resident parent (or her/his partner) becomes or stops being entitled to a benefit that qualifies her/him for the flat rate. | The day on which the change occurred.[76] |
| The CMS is superseding a decision given by the First-tier Tribunal or the Upper Tribunal following the CMS's having served notice that a test case which could have affected that decision was pending before the Upper Tribunal or a court. | The day on which the decision of the First-tier Tribunal or Upper Tribunal would have taken effect had it been decided in accordance with the decision in the test case.[77] |
| The CMS is superseding a decision of the First-tier Tribunal or the Upper Tribunal on the ground that it is wrong because of a misrepresentation about, or a failure to disclose, a material fact, and the decision is more advantageous to the person who misrepresented or failed to disclose than it would otherwise have been but for that error. | The date on which the First-tier Tribunal or Upper Tribunal decision took, or was to take, effect.[78] |
| A decision of the CMS is superseded because it is shown to have been wrong by the Upper Tribunal or a court. | The date of the relevant Upper Tribunal or court decision.[79] |

# Notes

1. **Changing a decision**
   1 Reg 27A CSMC Regs
   2 Reg 27A CSMC Regs
   3 *West v Secretary of State for Scotland*, 1992 SC 385, 1992 SLT 636, reported as *West v Scottish Prison Service*, 1992 SCLR 504
   4 r54.5 Civil Procedure Rules 1998, No.3132
   5 s27A Court of Session Act 1988
   6 s27B(1) Court of Session Act 1988
   7 *Council of Civil Service Unions v Minister for the Civil Service* [1984] 1 WLR 1174, [1984] 3 All ER 935

2. **Revisions**
   8 ss16 and 28G CSA 1991; reg 14(1)(a) and (d) CSMC Regs
   9 s16 CSA 1991
   10 Reg 14(2) CSMC Regs
   11 Reg 15 CSMC Regs
   12 Reg 15(4) CSMC Regs
   13 Reg 15(3) CSMC Regs
   14 Reg 15(5) CSMC Regs
   15 Reg 27A(4) CSMC Regs
   16 Reg 15(7) CSMC Regs
   17 See CIS/93/1992
   18 DWP, *Mandatory Consideration of Revision Before Appeal: government response to public consultation*, September 2012
   19 *R (CJ) and SG v SSWP (ESA)* [2017] UKUT 324 (AAC); *AO v SSWP and JA (CSM)* [2017] UKUT 499 (AAC)
   20 Reg 14(1)(c) CSMC Regs
   21 Reg 14(1)(e) CSMC Regs
   22 Reg 14(1)(b) CMSC Regs
   23 Reg 14(3) CSMC Regs
   24 Reg 14(1)(f) CSMC Regs
   25 Reg 14(1)(g) CSMC Regs
   26 Reg 14(3A) CSMC Regs
   27 Reg 14(4) CSMC Regs
   28 Regs 14(1)(a) and 27A CSMC Regs
   29 R(SB) 9/85
   30 R(SB) 2/92 (*Page and Davis v CAO*)
   31 CCS/15846/1996
   32 Reg 14(1)(b) CMSC Regs
   33 Reg 24(2) CSMC Regs
   34 Reg 57 CSMC Regs
   35 Reg 61 CSMC Regs
   36 R(I) 1/71
   37 s16(6) CSA 1991; Sch para 1(1) CSMC Regs

   38 Sch para 1(2) CSMC Regs
   39 Reg 26(1) CSMC Regs
   40 Reg 25(3) CSMC Regs
   41 s16(3) CSA 1991
   42 Reg 16 CSMC Regs
   43 r22(2) TP(FT) Rules

3. **Supersessions**
   44 s17(1) CSA 1991
   45 Reg 17(1)-(3) CSMC Regs
   46 s17(2) CSA 1991; reg 17(6) CSMC Regs
   47 R(A) 1/72; R(SB) 11/83
   48 *R v Gough* [1993] AC 646, [1993] 2 WLR 883, [1993] 2 All ER 724
   49 *Wednesbury Corporation v Ministry of Housing and Local Government (No.2)* [1965] 3 WLR 956, [1965] 3 All ER 571
   50 R(CS) 3/96; R(CS) 2/95; CCS/17/1994. These concerned the application of Art 141 of the EC Treaty (formerly Art 119), and Council Directives 75/117 and 79/7. CCS/6/1995
   51 Reg 17(4) CSMC Regs
   52 Reg 17(5) CSMC Regs
   53 Reg 23(1) and (2) CSMC Regs
   54 Reg 23(3) CSMC Regs
   55 Reg 59 CSMC Regs
   56 Reg 61(1) CSMC Regs
   57 Reg 59(1)(a) and (5) CSMC Regs
   58 Reg 25(3) CSMC Regs
   59 s17(2) CSA 1991; reg 17(6) CSMC Regs
   60 Reg 26(1) CSMC Regs
   61 Reg 24(2) CSMC Regs
   62 Regs 24(2) and 26(2) CSMC Regs
   63 Reg 27 CSMC Regs
   64 s17(4) CSA 1991
   65 Reg 18(4) CSMC Regs
   66 Reg 18(5) CSMC Regs
   67 Reg 18(6)(a) CSMC Regs
   68 Reg 18(6)(b) CSMC Regs
   69 Reg 18(6)(c) CSMC Regs
   70 Reg 18(2) CSMC Regs
   71 Reg 18(2) CSMC Regs
   72 Reg 18(3)(a) CSMC Regs
   73 Reg 18(3)(a) CSMC Regs
   74 Reg 18(3)(b) CSMC Regs
   75 Reg 18(3)(c) CSMC Regs
   76 Reg 18(3)(d) CSMC Regs
   77 Reg 30 CSMC Regs
   78 Reg 31 CSMC Regs
   79 Reg 32 CSMC Regs

# Chapter 10

· · · · · · · · · · · · · · · · · · · · · · · · · · · · · · · · · · · · · · · · · · · · · · · · ·

# Challenging a decision: appeals

**This chapter covers:**

## 1. Considering an appeal

Most decisions made by the Child Maintenance Service (CMS) can be appealed to an independent appeal tribunal: the First-tier Tribunal (Social Entitlement Chamber).

Before you can appeal, you must apply for a revision, asking the CMS to reconsider its decision. This is called a **'mandatory reconsideration'**. In order to be sure of having a right to appeal, you should request a mandatory reconsideration and should do so within the time limit for a revision (see p200).

If you appeal without first seeking a mandatory reconsideration, the CMS can treat the appeal as if it were a request for a mandatory reconsideration.[1] If the CMS does not do this, ask for a mandatory reconsideration as soon as possible, explaining why it is late, if necessary.

The CMS issues a letter, outlining its response to your request (a 'mandatory reconsideration notice'). Two copies are sent – you must send one of them to the First-tier Tribunal with the appeal.

**Note:** the CMS can correct an accidental error in a decision or in the record of a decision at any time (see p196).[2] A mandatory reconsideration of the corrected decision must be requested before an appeal to the First-tier Tribunal can be made.

## Who can appeal

Usually, anyone who is a party in a child support calculation (ie, a person with care, a non-resident parent and, in Scotland, a child applicant) has the right to appeal.[3]

Regardless of who appeals, all the parties in a child support calculation are also parties in the appeal and have the same rights, except that only the person making the appeal (the 'appellant') can ask to withdraw the appeal. Because an appeal can be withdrawn without the consent of any other party (see p222), it is best for each person who wishes to challenge a decision to bring her/his own appeal. The appeals can be heard together.

The CMS may also refer an application for a variation to the First-tier Tribunal in certain cases (see p114).

If a person with a right of appeal dies, the executor or administrator of her/his estate can continue with any appeal that is already underway.[4]

## Decisions that cannot be appealed

Only decisions and, in some cases, refusals to make decisions, can be appealed. It is not possible to appeal if no decision has been made – eg, because of a delay. Similarly, decisions about fees and some decisions about the method of collection or the enforcement of payment cannot be appealed. Decisions about the ending of liability in '1993 rules' and '2003 rules' cases as part of the transition to the '2012 rules' scheme (see p1) also cannot be appealed.[5] If you are uncertain whether you can appeal against a decision, get advice straight away. If a decision cannot be appealed, you can ask the CMS to reconsider and send any further information if appropriate. However, the CMS is not required to reconsider. Your only legal remedy is to seek a judicial review (see p198). If there is a delay in making a decision, or some other kind of poor service from the CMS, you may also wish to complain (see Chapter 11).

## Parentage disputes

If someone denies when s/he appeals, or during the course of the appeal, that s/he is the parent of a child named in the child support application, the appeal is not dealt with by the First-tier Tribunal, but by the family court (in England and Wales) or sheriff court (in Scotland).[6] If there are other grounds for appeal apart from the dispute about parentage, the tribunal deals with those issues and the parentage issue is dealt with by the court. If the appeal is sent to the tribunal and it involves a denial of parentage, the tribunal should transfer that issue to the court.[7] For more information about parentage disputes, see p42.

# 2. Appealing to the First-tier Tribunal

When the Child Maintenance Service (CMS) makes a decision, each party (ie, the person with care and non-resident parent, and, in Scotland, child applicant) must be sent a notice of that decision and information on the right to challenge it.[8]

If you are unhappy with a decision, you must first ask the CMS to reconsider it (see p211). Once you have received the mandatory reconsideration notice, if you are still unhappy you can appeal by sending a notice of appeal directly to the First-tier Tribunal. Form SSCS2 should be used, if possible, which is available from the gov.uk website.[9] Take care to provide all the required information.

The notice of appeal must include:[10]
- your name and address;
- the name and address of any representative (see p221);
- an address to which documents about the appeal may be sent or delivered;
- the name and address of any 'respondent' (ie, the other party), if you know it;
- the grounds of the appeal – ie, the reasons why you disagree with the CMS.

You must also send a copy of:[11]
- the mandatory reconsideration notice;
- any statement of reasons sent by the CMS for the decision; *and*
- any available documents supporting the appeal that have not already been supplied to the CMS or the other party.

The appeal will not be accepted by the First-tier Tribunal unless the mandatory reconsideration notice is included. Documents supporting the appeal are normally accepted by the tribunal after the notice of appeal has been sent, but should be sent as soon as practicable.

If there was a long delay before the CMS sent you the mandatory reconsideration notice and you think you have been placed at a disadvantage (eg, if it is now more difficult to obtain evidence), tell the tribunal.[12]

There are strict time limits for making an appeal, which can be extended in certain circumstances (see below).

There is a CMS leaflet that explains the appeal process.[13]

## Time limits

An appeal must normally be received by the First-tier Tribunal within one month of your being sent the mandatory reconsideration notice.[14] The tribunal can extend this time limit, but there is still an absolute time limit within which you must appeal (see below).

**Time limits**
'**Month**' means a complete calendar month from the day of notification.[15]

When calculating time, if something has to be done by a certain day, it must be done by 5pm that day. If a time limit ends on a day other than a working day, it must be done by the next working day to meet the time limit.[16] A notice of a decision counts as having been sent on the second day after the day it was posted.[17]

If you are appealing against a refusal to revise a decision following a late application for a revision (see p200) where time was not extended, this one-month time limit runs from the date of notification of the original decision, not the date on which the CMS notified you of its refusal to revise. However, if the CMS refused to revise a decision following an application for a revision that was made within the time limit (see p200) or the extended time limit, the one-month time limit runs from the date on which the notice of refusal to revise was issued.

**Note:** if you have difficulty meeting a time limit for any reason related to coronavirus (COVID-19), explain that to HM Courts and Tribunals Service (HMCTS) as soon as possible. Tribunals are instructed to look sympathetically on any requests for extension of time for reasons related to coronavirus.[18]

## Late appeals

If an appeal is not made within the one-month time limit, the First-tier Tribunal can extend the time limit, provided neither the CMS nor the other party objects.[19] The time limit can only be extended by 12 months – ie, there is an absolute time limit of 13 months from the date of the mandatory reconsideration notice being sent in which to appeal.[20] **Note:** in very exceptional circumstances (eg, if you did not receive notice of the decision), it may be possible to argue that the tribunal has discretion to accept an appeal outside this absolute time limit. You must show that you did everything you could have done to appeal in time.[21]

If you appeal outside the one-month time limit and the CMS or the other party objects, the tribunal decides whether the appeal should go ahead. It should bear in mind the overriding objective that appeals should be dealt with fairly and justly (see p217). It does not have to be satisfied that there are special reasons for why the appeal is late.[22] There is no guarantee that the tribunal will admit a late appeal, so make sure you appeal in time wherever possible.

If a notice of appeal is submitted outside the time limit, in addition to the information listed on p213, it must also include the reasons why it is late and a request for it to be accepted.[23] It is best to include as much detail as possible about why there may be special reasons for the appeal being late and why it would be fair for it still to be admitted.

If the First-tier Tribunal decides that an appeal cannot go ahead because it was made outside the time limit, you can appeal to the Upper Tribunal (see p231) against this decision.[24]

## After an appeal is made

When the First-tier Tribunal receives your appeal, the regional office of HMCTS sends you an acknowledgement. This advises you that HMCTS has also sent a copy of the appeal and any accompanying documents to the CMS and the other party(ies).[25] HMCTS checks that the appeal is validly made – ie, that the correct information has been included, the appeal has been made on time and the form has been signed. If the appeal is not validly made, HMCTS returns it to you and you have 14 days to complete it properly or provide the required information. If you do not do so, the appeal may be 'struck out' (see p220).[26]

HMCTS informs you that a hearing can be arranged at the nearest appeals venue. If it is not the most convenient venue for you, request that the venue be changed to a different one. This should be done promptly, as the later the request is left the more likely it is to be refused. In general, a request for a change of venue made in good time is likely to be agreed by HMCTS.

When the CMS receives a copy of the appeal, it may revise the decision. If it is revised and the revised decision is more advantageous to the person appealing, the appeal lapses. See p203 for further information.

If the CMS does not revise the decision (or revises the decision but the revised decision is not more advantageous to the person appealing), it should prepare a 'response' to the appeal. This should be sent to the tribunal, and copied to you and the other parties as soon as reasonably practical. Before sending the response, the CMS should check with you and any other party whether you (s/he) want your (her/his) address, or any information that could lead to it being identified, removed from the papers (see below).[27]

The CMS must send the response to the tribunal within 42 days of the date on which the CMS received the copy of the notice of appeal.[28] The response should state:[29]

- the name and address of the official who made the decision;
- the name and address of that official's representative (if any) – known as a 'presenting officer';
- an address where documents for the CMS can be sent or delivered;
- the name and address of the other party(ies) and her/his representative (if any).

The response should explain what parts of the grounds put forward for the appeal the CMS disagrees with, and why.[30] The response may also indicate whether the CMS thinks the case requires a hearing or could be decided by just considering the papers.[31]

The response must have the following attached to it:[32]

- a copy of any written record of the decision being appealed, and any statement of reasons for it, if they were not already sent with the appeal;
- copies of all documents the CMS has that are relevant to the case.[33]

If any delay in the CMS sending the response to the tribunal is causing hardship, you can apply to the tribunal for a direction instructing the CMS to provide the response.

Once you and the other party(ies) receive the copy of the response from the CMS, you (s/he) can make a written submission and supply any further documents in reply. This is your opportunity to explain your case in detail, and to provide any documents or other evidence to back it up. Your written submission should be sent to the tribunal within one month of receiving the CMS's response. The tribunal sends a copy of any written submission to the CMS and other parties.[34]

Although this one-month time limit is in the rules, it is unlikely that the tribunal will refuse to accept further evidence and submissions after this, especially if there is to be an oral hearing (see p224) at which submissions and further evidence may be expected to be presented. It is more helpful to the tribunal to send evidence ahead of the hearing, even if this is late, than to present it on the day of the hearing, especially if there is a large quantity of evidence (which is likely to lead to an adjournment of the hearing and further delay).

### Confidentiality

If either the person with care or non-resident parent wants her/his address, or the address of the child, to be kept confidential, s/he should inform the CMS or tribunal on the notice of appeal, or within 14 days of receiving an appeal enquiry form.[35] The CMS and tribunal must take appropriate steps to ensure that this information (or any information that would help identify this) is not revealed to another party.

## 3. **Tribunal procedures**

Both the First-tier and Upper Tribunal have procedural rules setting out their powers and how they should deal with appeals. There are also practice directions and practice statements, which set out how they should conduct themselves. The rules are similar for both the First-tier and Upper Tribunal and so this section applies to both (and explains where there are differences). The rules about hearings and decisions are also part of the procedural rules (see p224 and p227). Caselaw has also established a number of principles on how appeals should be conducted.

If the tribunal fails to follow the correct procedure, this may be grounds for appealing against a decision it reaches, as a breach of the procedural rules could mean that the decision is based on an error of law.[36] A complaint can also be made to HM Courts and Tribunals Service (HMCTS). For details of how to complain to HMCTS, see CPAG's *Welfare Benefits and Tax Credits Handbook*. A failure to follow procedure could also be challenged by a judicial review (see p198).

If a party to the appeal fails to comply with the rules, a practice direction or a direction, the tribunal may take any action which it considers just (including striking out the appeal – see p220).[37] The Upper Tribunal has more extensive powers to deal with failure to comply with the rules. The First-tier Tribunal may refer a person to the Upper Tribunal for it to deal with the issue.[38]

Legally qualified members of HMCTS staff ('registrars') and other appropriately trained staff ('caseworkers') can make many of the decisions about a case and how it is handled (but not final decisions on an appeal). They must act under the supervision of a judge and in accordance with relevant guidance. A party to the appeal can, within 14 days of being sent a notice of any decision made by a member of staff, apply in writing for the decision to be considered again by a judge.[39]

## The overriding objective: fair and just

The overriding objective of the procedural rules is to enable the tribunal to deal with appeals 'fairly and justly'.[40] Whenever the tribunal exercises a power under the rules (eg, to admit or not admit a late appeal, or to strike out an appeal), it must consider whether it would be fair and just. Similarly, when the tribunal interprets what the rules mean or what the practice directions say, it must try to come to the interpretation which enables an appeal to be dealt with in a way which is fair and just.[41]

It is important to bear this overriding objective in mind in any dealings with the tribunal.

The rules set out some of the things that must be taken into account when deciding whether a particular interpretation of the rules is fair and just, or in deciding whether it would be fair and just to exercise a power in a particular way.[42] The tribunal should:

- deal with the case in a way which is proportionate to its importance, the complexity of the issues, the anticipated costs and the resources of the parties;
- avoid unnecessary formality and be flexible in the proceedings;
- ensure, so far as practicable, that all the parties are able to participate fully in the proceedings;
- use any special expertise of the tribunal effectively; *and*
- avoid delay, so far as it is compatible with the proper consideration of the issues.

**Note:** this list is not exhaustive. Other matters can still be taken into account when considering what is fair and just in a particular case.[43]

The parties to an appeal also have a duty to assist the tribunal in dealing with cases fairly and justly.[44]

## Directions

Tribunals can give a wide range of directions in order to manage an appeal. These must be consistent with the overriding objective to deal with cases fairly and justly (see p217).

The tribunal can give directions to:

- extend or shorten the time for complying with any rule or direction;
- consolidate or hear together two or more appeals that raise common issues, or treat one as a lead case;
- permit or require a party to amend a document;
- permit or require a party or another person to provide documents, information, evidence or submissions. There are more specific powers to obtain evidence (see below);
- deal with an issue in the proceedings as a preliminary issue – eg, to decide precisely what decision is under appeal or whether the tribunal has jurisdiction;
- hold a hearing to consider any matter. This could include, for example, a preliminary hearing to decide what further evidence is needed and who should provide it, how much time the final hearing needs or whether the appeal should be 'struck out' because of a failure to comply with a direction;
- decide the form of any hearing (eg, the order in which parties speak or give evidence and who questions the appellant), and how to manage the hearing if one parent is concerned s/he will be intimidated by the other – eg, warning all parties in advance about behaviour, or organising the hearing so that the parties are not in the same room at the same time;[45]
- postpone or adjourn a hearing – eg, to enable further evidence to be produced;
- require a party to produce a 'bundle' (an indexed set of documents relating to the appeal) for a hearing. The tribunal must take into account the resources of the parties when issuing a direction;
- 'stay' (or, in Scotland, 'sist') proceedings. This allows the tribunal to put the case on hold pending the outcome of another appeal in which it is expected that legal issues will be decided that are relevant to the outcome;
- transfer proceedings to another court or tribunal – eg, if parentage is disputed;
- suspend the effect of its decision pending an application for permission to appeal against it.

A direction can be given at any time, either on the initiative of the tribunal or following an application by a party to the appeal.[46] You can apply for a direction either orally at a hearing or by writing to the tribunal, and must include the reason for seeking it. Unless it considers there is a good reason not to do so, the tribunal must send a written notice of any direction to every party and to anyone else affected by it.

If you are unhappy with a direction, you can apply for another direction which amends, suspends or sets aside the earlier direction.

If you fail to comply with a direction, the appeal could be 'struck out' (see p220) or you may be barred from taking part in any hearing (see p220).

It may be possible to appeal to the Upper Tribunal about the content of a particular direction – eg, to exclude or include certain evidence.[47]

## Evidence

The tribunal can give directions about:[48]
- issues on which it requires evidence or submissions;
- the nature of the evidence or submissions it requires, and the manner in which, and time at which, they are to be provided;
- whether the parties are permitted or required to provide expert evidence;
- any limit on the number of witnesses whose evidence a party may put forward.

The tribunal can exclude evidence if:
- it was not provided within a time limit set in a direction or practice direction;
  *or*
- it does not comply with a direction or a practice direction in some other way;
  *or*
- it would be unfair to admit it.

### Harmful evidence

If you are a party to the appeal (ie, a person with care or non-resident parent, or, in Scotland, a child applicant) and have told the Child Maintenance Service (CMS) or tribunal that you would like your address, or the address of a child, to be kept confidential, the tribunal and CMS must ensure that it (or information that could be used to identify it) is not revealed to other parties.[49] The tribunal can also order that documents or information should not be be disclosed, or that any matter which could allow the public to identify the people involved should not be disclosed.[50]

The tribunal can also direct that a particular person not get a document or information if this would be likely to cause her/him or another person serious harm.[51]

You can request the tribunal to direct that a particular document or piece of information that you must provide be withheld from another party. You must send a copy of it to the tribunal and explain why it should not be disclosed.[52]

The tribunal can, however, disclose the document or information to the party's representative if it is satisfied that s/he will not disclose the document to another person without the consent of the tribunal and that such disclosure is in the interests of justice.[53] If any evidence is withheld, the tribunal must still ensure that there is a fair hearing and that each party has sufficient information to conduct the case. Evidence should not be withheld from the tribunal itself.[54]

## Witnesses

The tribunal can summon (in Scotland, 'cite') witnesses and order other documents to be produced.[55] The tribunal may require someone to attend as a witness at a hearing, and answer any questions and provide documents related to the proceedings.

The tribunal must give at least 14 days' notice of the hearing (or a shorter period if the tribunal directs this). If the person summoned is not a party to the proceedings, her/his expenses are paid.

**Note:** the tribunal cannot summon a child if this would be detrimental to her/his welfare. The tribunal must consider how to assist any children under 18, or vulnerable or sensitive witnesses, to give evidence (including, for example, by telephone or video link).[56]

## Costs

Neither the First-tier Tribunal nor the Upper Tribunal can award costs, except if the Upper Tribunal is considering a judicial review (see p231).[57]

## Striking out an appeal

In certain circumstances, the tribunal can dismiss an appeal, or part of an appeal, without considering it. This is known as **'striking out'** an appeal.

The tribunal *must* strike out an appeal, or part of an appeal, if:
- the person who appealed has failed to comply with a direction which stated that the appeal, or that part of the appeal, *would* be struck out for failure to comply;[58] *or*
- it does not have jurisdiction to decide the appeal (or that part of it) and has not transferred it to another tribunal or court.[59]

The tribunal *may* strike out an appeal, or part of an appeal, if:
- the person who appealed has failed to comply with a direction which stated that the appeal, or that part of the appeal, *could* be struck out for failure to comply; *or*
- that person has failed to co-operate with the tribunal to such an extent that the tribunal cannot deal with the proceedings fairly and justly;[60] *or*
- it considers that the appeal has no reasonable prospects of success.[61]

The tribunal must consider whether it would be fair and just to strike out the appeal.

The power to strike out an appeal because the person who appealed has failed to comply with a direction should be used in exceptional cases as a last resort.[62] If your appeal, or part of your appeal, is struck out for this reason, you can apply for it to be reinstated.[63] You should do this within one month of the tribunal sending you notice of the striking out.[64] This one-month time limit can be extended if the tribunal considers it fair and just to do so.[65] If an application to reinstate an appeal is rejected, a further application can be made if you have further evidence or circumstances have changed.[66]

It is not possible for an appeal, or part of it, to be reinstated if it is struck out for any other reason. However, before striking out an appeal, the tribunal must invite you to make representations.[67]

The tribunal must give a written notice of its decision to strike out an appeal, or part of an appeal, and should explain why it is doing so.[68] A party to the appeal can ask for a written statement of reasons for the decision and can seek permission to appeal to the Upper Tribunal against a striking-out decision by the First-tier Tribunal.[69]

**Note:** if the other party or the CMS (ie, the 'respondent') fails to comply with a direction, they can be '**barred**' from taking any further part in the proceedings .[70] When the tribunal 'bars' a respondent, it need not consider any response or other submission made by that respondent. A barred respondent can apply to be reinstated.

## Sending and receiving documents

If there is a time limit to provide a document, this starts to run from when the tribunal sends the request. The time limit is met when the tribunal receives the response. The tribunal can extend (or shorten) any time limit, and has powers to deal with any failure to comply with rules and directions (see p217).[71]

**Note:** during a period of disruption due to the outbreak of coronavirus (COVID-19), tribunals are instructed to look sympathetically on any requests for extension of time for reasons related to coronavirus.[72]

See p213 for details of how time limits are calculated.

You can deliver documents to the tribunal by hand, post or fax to the address (or number) specified. The tribunal may give directions permitting documents to be sent by other methods.[73]

If you provide a fax, email address or other method for receiving documents electronically, you must accept delivery of documents by that method unless you have explicitly stated that this is not acceptable.[74]

If a document is sent electronically, the recipient can request a hard copy and the sender must supply it. The request for a hard copy should be made as soon as reasonably practicable after receiving the document electronically.[75]

Each party should assume that the address provided by another party remains valid unless s/he has received written notice to the contrary.[76]

## Representatives

You can appoint a representative (whether legally qualified or not) to represent you in the proceedings. Once appointed, a representative can do anything permitted or required to be done by you (except sign a witness statement).[77]

When the tribunal receives the notice of the appointment of a representative, it must provide her/him with any documents required to be issued to you and need not send the documents to you.[78] Any other party to the appeal must also be notified of the appointment and must send any documents required to the representative.

Even if you have not appointed a representative, you can still be accompanied at the hearing. The companion may act as a representative or otherwise assist in presenting the case at the hearing, provided the tribunal agrees.[79]

## Withdrawing an appeal

You can withdraw all, or part, of your appeal by writing to the tribunal before the hearing, or in person at the hearing.[80]

The tribunal's consent is not required for an appeal to be withdrawn before the hearing, unless it has already given a direction that withdrawal can only be with its consent.[81] If you wait until a hearing to withdraw, you can only do so with the tribunal's consent.[82] In the Upper Tribunal, consent is always needed to withdraw an appeal (even if the request is made in writing in advance), unless the case is still at the stage of awaiting permission to appeal.[83]

Once an appeal has been withdrawn, it can be reinstated if you request this in writing within one month of the notice of withdrawal being received by the tribunal, or within a month of the date of the hearing at which the appeal was withdrawn.

When an appeal is withdrawn, the tribunal must notify the other parties.

---

# 4. **Preparing a case**

The First-tier Tribunal may be the first chance for an independent evaluation of the decision being appealed. It may also be the last chance because its decision can only be appealed further to the Upper Tribunal on a point of law. Therefore, each party (ie, the person with care and non-resident parent, and, in Scotland, a child applicant) should make sure that the First-tier Tribunal knows the facts and arguments about the case. You may wish to attend the hearing (see p224) to put forward your views and evidence, even if you are not the person who appealed. You should also consider getting advice and asking an adviser to assist in preparing the case and to represent (see p221) you at the hearing.

## Considering the facts and law

- Read the response from the Child Maintenance Service (CMS) and any other documents to see whether it now accepts some of the arguments it previously rejected or ignored. Just because the CMS accepts part of a person's case does not mean that the tribunal will, especially if the other party disputes it.

- Check the law using this *Handbook, Child Support: the legislation* (see Appendix 4) and other sources. If the CMS quotes a decision of the Upper Tribunal (or of the previous commissioners), consider getting a copy. HM Courts and Tribunals Service (HMCTS) does not have copies of unreported decisions (those considered less legally significant), so if an unreported decision is to be relied on by the CMS, a copy should be supplied to the parties and to the tribunal. If you wish to quote an unreported decision, you should supply copies to everyone, preferably by sending a copy to the tribunal clerk in advance of the hearing. A party (including the CMS) can quote the CMS's internal procedural guidance, but it is important to remember that this guidance is not legally binding.
- Check the documents attached to the response. If anything relevant is missing, write to the tribunal asking it to direct the CMS to provide it.

The CMS must provide a response to an appeal within 42 days (see p215). If the CMS delays producing its response, you can write to the tribunal, asking that your appeal be heard. This may mean that the tribunal does not have all the evidence the CMS has. However, you (or the other party) can ask the tribunal to direct the CMS (see p218) to provide copies of all the papers, explaining why these are needed.

## Further evidence

- Consider whether you have (or can get) any further relevant written evidence. This can be sent to the First-tier Tribunal at any stage, but it is best to do this soon after the response is sent out, so papers can be copied to the other parties. If evidence or unreported caselaw decisions are produced at the hearing or sent in shortly before, this may cause a postponement or an adjournment.
- Check how best to explain the facts and law at the hearing. For example, telling the tribunal 'I look after the child from Friday night to Monday night' may be the best evidence of those facts.
- Decide whether to call any witnesses at the hearing (see p220).

Information relating to court proceedings concerning children heard in private or ancillary relief proceedings (ie, dealing with money and property) can be disclosed to the tribunal by any party without permission being sought, provided the court does not direct otherwise.[84] This means that one parent can supply information about the finances of the other parent, to which s/he admitted in the course of divorce proceedings.

## Obtaining information and evidence

If you would like another person to provide further information or documents, you can write to the First-tier Tribunal requesting that s/he be directed to provide these. It is best to send a prepared list to HMCTS, which is as precise as possible and explains why the documents are needed. For example, if a parent with care believes that a non-resident parent has undisclosed income, s/he could ask for bank statements for a certain period. A person who is not a party (eg, an employer) cannot be directed to provide evidence, but can be ordered to attend as a witness and produce documents (see p220). This should be done before the full hearing so all the parties can consider that evidence.

If a person fails to comply without a good explanation, the tribunal may decide that s/he has something to hide and so may not believe her/his evidence.[85] If s/he is the person appealing, the appeal can be 'struck out' (see p220).

## 5. **Hearings**

*Future changes*

The government plans to make all First-tier Tribunals digital by default and to pilot online dispute resolution. Appeals will be made online and the progress of a case will be tracked by text, email or online. There will be online hearings and hearings by telephone or video conference. Online submission of appeals and online appeal hearings are currently being tested, along with a text and email notification service. Also being tested is 'continuous online appeal resolution', where parties can upload documents and submissions and answer questions posted by the tribunal online. The government also says that, in future, there will no longer be an automatic right to an oral hearing. Some of the procedures outlined in this section are, therefore, likely to change.

**The First-tier Tribunal** must hold an oral hearing before making a final decision in an appeal unless:[86]
- it is 'striking out' the proceedings (see p220);
- it considers that it can decide the matter fairly and justly without one, and none of the parties object;[87]
- it is deciding whether to accept an application for permission to appeal, set aside a decision or correct a decision;
- it is making a consent order (see p229).

An oral hearing includes one conducted by video link, telephone or other instant two-way communication.[88]

**The Upper Tribunal** may decide any case without a hearing, but must consider a party's views when deciding whether to hold a hearing.[89]

If there is not a hearing, the tribunal makes its decision by considering what has been said on the appeal form, any other evidence provided by the parties, and the response from the Child Maintenance Service (CMS). This is known as a 'paper hearing'.

Note: temporary rules relating to disruption due to the outbreak of coronavirus (COVID-19) give tribunals more flexibility in relation to hearings. The First-tier Tribunal and Upper Tribunal can direct that all or part of a hearing is to be conducted remotely by live video or audio link.[90] The arrangements must allow each person taking part in the hearing to be able to see or hear all the other people taking part. The tribunal may direct that all or part of the hearing is broadcast to designated premises in such a way as to be public, and may direct that the hearing be recorded. If it is not practicable for a court or tribunal venue to be accessed by anyone other than those directly involved in the hearing, the tribunal may also direct that all or part of the hearing is to be private. If it is held in private, the tribunal must direct that it is recorded.[91] Unauthorised recording or transmission of a hearing is an offence. A tribunal can also decide an appeal without a hearing if it considers that the matter is urgent, it is not practicable to hold a hearing (including a live video or audio hearing) and it is in the interests of justice to decide the appeal without a hearing. For an initial period of six months from 19 March 2020, appeals are normally expected to be decided without a hearing wherever possible. Upper Tribunal appeals will normally be decided without a hearing. If the parties in a First-tier Tribunal case have not already consented to the appeal being decided without a hearing, the tribunal judge can decide whether doing so would be appropriate. If the tribunal considers it can decide the appeal without a hearing, it will send a provisional decision to the parties and ask whether they consent to a final decision being made in those terms. If a party does not agree and confirms that s/he requires a hearing, that is likely to take place remotely where arrangements can be made.[92]

## Notice

If an oral hearing is to be held, the tribunal must give reasonable notice of the time and place, and of any changes to the arrangements.[93] This must be at least 14 days, although shorter notice can be given with the parties' consent or in urgent or exceptional circumstances (if shorter notice is given, it must still be reasonable).[94] Papers, including evidence sent to the tribunal, should be sent to all the parties in good time before the hearing.[95]

## Attending a hearing

Generally, all hearings must be held in public and each party has a right to attend. However, the tribunal may direct that all, or part, of a hearing is to be held in private and may determine who is allowed to attend.

Even in a public hearing, the tribunal may exclude from all or part of it:[96]
- anyone whose conduct is disrupting, or is likely to disrupt, the hearing;
- anyone whose presence is likely to prevent another person from giving evidence or making submissions freely;

- anyone who should be excluded in order to prevent her/him hearing information that is likely to cause harm;
- anyone whose attendance would defeat the purpose of the hearing;
- a witness in the proceedings.

If a party fails to attend a hearing and the tribunal is satisfied that s/he has been notified or that reasonable steps to notify her/him have been taken, it may proceed with the hearing if it is in the interests of justice.[97] If you arrive late, after the tribunal has decided to proceed in your absence, it should still consider whether to allow you to participate or whether to adjourn the hearing to allow you the opportunity to attend.[98]

If you choose not to attend, you cannot then claim that the tribunal has acted unfairly if it decides the case on evidence given at the hearing that you have not had a chance to contest.[99]

## Composition of the tribunal

When the First-tier Tribunal deals with a case involving a child support decision, it usually comprises a single member, called a 'tribunal judge'.[100] The judge is legally qualified.[101] If the appeal raises difficult issues about financial accounts, the First-tier Tribunal can include a financially qualified member (a 'tribunal member') – ie, a chartered or certified accountant.[102] If there is one or more other members, the judge is the 'presiding member', can regulate the proceedings and has the casting vote.[103]

The Upper Tribunal almost always comprises a single judge, who is legally qualified. If the case is particularly difficult or there is conflicting caselaw, there may be a panel of two or three judges.[104]

If an appeal is meant to be heard by a tribunal of two or more members but some of them are absent, the hearing can still go ahead, but only if all the parties and the CMS agree.[105]

**Note:** during a period of disruption due the outbreak of coronavirus (COVID-19), a tribunal judge may direct that the composition of a tribunal is to be different from usual if s/he considers that the case could not proceed, or would be subject to unacceptable delay, if the usual composition was required.[106]

## The venue

There should normally be separate waiting rooms available at the hearing venue for the non-resident parent, parent with care and the CMS presenting officer. If you are worried about this, check with HM Courts and Tribunals Service (HMCTS) whether there are separate waiting areas available before the hearing and, if not, explain any problems this may cause. If the other party or witness could become violent, tell the tribunal clerk as soon as possible and ask what steps will be taken.

The hearing is usually held in the appellant's area. Expenses, including travel expenses, subsistence and some compensation for loss of earnings, can be claimed by those who attend as a party, witness or unpaid representative. The tribunal clerk will give you a claim form. Keep any receipts.

If it is difficult for you to attend the hearing (eg, because of disability), inform the tribunal clerk. An alternative venue may be possible, but convenience to the other parties to the appeal is also considered. If you are unable to attend a hearing at a venue, in rare cases a hearing may be arranged in your home. You may also be able to arrange to participate via video link, telephone or other means of instantaneous two-way electronic communication. Contact the tribunal to see whether this is possible.

### Conduct of the hearing

The First-tier Tribunal attempts to be informal. Its member(s) usually sit on one side of a table. The tribunal clerk (who does not take any part in making the decision) shows the parties into the room. The parties usually sit on the other side of the table from the tribunal. The presenting officer (an official representing the CMS) usually sits between the parties. The judge introduces everyone and explains the tribunal's role.

Hearings can take an hour or longer. Each party can address the tribunal, give evidence, call witnesses and put questions to any other party, the presenting officer and witnesses. The order in which the parties present their cases is up to the judge. The CMS is there to explain the decision, not to argue for the CMS. The presenting officer has a role, for example, to inform the tribunal about CMS procedures. It is rare for the presenting officer to call any witnesses. The tribunal may require any witness, including a party, to take an oath or affirmation.

Ask the judge for clarification if you are unclear about what is happening or about anything that has been said.

If you need an interpreter, the tribunal will arrange this if you request it in good time.

The tribunal can adjourn a hearing at any point – eg, if more documents are needed. It should adjourn a hearing if, for example, one party is unable to attend and her/his evidence could play an important part in its reaching a decision.[107] If evidence has been taken, a new panel hearing the case must be made up of either exactly the same, or entirely different, members.

# 6. **Decisions of the First-tier Tribunal**

After the hearing, the First-tier Tribunal considers the case and makes its decision. If the tribunal reaches a different conclusion from that of the Child Maintenance

Service (CMS), it allows the appeal. **Note:** it may make a decision that is less advantageous to the person appealing.[108]

If the appeal is allowed, the decision of the tribunal replaces that of the CMS. If the appeal is dismissed, the decision of the CMS remains in force.

In making its decision, the tribunal looks afresh at the situation on the date of the CMS decision that is being appealed.[109] It cannot take into account any change of circumstances that has occurred after the date of the decision, although it can take account of evidence that is relevant to the period up to the date of the decision, but which only became available later.[110] If it decides to allow the appeal because the decision was wrong on the facts at the time it was made, it cannot then direct how the CMS should deal with a later change of circumstances.

The whole appeal process can take some time, so if circumstances change while waiting for an appeal to be decided, a person with care or non-resident parent (or child applicant in Scotland) may also wish to make a new child support application or request a supersession.

The tribunal can consider any evidence and arguments, including those rejected or overlooked by the CMS and those which have not been used before.[111] The tribunal does not have to consider any issue not raised in the appeal.[112] However, it is 'inquisitorial', which means that it can consider legal arguments and factual questions on its own initiative, if appropriate, but should give its reasons for doing so.[113] The tribunal must decide what it believes are the relevant facts by evaluating all the relevant available evidence.[114] The tribunal can draw conclusions from the failure of a party to provide evidence.[115]

The tribunal can make a provisional decision, which will become final in specified circumstances. This may be done, for example, if it wants to give one last chance to a party to provide certain information within a specified time. The time limit for any further appeal runs from the date of the final decision.[116]

## Decision notices

Usually, the parties are invited to wait outside the hearing room and then asked back in to be told the decision. The First-tier Tribunal must also give a decision notice to the parties (unless it decides to withhold harmful information) as soon as reasonably practicable, stating:[117]

- its decision;
- any right to apply for reasons for the decision;
- any right of appeal against the decision, together with information about the time and manner in which such an appeal must be made.

The tribunal can decide to issue a full statement of the reasons for its decision, either verbally at the hearing or in writing to each party.[118] If it does not do this, you can apply for a written statement of reasons, provided this is received by the tribunal within a month of the decision notice being given or sent to the parties.[119]

Unless the decision was a consent order (see below), the tribunal must send this within one month of receiving the application, or as soon as reasonably practicable after that.[120]

## Record of proceedings

The presiding member of the First-tier Tribunal must keep a record of proceedings. This should include any evidence taken, submissions made and any procedural issues – eg, if a party asked for an adjournment.[121]

The record must be kept by HM Courts and Tribunals Service for at least six months from whichever is the later of:[122]

- the date of the decision;
- the date the reasons for the decision were given;
- the date the decision was corrected;
- the date a refusal to set aside was made; *or*
- the date of the determination of an application for permission to appeal (unless the documents are sent to the Upper Tribunal before the six months expire).

You can request a copy of the record of proceedings within this six-month period and it must be provided.

## Consent orders

If all the parties agree, they can request that the tribunal make an order disposing of (ie, cancelling) the proceedings with their consent. It only does so if it considers that it is appropriate.[123] The tribunal may simply make a decision on the appeal in the usual way. Dealing with an appeal by a consent order is only appropriate if it is clear that all parties have fully understood its implications.[124]

If a consent order is made, there does not have to be a hearing and no reasons for the order need to be given. Before agreeing to request a consent order, get independent advice.

# 7. Changing a First-tier Tribunal decision

If you are a party to the appeal (ie, a person with care or non-resident parent or, in Scotland, a child applicant), you or the Child Maintenance Service (CMS) can apply to have the First-tier Tribunal's decision changed. A First-tier Tribunal can change its decision by:[125]

- correcting an accidental error (see below);
- 'setting aside' the decision (see below);
- reviewing the decision (see p230);
- allowing an appeal to the Upper Tribunal (see p231).

**Note:** an application for any of the above can be treated by the tribunal as an application for any of the others.

## Correcting an error

The First-tier Tribunal can, at any time, correct a clerical mistake or accidental slip or omission in a decision, direction or any document it produces (but not the decision itself) by sending a notice of the amended decision or direction to all parties.[126]

## Setting aside the decision

A decision, or part of a decision, can be 'set aside' (ie, cancelled) by the First-tier Tribunal if it considers it to be in the interests of justice to do so. It can do this if:[127]
- a document relating to the proceedings was not sent to or received by the tribunal, a party or representative at an appropriate time; *or*
- a party or representative was not present at the hearing; *or*
- there has been some other procedural irregularity.

An application for a set-aside must be received within one month of being sent the decision by the tribunal.

If the decision is set aside, the appeal is heard again, usually by a differently constituted tribunal, and a new decision is made. You should be given the opportunity to have an oral hearing, even if the appeal was previously decided on the papers.[128]

If an application for permission to appeal has been made to the First-tier Tribunal and all the parties (including the CMS) argue that the decision is an error of law, it will be set aside and referred to a differently constituted First-tier Tribunal to determine.[129]

## Reviewing a decision

A First-tier Tribunal can 'review' its decision.[130] It must consider whether to do so before considering whether to grant permission to appeal to the Upper Tribunal and so, in practice, every application for permission to appeal is effectively an application for a review.

The tribunal can only review a decision if an application for permission to appeal has been made and it considers that there is an error of law.

If the tribunal considers that it is appropriate to amend the reasons for its decision, you should be given an opportunity to make suitable representations. The notice sent to you and the other parties should identify the error of law and the course of action the tribunal proposes to take.[131]

**Note:** a decision that has been reviewed can still be appealed to the Upper Tribunal. The First-tier Tribunal must notify the parties of the outcome of any review and of any right of appeal against it.

# 8. **Appealing to the Upper Tribunal**

Any party, including the Child Maintenance Service (CMS), can appeal to the Upper Tribunal against a final decision of the First-tier Tribunal. An appeal will only succeed if there is an error of law in the First-tier Tribunal's decision. See p205 and CPAG's *Welfare Benefits and Tax Credits Handbook* for information about when a decision contains an error of law. The tribunal's statement of reasons should include enough detail to allow all the parties to understand how the main issues in the case were decided.[132]

The Upper Tribunal can give the decision it thinks the First-tier Tribunal should have given. Alternatively (particularly if it thinks the First-tier Tribunal did not consider all the relevant facts or evidence properly), it may refer the case back to the First-tier Tribunal for a new decision to be made. If a case is referred back, the new First-tier Tribunal must apply the law in the way that the Upper Tribunal has instructed.

Before an appeal can be dealt with by the Upper Tribunal, you must apply for permission to appeal from the First-tier Tribunal. If this is refused, you can apply for permission directly to the Upper Tribunal. Permission should only be granted if it is arguable that there is an error of law in the First-tier Tribunal decision.

**Note:** a decision of the First-tier Tribunal which is a procedural decision or ruling (against which there is normally no right of appeal) can be challenged by judicial review. The case is normally heard by the Upper Tribunal. See CPAG's *Welfare Benefits and Tax Credits Handbook* for details.

## Applying to the First-tier Tribunal for permission to appeal

You must first apply to the First-tier Tribunal for permission to appeal to the Upper Tribunal. An application must be in writing and be received by the tribunal within one month of being sent the following, whichever is the latest:[133]
- a written statement of reasons for the decision;
- following a review, a notice that the reasons for the decision were amended or the decision corrected;
- a notice that an application for the decision to be set aside made within the time limit was refused.

The application must state:[134]
- the decision of the First-tier Tribunal to which it relates;
- the alleged errors of law in the decision; *and*
- the result sought.

If you apply late, you must explain why and include a request for an extension of time.[135] The First-tier Tribunal can extend the time limit, but there is no guarantee that you will be given longer, so you should apply within the time limit wherever possible.

**Note:** if you have difficulty meeting a time limit for any reason related to the outbreak of coronavirus (COVID-19), explain that to HM Courts and Tribunals Service (HMCTS) as soon as possible. Tribunals are instructed to look sympathetically on any requests for extension of time for reasons related to coronavirus.[136]

Usually, it is necessary to have obtained the full statement of reasons for a decision before seeking permission to appeal. If you have not requested a statement of reasons, the First-tier Tribunal must treat the application as an application for a statement of reasons (see p228), rather than as an application for permission to appeal.[137] If reasons are issued, you must then make a new application for permission to appeal. If a request for a statement of reasons has been refused because it was made late, the First-tier Tribunal can only grant permission to appeal if it is in the interests of justice to do so.[138]

When considering an application, the First-tier Tribunal must consider whether to review its decision.[139] If it has not changed the decision (or part of it) on review, it must consider whether to grant permission to appeal in respect of its decision, or the unchanged part of it.

The First-tier Tribunal must send a record of its decision on the application for permission to appeal to the parties.[140] If permission is refused, the notice must include the reasons for this. It must also include notice of the right to apply directly to the Upper Tribunal for permission to appeal, and details of how to do so.[141]

The First-tier Tribunal may grant permission to appeal against part of a decision. If this is the case, you may wish to file that appeal with the Upper Tribunal, and also to seek permission directly from the Upper Tribunal to appeal about the parts of the decision for which permission has not been granted.

## Applying to the Upper Tribunal for permission to appeal

If permission to appeal has been refused (in whole or in part), or an application has not been admitted, by the First-tier Tribunal, you can apply to the Upper Tribunal for permission.[142]

The application to the Upper Tribunal must be made in writing and within one month of being sent the refusal of permission.[143] If made late, the application must include an explanation for why it is late. The Upper Tribunal can extend the time limit, but there is no guarantee that you will be given longer, so you should apply within the time limit wherever possible.[144] If the earlier application for a written statement of reasons to the First-tier Tribunal or the application for permission to appeal to the First-tier Tribunal was made late, you must give an explanation. It can only be considered if the Upper Tribunal considers it in the interests of justice to do so.[145]

**Note:** if you have difficulty meeting a time limit for any reason related to coronavirus (COVID-19), explain that to HMCTS as soon as possible. Tribunals are instructed to look sympathetically on any requests for extension of time for reasons related to coronavirus.[146]

The application must include details of:[147]

- your name and address and any representative;
- an address for sending or delivering documents;
- details (including a full reference) of the decision challenged;
- the grounds for the appeal;
- whether you want a hearing of the application.

The application must include copies of:[148]

- the written record of the decision challenged;
- the written statement of reasons for the decision (if it exists);
- the First-tier Tribunal's notice refusing permission to appeal or refusing to admit the application.

Using Form UT1, *Application for Permission to Appeal to an Upper Tribunal Judge and Notice of Appeal,* should ensure that your application is correctly made.[149]

The Upper Tribunal must send you (but not the other parties) its reasons for refusing an application.[150] There is no right of appeal against a decision of the Upper Tribunal to refuse permission to appeal.[151] Your only legal remedy is to seek a judicial review (see p235).

The Upper Tribunal must send notice of permission to appeal to all the parties.[152] If this happens, generally the application for permission is treated as the notice of appeal. The Upper Tribunal sends a copy of this to all the parties and explains that it is treating the application for permission as the actual appeal.[153] If the parties agree, the Upper Tribunal can then determine the appeal without the need for any further response from them.[154]

## Notice of appeal

If the First-tier Tribunal grants you permission to appeal, you should send a notice of appeal to the Upper Tribunal. You are sent Form UT1 on which to do this.

If you have received permission to appeal directly from the Upper Tribunal, that is usually treated as the notice of appeal, unless the Upper Tribunal directs otherwise.[155]

The notice of appeal must be received by the Upper Tribunal within one month of your being sent the notice of permission to appeal by the First-tier Tribunal.[156]

The same information and documents must be included with the notice of appeal as for an application for permission to appeal.[157]

Late notices of appeal must include a request for an extension of time and the reasons why the notice was not provided in time. The Upper Tribunal can extend the time limit, but there is no guarantee that you will be given longer, so you should send the notice of appeal within the time limit wherever possible.[158]

**Note:** if you have difficulty meeting a time limit for any reason related to coronavirus (COVID-19), explain that to HMCTS as soon as possible. Tribunals are instructed to look sympathetically on any requests for extension of time for reasons related to coronavirus.[159]

The Upper Tribunal must send a copy of the notice of appeal and accompanying documents to each party and to the CMS.[160]

## Responses and replies

Any other party can respond to the appeal, but does not have to unless directed to by the Upper Tribunal.[161]

A response must be in writing and received by the Upper Tribunal within one month of your being sent the notice of appeal (or the notice of a grant of permission to appeal, if this is treated as the notice of appeal). A late response must request an extension of the time limit and explain why it is late.[162]

The response must state:[163]

- the name and address of the respondent and any representative;
- an address for sending or delivering documents;
- whether the respondent opposes the appeal;
- the grounds on which the respondent intends to rely in the appeal;
- whether the respondent wants a hearing.

The Upper Tribunal must provide a copy of the response to the appellant and the other parties.[164]

The person who appealed may then reply to the response, but does not have to unless directed to by the Upper Tribunal. The reply must be received within one month of your being sent the response and is then copied to the other parties by the Upper Tribunal.[165]

## Decisions of the Upper Tribunal

The Upper Tribunal's decision may replace the decision of the First-tier Tribunal (or it can direct that the case be reconsidered by a new First-tier Tribunal).

The Upper Tribunal may announce its final decision verbally at a hearing (although holding an oral hearing is far less common than at the First-tier Tribunal (see p224) and announcing the decision verbally after a hearing is also less common). The Upper Tribunal must then (unless it decides to withold harmful information) provide the parties with a notice stating its decision and details of any further rights of review and appeal. The Upper Tribunal must always give reasons for its decision, unless it was made with the consent of the parties or the parties have consented to a decision being given without reasons.[166]

If the proceedings are recorded, this should be kept for six months. You can apply for a transcript, but will have to pay for it unless you have challenged or intend to challenge the decision, the transcript is necessary in order to bring that challenge, and the Upper Tribunal is satisfied that you cannot afford to pay.

## Challenging an Upper Tribunal decision

**Note:** you should get legal advice if you are considering whether to challenge an Upper Tribunal decision.

Upper Tribunal decisions can be changed by:

- correcting an accidental error (see p230);[167]
- 'setting aside' the decision (see p230);[168]
- appealing to the Court of Appeal (in Scotland, the Court of Session). Permission is needed for this, and the appeal must be on the grounds that the Upper Tribunal made an error of law. An application for permission must first be made to the Upper Tribunal.[169] This is similar to the procedure for applying for permission from the First-tier Tribunal, except that the time limit is three months. The Upper Tribunal must consider a review (see below) before deciding whether to grant permission. If the Upper Tribunal refuses permission, the request can be made directly to the Court of Appeal/Court of Session. The Upper Tribunal's refusal decision should include a statement of reasons, details of the relevant court and the time limit for applying.[170] Permission can only be granted if the Upper Tribunal or court considers the appeal would raise an important point of principle or practice, or there is some other compelling reason to grant it;[171]
- reviewing the decision (see p230). The procedure is as for the First-tier Tribunal, except that the Upper Tribunal can only review the decision if it overlooked a legislative decision or binding legal authority which could have affected it or, since giving its decision, a court has made a decision that could have affected it.[172]

The Upper Tribunal may treat an application for a decision to be corrected, set aside or reviewed, or an application for permission to appeal against a decision, as an application for any one of these things.[173]

A decision of the Upper Tribunal that cannot be appealed (eg, a refusal to grant leave to appeal from the First-tier Tribunal to the Upper Tribunal) can be challenged by applying for a judicial review (see p198) to the High Court (in England and Wales) or the Court of Session (in Scotland). This can only be done if the case would raise some important point of principle or practice, or if there is some other compelling reason.[174]

For further details about challenging Upper Tribunal decisions, see CPAG's *Welfare Benefits and Tax Credits Handbook*.

## 9. **Test case rules**

Special rules apply if a court or Upper Tribunal decision on a 'test case' is pending, or an Upper Tribunal or court decision on a test case has been made. A 'test case' is one in which a person is challenging the Child Maintenance Service's (CMS's) interpretation of the law in a way that affects other cases more generally, even if it is the CMS's own appeal and even if the person does not consider the case to be a test case.

These rules apply to child support calculation decisions, revision and supersession decisions, and appeals to the First-tier or Upper Tribunal.

### If there is a test case pending

If an appeal in what could be a test case is still pending before the Upper Tribunal or a court, the CMS can:[175]

- postpone making a decision on an application, revision or supersession in any other case which might be affected by the decision in that appeal until the test case appeal has been decided; *or*
- make a decision as if the test case had already been decided in a way that would result in the lowest possible amount of child support being payable in a case that might be affected by the decision. This only applies if there is no calculation in force in the case that might be affected by the test case decision.[176]

An appeal is 'pending' before a court if:[177]

- an appeal (including an application for judicial review) about child support has been made to the High Court, Court of Appeal, Court of Session or Supreme Court, but has not been determined;
- an application for permission to make such an appeal (or judicial review) has been made, but has not been determined;
- the CMS has certified in writing that it is considering making such an appeal or application and the time for appealing or applying has not expired, and the CMS considers that the appeal might result in the non-resident parent having no, or less, liability for child support.[178]

An appeal also counts as pending if a court (but not the Upper Tribunal) has referred a question to the Court of Justice of the European Union for a preliminary ruling.

If the CMS does not make an application or appeal in time on the test case, it can no longer postpone making a decision on other cases.

A decision to suspend or make a decision on the assumption that the CMS will win the test case is a discretionary one. The CMS must, therefore, take into account the welfare of any child likely to be affected by the decision when making it.

### How a pending test case affects similar cases

If a test case pending before a court may affect a similar case awaiting a decision from the First-tier Tribunal or Upper Tribunal, or there is a possibility that the CMS may appeal, the CMS may:[179]

- direct the tribunal to refer the similar case to the CMS. The CMS makes no decision until the test case is decided. It then revises the CMS decision under appeal or supersedes the tribunal decision under appeal; *or*
- direct the tribunal to deal with the case itself. The tribunal must then either:
  - postpone its decision until the test case is decided; *or*
  - decide the appeal as if the test case appeal has already been decided against the person who appealed in the similar case. It should only do this if it considers that it is in the appellant's interests. If the test case is later decided in that person's favour, the CMS supersedes the tribunal decision in the similar case.

## Test case decisions

If a decision of the Upper Tribunal or court interprets child support law in the same way as the CMS, the CMS must usually apply that interpretation in the period before the decision was given. This usually requires the CMS to supersede all decisions which are affected.

However, if the Upper Tribunal/court rejects the CMS's interpretation of the law, that test case decision only has effect from the date it is made.[180] For the period before that date, the CMS (and either tribunal) assumes that it was right in its interpretation of the law when making the original decision which led to the appeal.[181]

This rule does not apply to:

- an application for child support made on or before 1 June 1999;[182]
- a revision or supersession of any decision made on or before 1 June 1999;[183]
- a decision in a case where the CMS had suspended a decision under the rules on pending test cases (see p236);[184]
- a revision or supersession decision in a case where the CMS had required the First-tier or Upper Tribunal to refer the case to the CMS, or deal with it on the assumption that the test case had already been decided against the appellant.[185]

# Notes

## 1. Considering an appeal

1 s20(4)(c) CSA 1991; reg 14A(4) CSMC Regs
2 Reg 27A(1) CSMC Regs
3 s20 CSA 1991
4 Reg 12(1) CS(MPA) Regs
5 *TB v SSWP and others (CSM)* [2019] UKUT 79 (AAC)
6 **EW** Arts 3 and 4 CSA(JC)O
  **S** Arts 2, 3 and 4 CSA(JC)(S)O
7 r5(3)(k) TP(FT) Rules

## 2. Appealing to the First-tier Tribunal

8 s20(3) CSA 1991; regs 24-26 CSMC Regs
9 gov.uk/government/organisations/hm-courts-and-tribunals-service
10 r22(3) TP(FT) Rules
11 r22(4) TP(FT) Rules
12 *MM v SSWP (PIP)* [2016] UKUT 36 (AAC)
13 CMS leaflet CMSB011GB, *What To Do If You're Unhappy With the Child Maintenance Service,* September 2018
14 r22(2)(d) and Sch 1 TP(FT) Rules
15 R(IB) 4/02
16 r12 TP(FT) Rules. The same rules about calculating time apply to the Upper Tribunal: r12 TP(UT) Rules.
17 Reg 7(2) CSMC Regs
18 Statement from the President of the Upper Tribunal Administrative Appeals Chamber, *Contingency Arrangements,* 20 March 2020
19 r22(8) TP(FT) Rules
20 r22(8) TP(FT) Rules
21 *KK v Sheffield City Council (CTB)* [2015] UKUT 367 (AAC); *PM v SSD (AFCS)* [2015] UKUT 647 (AAC); *PH and SM v SSWP (DLA) (JSA)* [2018] UKUT 404 (AAC)
22 rr2(1), (2) and (3)(a) and 5(3)(a) TP(FT) Rules; *Information Commissioner v PS* [2011] UKUT 94 (AAC); *CD v First-tier Tribunal (CICA)* [2010] UKUT 181 (AAC), reported as [2011] AACR 1
23 r22(6) TP(FT) Rules
24 *LS v London Borough of Lambeth (HB)* [2010] UKUT 461 (AAC)
25 r22(7) TP(FT) Rules
26 CMS leaflet CMSB011GB, *What To Do If You're Unhappy With the Child Maintenance Service,* September 2018
27 CMS leaflet CMSB011GB, *What To Do If You're Unhappy With the Child Maintenance Service,* September 2018
28 r24(1)(b)(ii) TP(FT) Rules
29 r24(2)(a)-(d) TP(FT) Rules
30 r24(2)(e) TP(FT) Rules
31 r24(3) TP(FT) Rules
32 r24(4) TP(FT) Rules
33 *TR v SSWP and PW (CSM)* [2013] UKUT 80 (AAC)
34 r24(6) and (7) TP(FT) Rules
35 r19(2) and (3) TP(FT) Rules

## 3. Tribunal procedures

36 R(IS) 11/99; *KB v SSWP (DLA)* [2011] UKUT 388 (AAC)
37 r7 TP(FT) Rules; r7 TP(UT) Rules
38 s25 TCEA 2007; r7(3) TP(FT) Rules; r7(3) and (4) TP(UT) Rules
39 r4 TP(FT) Rules; Courts and Tribunals Judiciary Practice Statement, *Authorising Tribunal Caseworkers First-tier Tribunal (Social Entitlement Chamber) to Carry Out Functions of a Judicial Nature,* 16 July 2018; Courts and Tribunals Judiciary Practice Statement, *Delegation of Functions to Registrars First-tier Tribunal (Social Entitlement Chamber),* 1 December 2016
40 r2 TP(FT) Rules; r2 TP(UT) Rules
41 r2(3) TP(FT) Rules; r2(3) TP(UT) Rules
42 r2(2) TP(FT) Rules; r2(2) TP(UT) Rules
43 *MS v SSWP* [2009] UKUT 211 (AAC)
44 r2(4) TP(FT) Rules; r2(4) TP(UT) Rules
45 *WA v SSWP and P (CSM)* [2016] UKUT 86 (AAC)
46 r6(1) TP(FT) Rules; r6(1) TP(UT) Rules
47 *LM v London Borough of Lewisham* [2009] UKUT 204 (AAC)
48 r15 TP(FT) Rules; r15 TP(UT) Rules
49 r19(3) TP(FT) Rules; r19(2) and (4) TP(UT) Rules
50 r14(1) TP(FT) Rules; r14(1) TP(UT) Rules
51 r14(2) TP(FT) Rules; r14(2) TP(UT) Rules
52 r14(3) TP(FT) Rules; r14(3) TP(UT) Rules
53 r14(5) and (6) TP(FT) Rules; r14(5) and (6) TP(UT) Rules

54 R(CS) 3/06

55 r17 TP(FT) Rules; r17 TP(UT) Rules

56 Tribunals Judiciary Practice Direction, *First-tier and Upper Tribunal: child, vulnerable adult and sensitive witnesses,* 30 October 2008; *SW v SSWP (DLA)* [2015] UKUT 319 (AAC); *LO'L v SSWP (ESA)* [2016] UKUT 10 (AAC), reported as [2016] AACR 31

57 r10 TP(FT) Rules; r10 TP(UT) Rules

58 r8(1) TP(FT) Rules; r8(1) TP(UT) Rules

59 r8(2) TP(FT) Rules; r8(2) TP(UT) Rules

60 r8(3)(b) TP(FT) Rules; r8(3)(b) TP(UT) Rules

61 r8(3)(c) TP(FT) Rules; r8(3)(c) TP(UT) Rules

62 *DTM v Kettering Borough Council (CTB)* [2013] UKUT 625 (AAC)

63 r8(5) TP(FT) Rules; r8(5) TP(UT) Rules

64 r8(6) TP(FT) Rules; r8(6) TP(UT) Rules

65 rr2(1) and (3)(a) and 5(3)(a) TP(FT) Rules; rr2(1), 3(a) and 5(3)(a) TP(UT) Rules

66 *R (BD) v First-tier Tribunal (CIC)* [2013] UKUT 332 (AAC)

67 r8(4) TP(FT) Rules; r8(4) TP(UT) Rules

68 *RN v SSWP (RP)* [2013] UKUT 461 (AAC)

69 *Synergy Child Services Ltd v Ofsted* [2009] UKUT 125 (AAC); *LS v London Borough of Lambeth (HB)* [2010] UKUT 461 (AAC), reported as [2011] AACR 27

70 r8(7) and (8) TP(FT) Rules; r8(7) and (8) TP(UT) Rules

71 rr5(3)(a) and 7 TP(FT) Rules; rr5(3)(a) and 7 TP(UT) Rules

72 Statement from the President of the Upper Tribunal Administrative Appeals Chamber, *Contingency Arrangements,* 20 March 2020

73 r13(1) TP(FT) Rules; r13(1) TP(UT) Rules

74 r13(2) and (3) TP(FT) Rules; r13(2) and (3) TP(UT) Rules

75 r13(4) TP(FT) Rules; r13(4) TP(UT) Rules

76 r13(5) TP(FT) Rules; r13(5) TP(UT) Rules

77 r11(5) TP(FT) Rules; r11(3) TP(UT) Rules

78 r11(6) TP(FT) Rules; r11(4) TP(UT) Rules

79 r11(7) and (8) TP(FT) Rules; r11(5) and (6) TP(UT) Rules

80 r17 TP(FT) Rules; r17 TP(UT) Rules

81 *WM v SSWP (DLA)* [2015] UKUT 642 (AAC)

82 r17(1)(b), (2) and (3)(b) TP(FT) Rules

83 r17(1) and (2) TP(UT) Rules

## 4. **Preparing a case**

84 r5 Family Proceedings Courts (Child Support Act 1991) Rules 1993, No.627; r10.21A Family Proceedings Rules 1991, No.1247

85 CCS/3757/2004

## 5. **Hearings**

86 r27 TP(FT) Rules

87 *MM v SSWP (ESA)* [2011] UKUT 334 (AAC); *JP v SSWP (IB)* [2011] UKUT 459 (AAC)

88 r1(3) TP(FT) Rules; r1(3) TP(UT) Rules

89 r34 TP(UT) Rules

90 ss29ZA-ZD TCEA 2007, as inserted by s55 and Sch 25, para 2, of the Coronavirus Act 2020 until the expiry of the 2020 Act (being 25 March 2022 unless provision is made under the Act for its expiry, or the expiry of any provision of it, earlier or later than that date).

91 rr5A, 30(3A) and 30A TP(FT) Rules and rr5A, 37(2ZA) and 37A TP(UT) Rules, as inserted by rr4 and 5 of the Tribunal Procedure (Coronavirus) (Amendment) Rules 2020, No.416 from 10 April 2020 until s55(b) of the Coronavirus Act 2020 expires for all purposes.

92 Tribunal Judiciary Pilot Practice Direction, *Contingency Arrangements in the First-tier Tribunal and the Upper Tribunal,* 19 March 2020

93 r29(1) TP(FT) Rules; r36(1) TP(UT) Rules

94 r29(2) TP(FT) Rules; r36(2)(b) TP(UT) Rules. The only other exception to this is when the Upper Tribunal is conducting a hearing of an application for permission to bring judicial review, in which at least two working days' notice must be given. Such proceedings are outside the scope of this *Handbook.*

95 CCS/1925/2002

96 r30 TP(FT) Rules; r37 TP(UT) Rules

97 r31 TP(FT) Rules; r38 TP(UT) Rules

98 *AK v HMRC (TC)* [2016] UKUT 98 (AAC)

99 CCS/1689/2007; CCS/2901/2001; CCS/2676/2001

100 Art 2 FT&UT(CT)O; Tribunals Judiciary Practice Statement, *Composition of Tribunals in Social Security and Child Support Cases in the Social Entitlement Chamber on or after 1 August 2013,* July 2013, para 6

101 Sch 2 para 1(2) TCEA 2007

102 Tribunals Judiciary Practice Statement, *Composition of Tribunals in Social Security and Child Support Cases in the Social Entitlement Chamber on or after 1 August 2013*, July 2013, para 7

103 Tribunals Judiciary Practice Statement, *Composition of Tribunals in Social Security and Child Support Cases in the Social Entitlement Chamber on or after 1 August 2013*, July 2013, para 12; Art 8 FT&UT(CT)O

104 Tribunals Judiciary Practice Statement, *Composition of Tribunals in Relation to Matters that Fall to be Decided by the Administrative Appeals Chamber of the Upper Tribunal on or after 26 March 2014*, March 2014, para 3a; Arts 3 and 4 FT&UT(CT)O

105 Sch 4 para 15(6) TCEA 2007; *PF v SSWP (ESA)* [2015] UKUT 553 (AAC)

106 Tribunals Judiciary Pilot Practice Direction, *Panel Composition in the First-tier Tribunal and the Upper Tribunal*, 19 March 2020 (for an initial pilot period of six months, but may be reviewed or revoked within that period).

107 *DC v SSWP (ESA)* [2015] UKUT 150 (AAC)

### 6. Decisions of the First-tier Tribunal

108 R(IB) 2/04

109 s20(7) CSA 1991

110 s20(7)(b) CSA 1991; R(CS) 1/03; *MT v SSWP and MB (CSM)* [2015] UKUT 492 (AAC)

111 CCS/16351/1996; *MB v CMEC* [2009] UKUT 29 (AAC), para 16

112 s20(7)(a) CSA 1991

113 R(IB) 2/04; *A P-H v SSWP (DLA)* [2010] UKUT 183 (AAC); *JW v SSWP & MC & JC (CSM)* [2013] UKUT 407 (AAC), reported as [2014] AACR 8; *JR v SSWP and TR (CSM)* [2015] UKUT 582 (AAC); *ET v SSWP (PIP)* [2017] UKUT 478 (AAC)

114 CCS/2861/2001

115 CCS/3757/2004

116 *AB v CMEC (CSM)* [2010] UKUT 385 (AAC)

117 r33 TP(FT) Rules

118 r34(2)(b) TP(FT) Rules

119 r34(3) and (4) TP(FT) Rules

120 r34(5) TP(FT) Rules

121 Tribunals Judiciary Practice Statement, *Record of Proceedings in Social Security and Child Support Cases in the Social Entitlement Chamber on or after 3 November 2008*, November 2008

122 *DT v SSWP* [2015] UKUT 509 (AAC)

123 r32 TP(FT) Rules; r39 TP(UT) Rules; *AW v SSWP and AL (CSM)* [2017] UKUT 235 (AAC)

124 *MM v SSWP and IJ (CSM)* [2015] UKUT 590 (AAC)

### 7. Changing a First-tier Tribunal decision

125 Not including judicial review of non-appealable decisions.

126 r42 TP(FT) Rules; *AS v SSWP (ESA)* [2011] UKUT 159 (AAC); *CG v SSWP (DLA)* [2011] UKUT 453 (AAC)

127 r37 TP(FT) Rules

128 CIB/4193/2003

129 s23A CSA 1991

130 Introduced by s9 TCEA 2007; see also r40 TP(FT) Rules

131 *JS v SSWP (DLA)* [2013] UKUT 100 (AAC), reported as [2013] AACR 30

### 8. Appealing to the Upper Tribunal

132 *MW v SSWP (II)* [2011] UKUT 465 (AAC)

133 r38(2) and (3) TP(FT) Rules

134 r38(6) TP(FT) Rules

135 r38(5) TP(FT) Rules

136 Statement from the President of the Upper Tribunal Administrative Appeals Chamber, *Contingency Arrangements*, 20 March 2020

137 r38(7) TP(FT) Rules

138 r38(7)(c) TP(FT) Rules

139 r39(1) TP(FT) Rules

140 r39(3) TP(FT) Rules

141 r39(4) TP(FT) Rules

142 r21(2) TP(UT) Rules

143 r21(3)(b) TP(UT) Rules

144 r21(6) TP(UT) Rules

145 r21(7) TP(UT) Rules

146 Statement from the President of the Upper Tribunal Administrative Appeals Chamber, *Contingency Arrangements*, 20 March 2020

147 r21(4) TP(UT) Rules

148 r21(5) TP(UT) Rules

149 Form UT1 is available from gov.uk/ government/collections/administrative-appeals-chamber-upper-tribunal-forms

150 r22(1) TP(UT) Rules

151 *R (Cart) v Upper Tribunal and R (MR (Pakistan)) v Upper Tribunal and SSHD* [2011] UKSC 28, reported as [2011] AACR 38

152 r22(2)(a) TP(UT) Rules

153 r22(2)(b) TP(UT) Rules

154 r22(2)(c) TP(UT) Rules

155 r23(1) TP(UT) Rules

156 r23(2) TP(UT) Rules

157 r23(3) and (4) TP(UT) Rules

158 r23(5) TP(UT) Rules
159 Statement from the President of the
 Upper Tribunal Administrative Appeals
 Chamber, *Contingency Arrangements*,
 20 March 2020
160 r23(6) TP(UT) Rules
161 r24(1) TP(UT) Rules
162 r24(2) and (4) TP(UT) Rules
163 r24(3) TP(UT) Rules
164 r24(5) TP(UT) Rules
165 r25 TP(UT) Rules
166 r40 TP(UT) Rules
167 r42 TP(UT) Rules
168 r43 TP(UT) Rules
169 s13 TCEA 2007; rr44 and 45 TP(UT)
 Rules
170 r45(4) TP(UT) Rules
171 s13(6) and (6A) TCEA 2007; AUTCAO;
 r41.57(2) Court of Session Rules
172 r46 TP(UT) Rules
173 r48 TP(UT) Rules
174 *Eba v Advocate General for Scotland*
 [2011] UKSC 29; *R (Cart) v Upper
 Tribunal and R (MR (Pakistan)) v Upper
 Tribunal and SSHD* [2011] UKSC 28,
 reported as [2011] AACR 38

## 9. Test case rules
175 s28ZA(1) and (2) CSA 1991
176 Reg 28(1) CSMC Regs
177 s28ZA(4) and (5) CSA 1991
178 s28ZA(4)(c) CSA 1991; reg 28(2) CSMC
 Regs
179 s28ZB CSA 1991
180 s28ZC(1) and (3) CSA 1991; regs 30-32
 CSMC Regs
181 s28ZC(1) and (3) CSA 1991
182 s28ZC(1)(b)(i) CSA 1991
183 s28ZC(1)(b)(ii) and (iii) CSA 1991
184 s28ZC(2)(a) CSA 1991
185 s28ZC(2)(b) CSA 1991

# Chapter 11

# Complaints

**This chapter covers:**
1. Grounds for a complaint (below)
2. Compensation payments (p243)
3. Complaining about the Child Maintenance Service (p244)
4. Complaining about Child Maintenance Options (p246)
5. Complaining about Jobcentre Plus (p246)
6. Complaining to the Independent Case Examiner (p247)
7. Using your MP (p248)
8. Complaining to the Ombudsman (p248)

## 1. Grounds for a complaint

If you disagree with a decision about child support, you can usually challenge it by applying for a revision and then appealing (see Chapters 9 and 10).

If you are unhappy about how you have been treated, you can make a complaint. A complaint is a separate process from a revision or an appeal, and does not necessarily lead to a decision being changed. You can complain about any aspect of the administration of the statutory child support scheme – eg, a delay in dealing with your case, poor administration, the behaviour of staff, incorrect information or advice provided by officials or the way in which a particular policy or practice has affected you.

In some cases, it may be appropriate to challenge a decision as well as making a complaint – eg, if you think that child support has been wrongly calculated and you want to challenge the decision, but you also wish to complain about a delay in making the calculation or some other aspect of the way your case has been handled or you have been treated.

A complaint may be appropriate if there is no right to appeal against the decision in question (see p198). In this situation, judicial review may also be possible (instead of, or as well as, making a complaint). Get legal advice if you are considering a judicial review (see also p198).

It may be appropriate to seek a compensation payment for any loss related to a complaint (see p243).

The Parliamentary and Health Service Ombudsman (see p248) has a website (ombudsman.org.uk/making-complaint) to encourage and assist people to complain about government departments and agencies.

## Who the complaint is about

It is important to be clear which organisation has caused the problem. In most cases, this will be the Child Maintenance Service (see p244). You can also complain about the standard of service provided by Child Maintenance Options (see p246). Problems concerning the deduction of payments from benefits may be caused by Jobcentre Plus, and complaints about any of its functions should be made to the Department for Work and Pensions (see p246). If there is a delay or poor administration of an appeal by HM Courts and Tribunals Service (HMCTS), or you are unhappy about the way you were treated by a tribunal judge or member, the complaint should be made to HMCTS. For information about making complaints to HMCTS, see CPAG's *Welfare Benefits and Tax Credits Handbook*.

## 2. **Compensation payments**

If you have not received prompt, courteous and efficient service, or have lost out because of an error, delay or poor standard of service by the Child Maintenance Service (CMS) or Jobcentre Plus, it may be appropriate to request compensation or a consolatory payment (see below) when making a complaint. Ex gratia payments can be made if someone has experienced a financial loss or significant delay, or has been caused severe distress or inconvenience.

A Department for Work and Pensions guide explains the rules on whether financial compensation should be paid and, if so, how much is appropriate. It is available on the gov.uk website[1] or on request from the CMS and Jobcentre Plus.

There is no legal right to these payments, but it can sometimes be useful to make it clear that financial compensation would help to resolve the complaint. The CMS cannot be sued for negligence.[2]

Compensation payments may be appropriate if there has been:

- significant delay – eg, in making calculations or reviewing liability;
- delays or errors in enforcement;
- delays in passing child support payments to the person with care;
- wrong identification of a non-resident parent;
- financial loss because of CMS or Jobcentre Plus error – eg, in bank, postal or telephone charges;
- other examples of gross inconvenience, embarrassment, breach of confidentiality or severe distress.

You should consider asking for a payment equal to any money you may have lost plus any additional expenses you have incurred, and an amount to compensate you for any hardship or distress. If you are not offered compensation, or you are not offered as much as you consider appropriate, you could consider taking the complaint further – ie, to the Independent Case Examiner (see p247) or the Ombudsman (see p248).

## Consolatory payments

Consolatory payments are smaller payments than compensation payments that can be made if action by the CMS or Jobcentre Plus has caused serious inconvenience because the same mistakes were made more than once, or the mistakes caused severe embarrassment or humiliation. Evidence of your (or a family member's) health being affected as a result may also be considered if it can be shown to be a direct result of errors made by the CMS or Jobcentre Plus. Consolatory payments are made in recognition of the effect of an error on someone's life and, therefore, it is possible to claim them even if there is no financial loss.

Many people experience inconvenience and frustration when using the CMS and Jobcentre Plus, and this alone is not enough to secure a consolatory payment.

Separate decisions are made on whether to award compensation or a consolatory payment, based on the facts of each case. In some cases, both may be paid. The *Financial Redress for Maladministration* guide covers both compensation and consolatory payments.[3]

---

# 3. **Complaining about the Child Maintenance Service**

Most complaints involving child support are made to the Child Maintenance Service (CMS). Complaints are likely to be about:
- standards of service, including delays, staff communications, poor administration and lost papers; *or*
- how discretionary decisions are made – eg, failure to follow guidance, following it too strictly or failing to take all the relevant circumstances into account. It may be appropriate to get advice on whether judicial review is also possible if you think a discretionary decision is unreasonable or unfair.

A complaint should be started by contacting the person who has been dealing with your case, or her/his manager. This information should be in letters sent by the CMS, along with telephone contact information. The complaint can be made by telephone or in writing. Records of all communications should be kept in case the complaint is taken further. A complaint made by letter should be clearly headed 'Complaint' – see Appendix 1 for the CMS address.

If the CMS officer or manager cannot resolve the complaint, it can be taken further by contacting the complaints resolution team at the office handling your case. Contact details should be given in any letters sent. The CMS calls this 'complaints stage 1'.

If there has been an unreasonable delay or you are still not satisfied with the outcome after the complaints resolution team has looked at your complaint, you can ask for a review. The CMS calls this review 'complaints stage 2'. The review is carried out by a senior CMS official and considers whether the complaint was dealt with properly and if anything else can be done. Contact details for requesting a review should be given in the letter from the complaints resolution team.

At each of these stages of the complaints procedure, your complaint should be acknowledged within two days and the CMS should normally resolve it within 15 working days. If it is expected to take longer, the CMS should keep you informed and agree a timescale with you.

More information about the complaints procedure is available in a CMS leaflet[4] or on the web at gov.uk/manage-child-maintenance-case.

If you are not satisfied that the complaint has been resolved, you can contact the Independent Case Examiner (see p247).

The final option is to complain, via your MP, to the Parliamentary and Health Service Ombudsman (see p248).

## Standards of service

When considering whether, or at what point, to make a complaint, it may be useful to be aware of the standards of service that the CMS says it will meet.

The CMS no longer publishes detailed information about its service standards. However, standards that should be expected include for the CMS to:

- start gathering information from the non-resident parent within four weeks of a child support application, if it has contact details;
- make an accurate decision on an application within 12 weeks (but in some cases, a decision may take up to 26 weeks);
- make payments to the person with care within a week of receiving the money from the non-resident parent, if the collection service is being used;
- take action to use a deduction from earnings order, where appropriate, within four months of a non-resident parent's first being informed of her/his liability;
- answer telephone calls within one minute;
- respond to letters, and either resolve complaints or agree on the next course of action, within three weeks of receiving them.

# 4. **Complaining about Child Maintenance Options**

The complaints process for the Child Maintenance Options service is similar to that for the Child Maintenance Service (see p244). A complaint should be started by talking to the person dealing with the enquiry, or to her/his manager. If the matter cannot be resolved, a complaint can be made by phone, through a live web-chat service or on an online enquiry form.[5] Make it clear that you want to make a complaint. Keep a record of any contact you make with Child Maintenance Options to complain.

If you are not satisfied after following this procedure, you can ask for a review. The complaints review team should look at the complaint again to see whether there is more that can be done. The review team aims to resolve complaints within 15 days.

Further details of the complaints process is available by telephoning 0800 988 0988 (Child Maintenance Choices in Northern Ireland: 0800 028 7439).

If you have gone through every stage of the complaints procedure and you are still not satisfied, you can complain to the Independent Case Examiner (see p247), or, via your MP, to the Parliamentary and Health Service Ombudsman (see p248).

# 5. **Complaining about Jobcentre Plus**

Other parts of the Department for Work and Pensions (DWP) have a similar complaints procedures to the Child Maintenance Service (CMS). If you are a non-resident parent, you may want to complain about the way in which child support payments have (or have not) been deducted from your benefit. If you disagree with the rate of child support you should be paying (and therefore with the deduction being made from benefit), you should challenge the decision of the CMS, not complain to Jobcentre Plus. A complaint to Jobcentre Plus can be made if it is about the administration of the deductions. Jobcentre Plus can make compensatory payments if appropriate.

See CPAG's *Welfare Benefits and Tax Credits Handbook* for more information about how to complain about any part of the DWP.

If you have gone through every stage of the DWP complaints procedure and you are still not satisfied, you can complain to the Independent Case Examiner (see below) or, via your MP, to the Parliamentary and Health Service Ombudsman (see p248).

**Note:** remember that some decisions about benefits can be challenged. It may be necessary to do this as well as, or instead of, complaining.

# 6. **Complaining to the Independent Case Examiner**

The Independent Case Examiner's (ICE's) office can help resolve situations where people believe that certain government agencies have not dealt with them fairly or resolved complaints to their satisfaction. ICE is an independent referee, completely separate from the Child Maintenance Service (CMS), Child Maintenance Options service, Jobcentre Plus or any other government department.

A complaint can only go to ICE after the CMS's (or other agency's) complaints procedure has been used and a final response received – ie, a decision on a review of the complaint (ie, a stage 2 complaint), which advises that the complaint can be made to ICE. The complaint to ICE must be made within six months of the final response. ICE cannot look at complaints made after this date.

ICE cannot consider a complaint which is being investigated, or which has been investigated, by the Parliamentary and Health Service Ombudsman (see p248). There may be a choice of complaining directly to the Ombudsman via an MP, but the Ombudsman's office usually encourages people to use ICE first.

Complaints can be made in writing (see Appendix 1 for the address) or by telephone on 0800 414 8529. Contact details are on the ICE website.[6] Include all the relevant facts and details of the complaint and responses you have received so far, including whether it is the CMS, Child Maintenance Options or Jobcentre Plus that you are complaining about, with details of the particular office being complained about, if possible. ICE can give further advice on making a complaint, or appoint a representative to act on your behalf, if required.

ICE first investigates and decides whether or not it can accept the complaint. It aims to decide this within two weeks. If ICE accepts the complaint, it attempts to settle it by suggesting ways in which you could come to an agreement with the CMS or Jobcentre Plus. It aims to resolve complaints this way within eight weeks of accepting them.

If this fails, ICE can then ask for all relevant information and attempts to settle the complaint. If this is not possible, an investigation is carried out and a formal report prepared setting out how the complaint arose and how it believes it should be settled. ICE aims to do this within 15 weeks, or 20 weeks if a report by ICE is required.

In 2018/19, ICE fully or partially upheld almost 70 per cent of the complaints relating to child support that it investigated.[7] If it makes a recommendation of action to the CMS or Jobcentre Plus, that is almost always followed.

If you are unhappy with the way that ICE has dealt with a complaint, you can use ICE's own complaints process. Details of ICE's standards of service are available on its website. If you remain unhappy, you can ask your MP to consider referring the case to the Parliamentary and Health Service Ombudsman (see below).

# 7. **Using your MP**

It may be appropriate to consult your MP at any stage of the complaints process. An MP may be able to provide advocacy or other support to get the matter resolved more quickly. However, consulting an MP is particularly important if you have been through the complaints process of the Child Maintenance Service (or Child Maintenance Options or Jobcentre Plus) without a satisfactory resolution, and even more so if you have used the Independent Case Examiner but still want to take matters further.

An MP may be able to advise on whether taking the complaint further is worthwhile. It may be that you are unhappy about an aspect of child support law, in which case a complaint is not appropriate. Whether the issue concerns law or procedure, an MP may be willing to take matters further to try to get legislation changed or practice improved. An MP may also refer the complaint to the Parliamentary and Health Service Ombudsman (see below).

You can find out who your MP is by using the constituency locator on the UK Parliament website, by phoning 020 7219 4272 or freephone 0800 112 4272 (NGT Text Relay 18001 then 0800 112 4272) or emailing hcenquiries@parliament.uk. Most MPs have local surgeries where they meet constituents. Alternatively, a complaint can be passed to the MP in writing. Contact details, including email addresses, for MPs are available on the UK Parliament website.[8]

# 8. **Complaining to the Ombudsman**

The Parliamentary and Health Service Ombudsman investigates complaints about a range of government departments and other public bodies.

Before using the Ombudsman, the organisation should have a full opportunity to respond to your complaint and put things right. For complaints about the Child Maintenance Service, Child Maintenance Options and Jobcentre Plus, the Independent Case Examiner (ICE) (see p247) can also be used. This does not need a referral from an MP, and the Ombudsman's office encourages people to use ICE first.

The first stage of using the Ombudsman is to download a complaints form from the Ombudsman website and send the complaint to your MP, asking her/him to consider the complaint, sign the form and send it to the Ombudsman. Normally, the Ombudsman does not investigate if the complaint is passed to an MP more than 12 months after the complainant became aware that s/he had a good reason to complain – ie, that there was a need to take the complaint further.

If the complaint is investigated, the MP is sent a full report. The Ombudsman may recommend an apology and possibly compensation. Ombudsman reports can also lead to changed practices and procedures in the agencies under investigation.

More information about the Ombudsman is available at ombudsman.org.uk or from the helpline on 0345 015 4033.

# Notes

### 2. Compensation payments
1 *Financial Redress for Maladministration: staff guide,* available at: gov.uk/government/publications/compensation-for-poor-service-a-guide-for-dwp-staff
2 *Rowley and others v SSWP* [2007] EWCA Civ 598
3 *Financial Redress for Maladministration: staff guide,* available at: gov.uk/government/publications/compensation-for-poor-service-a-guide-for-dwp-staff

### 3. Complaining about the Child Maintenance Service
4 CMS leaflet CMSB011GB, *What to Do if You're Unhappy With the Child Maintenance Service,* September 2018

### 4. Complaining about Child Maintenance Options
5 Contact details for Child Maintenance Options are available at: gov.uk/making-child-maintenance-arrangement/arrange-child-maintenance-yourself

### 6. Complaining to the Independent Case Examiner
6 gov.uk/government/organisations/independent-case-examiner
7 Independent Case Examiner for the DWP, *Annual Report, 1 April 2018 – 31 March 2019,* September 2019

### 7. Using your MP
8 members.parliament.uk/members/Commons

# Appendix 1

## Useful addresses

**Department for Work and Pensions**

gov.uk/government/organisations/
department-for-work-pensions

**Child Maintenance Options**

(England, Wales and Scotland)
Tel: 0800 988 0988
Welsh language line:
0800 408 0308

**Child Maintenance Choices**

(Northern Ireland)
Tel: 0800 028 7439
NGT text relay (if you cannot hear or
speak on the phone):
18001 then 0800 028 7439
cms_choices@nidirect.gsi.gov.uk
nidirect.gov.uk/contacts/
contacts-az/child-maintenance-
choices

**Child Maintenance Service**

Child Maintenance Service 21
Mail Handling Site A
Wolverhampton WV98 2BU
National enquiry line:
0800 171 2345
Textphone: 0800 232 1975
gov.uk/child-maintenance

**Northern Ireland Child Maintenance Service**

Child Maintenance Service 24
Mail Handling Site A
Wolverhampton WV98 2BU
Tel: 0800 232 1956
Textphone: 0800 232 1957
nidirect.gov.uk/contacts/child-
maintenance-service

**HM Courts and Tribunals Service**

Appeals should be sent to:

**England and Wales**

HMCTS SSCS Appeals Centre
PO Box 1203
Bradford BD1 9WP
General enquiries: 0300 123 1142
Welsh language: 0300 303 5170

**Scotland**

HMCTS SSCS Appeals Centre
PO Box 27080
Glasgow G2 9HQ
General enquiries: 0300 790 6234
Information about your nearest
tribunal venue can be found at:
courttribunalfinder.service.gov.uk/
search

## Upper Tribunal (Adminstrative Appeals Chamber)

gov.uk/courts-tribunals/upper-ibunal-administrative-appeals-chamber

### England and Wales

5th Floor
7 Rolls Buildings
Fetter Lane
London EC4A 1NL
Tel: 020 7071 5662
NGT text relay (if you cannot hear or speak on the phone):
18001 then 020 7071 5662
adminappeals@justice.gov.uk

### Scotland

George House
126 George Street
Edinburgh EH2 4HH
Tel: 0131 271 4310
Fax: 0131 271 4398
UTAACmailbox@gov.scot

### Northern Ireland

Tribunal Hearing Centre
2nd Floor
Royal Courts of Justice
Chichester Street

Belfast BT1 3JF
Tel: 028 9072 4883
tribunalsunit@courtsni.gov.uk
justice-ni.gov.uk/topics/courts-and-tribunals

## Independent Case Examiner

PO Box 209
Bootle L20 7WA
Tel: 0800 414 8529
NGT text relay (if you cannot hear or speak on the phone):
18001 then 0800 414 8529
ice@dwp.gov.uk
gov.uk/government/organisations/independent-case-examiner

## The Parliamentary and Health Service Ombudsman

Citygate
Mosley Street
Manchester M2 3HQ

Millbank Tower
30 Millbank
London SW1P 4QP
Tel: 0345 015 4033
Text 'call back' service:
07624 813 005
ombudsman.org.uk

# Appendix 2

## Statutes

A man is assumed to be the father of a child for child support purposes (see p44) if he is found to be the father by a court in England or Wales in proceedings under one of the following statutes.

s42 National Assistance Act 1948
Affiliation Proceedings Act 1957
s6 Family Law Reform Act 1969
Guardianship of Minors Act 1971
Children Act 1975
Child Care Act 1980
Children Act 1989
s26 Social Security Act 1986
s4 Family Law Reform Act 1987
s105 Social Security Administration Act 1992

A maintenance order only prevents an application to the Child Maintenance Service under section 4 or 7 of the Child Support Act 1991 (see p21) if it was made in proceedings under one of the following statutes. (This applies even if it was made under a statute that is now repealed.)

Conjugal Rights (Scotland) Amendment Act 1861
Court of Session Act 1868
Sheriff Courts (Scotland) Act 1907
Guardianship of Infants Act 1925
Illegitimate Children (Scotland) Act 1930
Children and Young Persons (Scotland) Act 1932
Children and Young Persons (Scotland) Act 1937
Custody of Children (Scotland) Act 1939
National Assistance Act 1948

Affiliation Orders Act 1952
Affiliation Proceedings Act 1957
Matrimonial Proceedings (Children) Act 1958
Guardianship of Minors Act 1971
Part II Matrimonial Causes Act 1973
Guardianship Act 1973
Children Act 1975
Supplementary Benefits Act 1976
Domestic Proceedings and Magistrates' Courts Act 1978
Part III Matrimonial and Family Proceedings Act 1984
Family Law (Scotland) Act 1985
Social Security Act 1986
Schedule 1 Children Act 1989
Social Security Administration Act 1992
Schedule 5, 6 or 7 Civil Partnership Act 2004

The court order usually states the legal provisions under which it was made.

# Appendix 3

## Information and advice

It may be easier to get a positive response from the Child Maintenance Service if you have obtained advice about your rights or have an adviser assisting you.

Unfortunately, CPAG is unable to deal with enquiries, either from advisers or members of the public, on child support issues.

The following may be able to help.

- Citizens Advice and other local advice centres provide information, and may be able to represent you. You can find your nearest office from citizensadvice.org.uk.
- Law centres can help with advice and representation, but may not cover child support problems and may limit their help to people who live and work in certain areas. You can check whether you are near a law centre from lawcentres.org.uk.
- Solicitors can give free legal advice to people on low incomes under the 'legal help' scheme (advice and assistance scheme in Scotland). This does not cover the cost of representation at an appeal hearing, but can cover the cost of preparing written submissions and obtaining evidence such as medical reports. However, solicitors do not always have a good working knowledge of the child support rules and you may need to shop around until you find one who does.
- find-legal-advice.justice.gov.uk can be used to find high-quality legal advisers in England and Wales, including advice agencies and solicitors.
- Local authority welfare rights workers provide an advice and representation service for benefit claimants in many areas.
- Lone-parent organisations may offer help and advice about child support, or it may help to talk to other parents about their experiences. For details of your local group and for helpline advice, contact: Gingerbread (helpline: 0808 802 0925; gingerbread.org.uk); One Parent Families Scotland (helpline: 0808 801 0323; opfs.org.uk).
- There are some groups supporting parents who may be able to provide advice. These include the National Association for Child Support Action (NACSA), Loverock House, Brettell Lane, Brierley Hill, West Midlands DY5 3JN (nacsa.co.uk). For general enquiry support, you can write, phone (01384

572525) or email (admin@nacsa.co.uk). A telephone advice line for advice on individual cases is available to subscribers.

* Many trade unions provide advice to members on child support.
* Local organisations for particular groups of people may offer help.

## Representation at appeals

Some parents may find it difficult to obtain representation at appeal hearings. Although many parents, especially with the help of Chapter 10, will be able to present their own case, it can be invaluable to obtain objective independent advice which draws on the legislation. An advice centre which has a copy of the legislation (see Appendix 4) and experience of representing at tribunals in other sorts of cases (eg, social security) may be able to provide a representative for a child support appeal.

# Appendix 4

## Useful publications

The Stationery Office (TSO) books are available from TSO bookshops or can be ordered from TSO Orders, 18 Central Avenue, St Andrew's Business Park, Norwich NR7 0HR (tel: 0333 202 5070; email: esupport@tso.co.uk; web: tsoshop.co.uk). Many publications listed are available from CPAG. See below for order details, or order from cpag.org.uk/shop.

### 1. Caselaw and legislation

All the legislation listed in Appendix 5 can be found at legislation.gov.uk. Most is updated.

*Child Support: the legislation*
E Jacobs (CPAG)
Legislation with detailed commentary. 14th edition main volume (summer 2019): £102 (£86.70 for CPAG members and Citizens Advice).

*Social Security Legislation, Volume I: Non-Means-Tested Benefits and Employment and Support Allowance*
D Bonner, I Hooker and R White (Sweet & Maxwell)
Legislation with commentary. 2020/21 edition (September 2020): £119 for the main volume.

*Social Security Legislation, Volume II: Income Support, Jobseeker's Allowance, State Pension Credit and the Social Fund*
J Mesher, P Wood, R Poynter, N Wikeley and D Bonner (Sweet & Maxwell)

Legislation with commentary. 2020/21 edition (September 2020): £119 for the main volume.

*Social Security Legislation, Volume III: Administration, Adjudication and the European Dimension*
M Rowland and R White (Sweet & Maxwell)
Legislation with commentary. 2020/21 edition (September 2020): £119 for the main volume.

*Social Security Legislation, Volume IV: Tax Credits and HMRC-administered Social Security Benefits*
N Wikeley and D Williams (Sweet & Maxwell)
Legislation with commentary. 2020/21 edition (September 2020): £119 for the main volume.

*Social Security Legislation, Volume V: Universal Credit*
P Wood, R Poynter and N Wikeley (Sweet & Maxwell)
Legislation with commentary. 2020/21 edition (September 2020): £119 for the main volume.

*Social Security Legislation – updating supplement (Sweet & Maxwell)*
The spring 2020 update to the 2019/20 main volumes: £75.

*Housing Benefit and Council Tax Reduction Legislation*
L Findlay, R Poynter, S Wright, C George, M Williams, S Mitchell and M Brough (CPAG)
Legislation with detailed commentary. 2020/21, 33rd edition (winter 2020): £128 including Supplement (£108.80 members). The 32nd edition (2019/20) is still available, £128 per set (£108.80 members).

## 2. Periodicals

*Welfare Rights Bulletin*
(CPAG, bimonthly).
Covers developments in social security law, including Upper Tribunal decisions, and updates this Handbook between editions. The annual subscription is £49 (£41.65 for members) but it is sent automatically to CPAG members and welfare rights subscribers (more information at cpag.org.uk/membership).

Articles on social security can also be found in *Legal Action* (Legal Action Group), AdviserNet(Citizens Advice) and the *Journal of Social Security Law* (Sweet & Maxwell).

## 3. Department for Work and Pensions publications

Many leaflets and factsheets explaining the statutory child support schemes are available through the gov.uk website (gov.uk/making-child-maintenance-arrangement). Other leaflets on child maintenance issues are available from Child Maintenance Options on 0800 988 0988.

Leaflets and most other Child Maintenance Service publications can also be obtained from the national enquiry line: 0800 171 2345.

Bulk copies of leaflets (more than 50 copies) can be ordered by advice agencies from APS. An order form is available at gov.uk/government/publications/dwp-leaflets-order-form.

Leaflets cover a wide range of subjects, including:
- how to apply;
- how child support is worked out and paid;
- how shared care and split care affect child support;
- what happens if someone denies s/he is a parent of a child;
- how the statutory child support services use personal information;
- what happens if the non-resident parent does not pay child support;
- information for a non-resident parent's employer;
- disputing decisions, making a complaint and appealing;
- changes that must be reported.

Where rules differ for each of the three statutory child support schemes, there are specific versions of the leaflets for each scheme.

## 4. Other publications: general

*Welfare Benefits and Tax Credits Handbook* (CPAG)
2020/21, April 2020: £65 (£55.25 members and Citizens Advice)/£15 for claimants.

*Welfare Benefits and Tax Credits Handbook Online* (CPAG)
Includes the full text of the *Welfare Benefits and Tax Credits Handbook* updated throughout the year. Annual subscription £65 per concurrent user (£55.25 members and Citizens Advice). Bulk discounts are available. More information at AskCPAG.org.uk.

*Council Tax Handbook* (CPAG)
13th edition, autumn 2020: £31 (£26.35 members and Citizens Advice).

*Debt Advice Handbook* (CPAG)
13th edition, March 2020: £29 (£24.65 members and Citizens Advice).

*Fuel Rights Handbook* (CPAG)
19th edition, March 2019: £29 (£24.65 members and Citizens Advice).

*Benefits for Migrants Handbook* (CPAG)
12th edition, winter 2020: £40 (£34 members and Citizens Advice).

*Student Support and Benefits Handbook* (CPAG)
17th edition, autumn 2020: £28 (£23.80 members and Citizens Advice).

*Benefits for Students in Scotland Handbook* (CPAG)
17th edition, autumn 2020: £31 (£26.35 members and Citizens Advice).
Available free online at AskCPAG.org.uk.

*Children's Handbook Scotland: a benefits guide for children living away from their parents* (CPAG)
13th edition, autumn 2020: £31 (£26.35 members and Citizens Advice).
Available free online at AskCPAG.org.uk.

*Universal Credit: what you need to know* (CPAG)
6th edition, autumn 2020: £15 (£12.75 members and Citizens Advice).

*Financial Help for Families: what you need to know*
2nd edition, autumn 2020: £15 (£12.75 members and Citizens Advice).

*Personal Independence Payment: what you need to know* (CPAG)
2nd edition, August 2016: £15 (£12.75 members and Citizens Advice).

*Winning Your Benefit Appeal: what you need to know* (CPAG)
3rd edition, July 2019: £15 (£12.75 members and Citizens Advice).

*Help with Housing Costs Vol 1: Guide to Universal Credit and Council Tax Rebates 2020/21* (Shelter/CIH)
June 2020: £43.50.

*Help with Housing Costs Vol 2: Guide to Housing Benefit 2020/21* (Shelter/CIH)
June 2020: £43.50.

*Disability Rights Handbook 2020/21* (Disability Rights UK)
May 2020: £36.

*Tribunal Practice and Procedure* (Legal Action Group)
5th edition, September 2019: £70.

*Disabled Children: a legal handbook* (Legal Action Group)
3rd edition, January 2020: £50.

For CPAG publications and most of
those in Sections 1 and 4, contact:
CPAG, 30 Micawber Street, London
N1 7TB, tel: 020 7812 5227, email:
bookorders@cpag.org.uk,
cpag.org.uk/shop

# Appendix 5

# Abbreviations used in the notes

| | |
|---|---|
| AAC | Administrative Appeals Chamber |
| AACR | Administrative Appeals Chamber Reports |
| AC | Appeal Cases |
| All ER | All England Reports |
| Art(s) | Article(s) |
| CA | Court of Appeal |
| CMLR | Common Market Law Reports |
| col | column |
| EC | European Commission |
| EHRR | European Human Rights Reports |
| EWCA Civ | England and Wales Court of Appeal (Civil Division) |
| EWFC | England and Wales Family Court |
| EWHC | England and Wales High Court |
| FCR | Family Court Reports |
| FLR | Family Law Reports |
| HL | House of Lords |
| HMCTS | Her Majesty's Courts and Tribunals Service |
| para(s) | paragraph(s) |
| r(r) | rule(s) |
| Reg(s) | Regulation(s) |
| s(s) | section(s) |
| SC | Supreme Court |
| Sch(s) | Schedule(s) |
| SCLR | Scottish Civil Law Reports |
| SLT | Scots Law Times |
| SP | Scottish Parliament |
| UKHL | United Kingdom House of Lords |
| UKSC | United Kingdom Supreme Court |
| UKUT | United Kingdom Upper Tribunal |

## Acts of Parliament

Legislative references are generally for '2012 rules' cases only, unless there is a particular reason also to refer to references for '1993 rules' or '2003' rules. Full sources for '1993 rules' cases can be found in the 2001/02 and 2002/03 editions, and for '2003 rules' cases in the 2013/14 edition, of this *Handbook*.

| | |
|---|---|
| AA 1976 | Adoption Act 1976 |
| A(S)A 1978 | Adoption (Scotland) Act 1978 |
| A&CA 2002 | Adoption and Children Act 2002 |
| A&C(S)A 2007 | Adoption and Children (Scotland) Act 2007 |
| CA 1989 | Children Act 1989 |
| C(S)A 1995 | Children (Scotland) Act 1995 |
| CMOPA 2008 | Child Maintenance and Other Payments Act 2008 |
| CPA 2004 | Civil Partnership Act 2004 |
| CSA 1991 | Child Support Act 1991 |
| CSPSSA 2000 | Child Support, Pensions and Social Security Act 2000 |
| DPMCA 1978 | Domestic Proceedings and Magistrates' Courts Act 1978 |
| ERA 1996 | Employment Rights Act 1996 |
| FL(S)A 1985 | Family Law (Scotland) Act 1985 |
| FLRA 1969 | Family Law Reform Act 1969 |
| HF&EA 1990 | Human Fertilisation and Embryology Act 1990 |
| HF&EA 2008 | Human Fertilisation and Embryology Act 2008 |
| ICTA 1988 | Income and Corporation Taxes Act 1988 |
| ITA 2007 | Income Tax Act 2007 |
| IT(EP)A 2003 | Income Tax (Earnings and Pensions) Act 2003 |
| IT(TOI)A 2005 | Income Tax (Trading and Other Income) Act 2005 |
| LR(PC)(S)A 1986 | Law Reform (Parent and Child) (Scotland) Act 1986 |
| MCA 1973 | Matrimonial Causes Act 1973 |
| MO(RE)A 1992 | Maintenance Orders (Reciprocal Enforcement) Act 1992 |
| SSA 1998 | Social Security Act 1998 |
| SSAA 1992 | Social Security Administration Act 1992 |
| SSCBA 1992 | Social Security Contributions and Benefits Act 1992 |
| TCEA 2007 | Tribunals, Courts and Enforcement Act 2007 |
| WRA 2012 | Welfare Reform Act 2012 |

## Regulations and other statutory instruments

Legislative references are generally for '2012 rules' cases only, unless there is a particular reason also to refer to provisions in the equivalent regulations for '1993 rules' or '2003' rules. Full sources for '1993 rules' cases can be found in the 2001/02 and 2002/03 editions, and for '2003 rules' cases in the 2013/14 edition, of this *Handbook*.

| | |
|---|---|
| AS(CSA)(AOCSCR) | Act of Sederunt (Child Support Act 1991) (Amendment of Ordinary Cause and Summary Cause Rules) 1993 No.919 |
| AS(CSR) | Act of Sederunt (Child Support Rules) 1993 No.920 |
| AUTCAO | The Appeals from the Upper Tribunal to the Court of Appeal Order 2008 No.2834 |
| CB Regs | The Child Benefit (General) Regulations 2006 No.223 |
| CS(AIAMA) Regs | The Child Support (Arrears, Interest and Adjustment of Maintenance Assessments) Regulations 1992 No.1816 |
| CS(APD) Regs | The Child Support (Applications: Prescribed Date) Regulations 2003 No.194 |
| CS(C&E) Regs | The Child Support (Collection and Enforcement) Regulations 1992 No.1989 |
| CS(CEOFM) Regs | The Child Support (Collection and Enforcement of Other Forms of Maintenance) Regulations 1992 No.2643 |
| CS(DEOAMMA) Regs | The Child Support (Deduction from Earnings Orders Amendment and Modification and Miscellaneous Amendments) Regulations 2016 No.982 |
| CS(DOF) Regs | The Child Support (Deduction Orders and Fees) (Amendment and Modification) Regulations 2016 No.439 |
| CS(MA) Regs 2018 | The Child Support (Miscellaneous Amendments) Regulations 2018 No.1279 |
| CS(MA) Regs 2019 | The Child Support (Miscellaneous Amendments) Regulations 2019 No.1084 |
| CS(MAJ) Regs | The Child Support (Maintenance Arrangements and Jurisdiction) Regulations 1992 No.2645 |
| CS(MCSC) Regs | The Child Support (Maintenance Calculations and Special Cases) Regulations 2000 No.2001/155 |
| CS(MOC&NCR) Regs | The Child Support (Meaning of Child and New Calculation Rules) (Consequential and Miscellaneous Amendment) Regulations 2012 No.2785 |
| CS(MPA) Regs | The Child Support (Management of Payments and Arrears) Regulations 2009 No.3151 |
| CS(NIRA) Regs | The Child Support (Northern Ireland Reciprocal Arrangements) Regulations 1993 No.584 |

| | |
|---|---|
| CS(V) Regs | The Child Support (Variations) Regulations 2000 No.2001/ 156 |
| CS(V)(MSP) Regs | The Child Support (Variations) (Modification of Statutory Provisions) Regulations 2000 No.3173 |
| CS(VP) Regs | The Child Support (Voluntary Payments) Regulations 2000 No.3177 |
| CSA(CA)O | The Child Support Act 1991 (Consequential Amendments) Order 1993 No.785 |
| CSA(JC)O | The Child Support Appeals (Jurisdiction of Courts) Order 2002 No.1915 |
| CSA(JC)(S)O | Child Support Appeals (Jurisdiction of Courts) (Scotland) Order 2003 No.96 |
| CSF Regs | The Child Support Fees Regulations 1992 No.3094 |
| CSF Regs 2014 | The Child Support Fees Regulations 2014 No.612 |
| CSI Regs | The Child Support Information Regulations 2008 No.2551 |
| CSM(CBR) Regs | The Child Support Maintenance (Changes to Basic Rate Calculation and Minimum Amount of Liability) Regulations 2012 No.2678 |
| CSMC Regs | The Child Support Maintenance Calculation Regulations 2012 No.2677 |
| FT&UT(CT)O | The First-tier Tribunal and Upper Tribunal (Composition of Tribunal) Order 2008 No.2835 |
| SS(C&P) Regs | The Social Security (Claims and Payments) Regulations 1987 No.1968 |
| TP(FT) Rules | The Tribunal Procedure (First-tier Tribunal) (Social Entitlement Chamber) Rules 2008 No.2685 |
| TP(UT) Rules | The Tribunal Procedure (Upper Tribunal) Rules 2008 No.2698 |
| UC,PIP,JSA&ESA(C&P) Regs | The Universal Credit, Personal Independence Payment, Jobseeker's Allowance and Employment and Support Allowance (Claims and Payments) Regulations 2013 No.380 |

# Index